GOD

GOD

A Story of Revelation

Deepak Chopra

HarperOne
An Imprint of HarperCollinsPublishers

HarperOne

HarperCollins books may be purchased for educational, business, or sales promotional use. For information please e-mail the Special Markets Department at SPsales@harpercollins.com.

HarperCollins website: http://www.harpercollins.com

HarperCollins®, ☰®, and HarperOne™ are trademarks of HarperCollins Publishers.

FIRST HARPERCOLLINS PAPERBACK EDITION PUBLISHED IN 2013

Library of Congress Cataloging-in-Publication Data

Chopra, Deepak.
God : a story of Revelation / by Deepak Chopra.
     p. cm.
ISBN 978–0–06–202069–7
1. Revelation. 2. God. 3. Spirituality. I. Title.
BL475.5.C46   2012
202'.117—dc23   2012017643

13 14 15 16 17 RRD(H) 10 9 8 7 6 5 4 3 2 1

Contents

Prologue

Like a car with two steering wheels, the world has been guided by two forces, the spiritual and the secular, that fight for control. The secular has seized the advantage today, but for many centuries the power lay with spirituality. Visionaries could shape the future as much as kings, often more. A king was anointed by God, but visionaries were visited by God. They heard his message personally before appearing in public to announce what God wanted people to do.

I became fascinated by the perplexing situation that visionaries find themselves thrust into. Very few asked for this power to affect other people. God wrenched them from the comfort of everyday life and guided their steps. The voice they heard in their heads wasn't their own, but divinely inspired. What was that like? On one hand, it must have been terrifying. In a world that made a spectacle of feeding martyrs to lions, crucifying saints as enemies of the state, and jealously guarding old religions, the voice of God could be pronouncing a death sentence. On the other hand, to experience the divine was ecstatic, as witnessed by the mystical poets in every culture who had a love affair with the divine. That mixture of rapture and torment became the seed of this book.

"God" is an empty term except as it finds expression through the revelations of all the saints, prophets, and mystics of history. They exist to plant the seeds of spirituality as direct experience rather than a matter of hope and faith. Yet no one can say that God was revealed in one consistent shape delivering one consistent message—quite the opposite. Somehow revelations can be divine and contradictory at the same time.

Why doesn't God just say what's on his (or her) mind and let it spread to every people? The contradiction in holy messages arose because of our own limitations. Let's assume that God is infinite. Our minds are not equipped to perceive the infinite. We perceive what we are prepared to see and know. Infinity reveals itself in bits and pieces tailored to each society, epoch, and habit of mind. We label as God mere glimpses of higher reality, like seeing one figure in Da Vinci's *Last Supper*. A glimpse fills us with wonder, but the whole thing has been missed.

With that in mind, I've turned this novel into a meditation about God in us. Only half is fictional, devoted to ten visionaries entranced by the words that God spoke to them. The other half consists of reflections on what God meant when he singled out these sages, seers, prophets, and poets. The message wasn't the same each time—Job in the Old Testament heard something very different from what St. Paul in the New Testament heard—yet one sees a pattern.

God evolves. That's why he keeps speaking and never grows silent. The very basic fact that God has shifted between "he," "she," "it," and none of the above shows how changeable the divine presence is. But to say that God evolves implies that he began in an immature state and then grew into fullness, when every faith holds that God is infinite to begin with. What actually evolved was human understanding. For thousands of years, perhaps as far back as cave dwellers, the human mind held a capacity for higher reality. Sacred paintings and statues are as ancient as civilization, preceding written language and probably even agriculture.

Nearness to God is a constant, not just in human history, but in human nature. If we are connected to our souls, the connection is permanent, even if our attention falters. We think that God changes, because our own perception waxes and wanes. The messages keep coming, though, and God keeps showing different faces. Sometimes the whole notion of the divine gets hidden, when secular forces snatch the steering wheel and attempt to drive alone. But the force of spirituality never fully surrenders. God stands for our need to know ourselves, and as awareness evolves, so does God. This journey never ends. At this moment somewhere in the world a person is waking up in the middle of the night hearing a message that feels uncanny, as if arriving from another reality. Actually, there must be many such visitations every night, and the people who step forth to announce what they've heard form a motley crew of crazies, artists, avatars, rebels, and saints.

I've always wanted to join this motley crew, and in the following pages I get to imagine that I belong with them. Don't we all, at some level, want to join the outsiders? Their stories tear at our hearts and uplift our souls. The lessons they learned took the human race down unknown roads. One could do worse than to jump the track of everyday life and follow them.

Deepak Chopra
April 2012

1

JOB

"I Am the Lord Thy God"

"Where does the world end?" the father asked.

His son, Job, wasn't prepared for being questioned. It was spring. Outside their tent the first warm breezes carried the pleasant noise of birds and frisky lambs. The boy's friends were kicking a leather ball across the fields.

"I asked you a question."

Job pulled at his sandal straps and stared at the carpeted dirt floor. "The world ends at the city walls, where the demons are locked out."

This seemed reasonable to a ten-year-old. He had been warned about demons very early, and their names, such as Moloch and Astaroth, stuck in his mind. Claws and fangs held a dread fascination. When the winter cold drove the shepherds back inside the city gates, Job felt trapped, but he was forbidden to venture where he might inhale a demon as easily as a gnat.

His father shook his head. "Try again. Where does the world end?"

A big man, Job's father loomed over him; he wore a menacing look, which was out of place in a weaver who was almost as easy with his children as a woman. This time, though, Job knew without thinking that the look was dangerous.

"The world ends where Judea meets the land of war," he replied. This had to be right. Their green valley, known as Uz, petered out into the brown scorching desert, like milk spilled from a jug that flows until the sand drinks it up. The difference was that the land of war drank blood.

But his father still loomed. "One last time, boy. Where does the world end?"

Now the boy was tongue-tied with bewilderment. He lowered his eyes. Suddenly, he was struck a hard blow on the side of his head, hard enough to hurl him flat on the ground, where he lay, very still. When he stopped seeing stars, Job stared at his father, who was bending over him, examining him the way you examine a wounded goat for maggots.

"The world ends here," his father grunted. He suspended his brawny arm over Job's face. "Don't ever forget my fist."

Why was he acting this way? There was no chance that the boy would cry. The blow was unfair. A pride known to small children rose in him. He had been insulted, and insults deserve contempt, not tears. But his father's fist remained clenched, and Job wouldn't risk a second blow. He bit his lip and wore a mask until his father, having made the point, straightened up and strode out of the tent without another word.

He had dropped something and left it behind. A scrap of cloth, fine white wool with a purple stripe in it. Job only just noticed it when his mother came rushing in, wringing her hands, which were wet from the washtub. There was no time to tell her what had happened. There wasn't time for a word, in fact, before her face crumpled and she let out a shriek. She grabbed up the scrap of cloth and pressed it to her cheek.

Job was stunned. His mother was a dignified woman, the kind who turned away rather than be watched suckling a baby. Job had never seen her anything but fully dressed. Suddenly she tore at her black shift and almost ripped it away from her breast. It took a moment before her strangled sobs formed into a word the boy could understand.

"Rebekah!"

His sister? Why would his mother call out her name? In his confusion, Job was lost until a fact dawned, a simple fact now full of terror. His older sister wore a fine white undergarment. Purple dye from Tyre was expensive, but she was betrothed, and the groom's mother had paid a visit. The two families were pleased with the match, and before she left, the groom's mother presented Job's mother with a ball of purple yarn. This was immediately woven into the hem of Rebekah's white skirt, so that when she walked, a flick of purple could be seen at her ankles.

"She's dead?" Job murmured, afraid to ask the question, but more afraid not to know. His sister had torn the scrap from her clothing—or someone else had.

His mother grabbed him to her breast and squeezed him tight. He squirmed, feeling the hot skin under her bodice. He could hardly breathe, but she wouldn't let go; the boy began to gasp.

"Job!"

His father's voice shouted for him. At the same time the sound of women running toward the tent made his mother's body slump. The running feet entered. Suddenly the boy was drowned in wailing.

His father shouted again, and Job broke free. Running outside, he looked over his shoulder. In the darkness of the tent his mother was enfolded by a dozen hands clutching at her, like a baby being yanked by midwives into a terrifying birth. Job wanted to protect his mother. He would have run back to tear her from the clutching hands except that his father whirled him around.

"You understand now?" his father demanded.

How could he possibly understand? Seeing his bewildered eyes, his father crouched down.

"God gave us this place and made it beautiful. But he didn't blind the eyes of strangers. They are jealous. They snatch away what is beautiful, and they know that they are evil, so they hide in the night."

Now it was dawning. Roads carried travelers past their city. Sometimes the strangers came in a trickle, as traders or pilgrims to Jerusalem. No, the pilgrims were not to be called strangers, only the others. But when the trickle became a torrent, armies tramped on the roads. The land of war was brought to their doorstep.

"A battle?" asked Job. He wasn't afraid. In two years he would have to stand ready at the city walls, in case the invaders from Persia or beyond killed the men and older boys. He was already armed with an iron-tipped stick. In two years he might even be as tall as a spear.

"Not a battle, my son. A raid, by cowards, by men worse than animals."

Whatever blow had fallen, it made his father suddenly weak-kneed, and as he reached to hold his boy's shoulders straight, his own hands trembled. He couldn't bear to let Job see his face creased with tears. The boy didn't know that this was the reason his father stood up and ran away without a word. Only he never forgot. The day his father struck him to the ground was the day his sister, Rebekah, died. Probably she had gone to the well with an empty jug balanced on her head to fill. Probably she was smiling and then vaguely disappointed when she found that no other women or girls were gathered there to gossip. Were the dun-colored wrens who dipped in and out of the water singing, or did they know?

Rebekah would have had a minute to guess why she found herself alone, would have thrown the jug to the ground and heard it shatter. In two or three steps, not enough to escape, the raiders would have been upon her. When the men of Uz went outside the walls later, to the spring that was circled with stones to make a well, they found drops of blood. The girl had struggled, and she had torn a scrap of cloth from her undergarment. It was white wool, woven by her father, but it could have been a note written in ink.

Forget me. I am defiled. We are lost to one another. Forget me, my dear ones.

The circle of wailing women didn't leave her mother's side. Job and his father slept outside the tent that night. The sky looked darker than the boy ever remembered it. He didn't remember falling asleep, but he woke up at dawn, seeing a shadowy figure emerge from the tent flap. Suddenly he had an image of his mother creeping away to drown herself in the well. It was a shallow well, but if she was determined and lay face down in it—

"Boy, wake up."

Job opened his eyes and realized that he had been having a bad dream. His father sat on the ground next to him; he handed his son a bowl of curds with grain mixed in. With a nod Job took it. He was sure when he had rolled up in a sheepskin to go to sleep that he would never want to eat again, but now he was ravenous. He scooped up the food with his cupped fingers, watching to see what his father would do next. A child, if well loved, will give a parent a second chance, but Job felt the bruised spot on the side of his head where it had hit the floor. He waited. At first his father sat motionless, as if deciding what kind of man he would turn into that day. His silence began to make Job nervous, until a moment later when his father arose and walked around to the other side of the tent, where his loom was set up. Then there was the familiar clacking sound of his work, a sound Job always found reassuring.

When he had finished eating, the boy walked to where the loom stood; in spring all the weavers worked out in the open if the weather was good. His father was the first one to start; the sun was still half sunk below the horizon. Job watched him without speaking. The rest of their lives would fall under the shadow of the raid. He didn't know particulars. Would they hold funeral rites without a body? Would a party of men strap spears to their pack animals and try to rescue her? For a long time his father threw the shuttle, saying nothing.

"God blesses his people."

When the sentence came out, Job was startled. He wondered if grief had turned his father's brain. The words were repeated, louder this time, as if his father wanted the surrounding tents to hear him.

"God blesses his people. We bring misfortune on ourselves. No one is without sin."

His father addressed no one in particular except, perhaps, the sky. Now he gazed at Job, as if noticing him for the first time.

"Do you understand?" he said.

The boy shook his head. Until the day before, he had considered his father perfect. The boy never thought about God; he had no need. His own father provided everything, knew everything. What was he saying, that he had caused the crime against Rebekah? From deep inside, Job wanted to cry, "Stop it! You didn't kill her." But he couldn't, because if he did, his father might strike him again, and he didn't know how hard the blow would be. There was another reason not to cry out. If his father wasn't responsible for this cruel twist of fate, there was only one other to blame.

In a dull voice his father said, "It's all right. I don't expect you to understand, but remember what I said to you this morning." He turned back to his weaving, and as his hands moved swiftly across the tautly stretched yarn, a change took place. His body relaxed; his face resumed the mild expression it always wore. Soon he whistled softly to himself, and you would not have known, unless you did know, that anything amiss had ever happened.

"My father was content. Do you know how that could be? One of you speak up. How can a man contentedly work the day after his daughter is stolen from him?"

Job was no longer a boy. He was a father himself now, with sons and daughters. The men around him remained quiet. A new baby had arrived. Job held him in his arms while he recounted the tale of Rebekah's disappearance. It was his custom to do this every time his wife bore him a son. The men had gathered for the circumcision rite, but the priest held the knife back while Job told his story.

The men, who had heard it before, could have answered Job, but they took pleasure in hearing him deliver the moral.

"My father was content because he knew that God would reward the righteous and punish the wicked. My sister was no exception. I pray she survived, but if not, God is lawful, always."

The men in the dark room with the shutters closed murmured their assent. "God is lawful," one repeated. Candles burned on the table where the newborn baby had been laid. He kicked his feet randomly, but didn't cry out. When the priest's knife touched him, he made a queer sound of surprise and distress. It was more like a small animal's cry, like a herding dog having its tail docked, than a human cry. The sound was the signal for Job's wife to rush in, swaddle the baby, whose face had turned bright red, and rush him away to be bathed and bandaged.

The solemn atmosphere turned when they left. The priest was the first to raise a cup of wine, and the men cheered, showering the new father with praise. But no one slapped him on the back. Job was not someone you took familiarities with. After the third cup the men knew without being told that they should leave. When they got home, they would be pestered by their wives. Were the wall hangings silk, the plates gold? How pretty were the servant girls? Don't tell me Job didn't look them over first. The rich are a law unto themselves.

One guest was exhausted, having stayed up all night to attend a difficult calving. He might have lost both mother and baby, but as it was, God willed that the calf was stillborn. So the man was angry as well as exhausted, and he could hardly hold his wine at the best of times.

"Your father had no right to strike you," he said. "I've known some sons to run away, or worse." The drunken guest pushed his face right up to Job's. The others looked on, startled and embarrassed.

Job regarded him tolerantly. "What would another son have done?"

"Don't ask me. But he wouldn't have cowered. If it was my father, he would have hidden the knives after that."

A sudden passion burned in the drunken guest's face. Without warning he turned and grabbed the priest's knife, which lay on the table waiting to be cleaned and blessed for the next rite.

"Hide your knives!" the drunk shouted. "Because I'm coming!"

As quickly as it came on him the passion faded. The drunken guest blinked and looked around in confusion, as if he had heard his words, but didn't know who had shouted them.

"Pardon," he mumbled. He dropped the knife, which clattered on the stone floor, and ran out without meeting anyone's gaze. Nobody spoke, waiting for Job's reaction. Not one of them owned what he owned, and most had borrowed money from his coffers, which always stood open.

"Is he the only one?" Job murmured quietly.

The men around him shuffled uncomfortably at this baffling question, but Job answered himself.

"You all wonder, and so did I. My sister was gone, and my father chose that very moment to strike me. I was young, but I knew about knives." Job smiled, as if revisiting an old impulse that had not quite died with time. "Even young boys help slaughter spring lambs."

"Your father was your father. He could do what he liked," said a close friend named Eliphaz.

"And that would have been good enough for you, if you were in my place?" asked Job.

"I *was* in your place. When my father was in a rage, he threw it in every direction," Eliphaz replied. More than a few heads nodded; there was a general murmur of agreement.

"Was your father's rage a kindness?" Job asked.

Eliphaz hesitated and then smiled. "You're full of mysteries today."

"So is the world, and so is God. But this is a mystery I solved," said Job. He didn't pause for a reaction. "What do we know about our Lord?" (There was no chance that Job would actually pronounce the name of God, which was forbidden.) "He told us himself. He is a jealous and angry God. Did not Moses receive that teaching? We have the law, so we know how to please God. Even when he is angry, he is just."

Job had wound himself up and could have delivered a sermon, but suddenly he stopped. He looked blank, like a man lost in thought or hearing voices, you couldn't tell which.

Quietly he continued, "To a boy, what is his father? God in the flesh. This is righteous. It is the law that fathers rule as God, and my father wanted to protect me. How far could his protection reach? Only as far as his arm. Beyond his fist I would be at the end of the world. I would fall into the same danger that snatched away my sister. The blow my father struck was pure love. I hated him in my heart until God showed me this meaning. Now I only wish I could have returned such love, the kind that is willing to be hated and yet cannot be stopped by hatred."

Some of his guests murmured at these words, deeply moved. But not all. Another friend, Bildad, was skeptical. "What is your teaching, that God strikes us down out of love? If so, what does he do when he hates us? Surely he condemns the sinners and rewards the righteous."

Before Job could reply, another friend, Zophar, jumped in. "This was only a child's lesson. When you were a boy, the world ended with your father's fist. Now you know better. There is no world out of reach of God's wrath."

Job looked at his friends soberly. All three were smiling. To be close to the rich, you must learn subtlety, and the first lesson is a concealing smile. The kind an assassin wears until he draws close enough to strike.

"What do you think of me, my friends, that I have never known suffering?"

"Money is like a feather bed, only softer," said Bildad, a favorite saying of his.

"This is a day of celebration. Let's not break our heads arguing over God," Zophar chimed in.

Job nodded. "There is no point in such arguments. What we know about God, we know. True?"

He bowed his head. Was he praying or being modest or feeling defeated? The room was dim. No one could tell. They were grateful simply to escape. Each departing guest grasped Job's hand warmly, but he never raised his face. Whatever he might be thinking, the voice in his head had run out of words.

A field hand stood dripping with sweat, holding out two blackened heads of barley. They were blighted, and the first thing Job asked was how far the sticky smut had spread. The field hand shrugged.

"Go ask my friends," Job said. "Their crops are planted close to mine. Show them what you've shown me. It's probably nothing, but ask if they are worried."

The field hand retreated with a bow. For some reason the two heads of blighted barley made an image that stuck in Job's mind. He wasn't concerned for himself. He owned the richest fields in the valley, and he always had a season's harvest stored in his granary. His neighbors were not so blessed; they lived from crop to crop. An hour later the field hand rushed back, shaking his head.

"Your friends, their grain is clean," he said, but he didn't look like a man delivering good news. He held a bulging sack close to his belly. With a gesture he let go. Out of the sack spilled a hundred heads of barley, all smutty and withered. They lay at Job's feet like charred caterpillars. His brow furrowed.

"Why didn't you bring this many before?" he asked.

"I brought all there was. This just happened. Whatever this is, it's moving fast." The field hand backed away a step, as if the grain really was plague-ridden.

Job was a mild man, as his father had been, but he shot the field hand a sharp look and ordered him to keep watch over the barley crop that night. He was to bring any news in the morning. But the blight moved with alarming speed. There was news before nightfall—one of Job's largest fields had turned to blackened stalks. Some invisible fire had killed his crop, and yet it stopped, as if by command, exactly where Job's land met his neighbor's. The people began to mutter. In their minds there was a fine line between ill fortune and being cursed. When the sun rose the next morning, the invisible fire had spread to two other fields, the best that Job farmed. The tips of the grain were charred already. The next field over, owned by his friend Eliphaz, stood untouched. The line between ill fortune and being cursed was crossed.

Job went to his wife, who was being dressed by a servant girl. "Leave off your jewelry, and if you go out, cover your head," he said. She looked at him, puzzled, and waved the girl away.

When they were alone his wife said, "Why do you ask this? Do you suspect me of something? I'm completely innocent."

Another husband would have wondered why such a thought leapt into her mind, but he was trusting. "My dear, there's something bad in the fields. God sees everything. If he is angry, let's show that we're not proud." Pride was the easiest sin for a rich man to fall into; Job had always kept that in mind. He didn't feel that he had sinned, but God looks into the deepest recesses of the heart. Being doubly careful, Job had even sanctified his sons' houses with offerings, just in case they had harbored evil thoughts.

Later that day Job wrapped himself in sackcloth and appeared at Eliphaz's door.

"You've heard?" he said.

"That your crops are wiped out? Everyone's heard." Eliphaz wore a grim look and invited Job to step over his threshold. Was there a slight hesitancy on his part? Job didn't notice; he was anxious for his friend's advice. He had done everything he could to appease the Lord. He hired priests to light their altars and sacrifice a dozen of Job's newborn animals. He ordered his sons and daughters to follow their father's example and wear rough sackcloth; the women walked to market with a streak of gray ash on their foreheads as a sign of atonement.

Eliphaz disagreed with this gesture. "You're advertising that you've sinned. People will turn on you. I know them."

Job shook his head. "To walk this earth advertises that we have all sinned. What matters is pleasing our Father."

Despite his penance, however, misfortune continued to rain down. Job's flocks took sick and died. Overnight the grain he had stored up in his granary withered away. What could it mean? Behind his back not everyone was entirely grief-stricken. Somehow they found the strength to survive a rich man's downfall. Eliphaz took Bildad aside. What was God saying to them?

Bildad shrugged. "Who am I, Moses? God sent him to Pharaoh to say that Egypt would be visited by ten plagues. I got no message."

Eliphaz twisted his mouth. "Only eight plagues to go."

His morbid joke didn't reach Job's ears. Envy and pity divided the people, but they were all aghast as Job's huge holdings of sheep and camels died. In the space of a month his yoked oxen fell to their knees while plowing and never got up again. A few surmised that demons were responsible, not the wrath of God, until the calamity of calamities befell. Job gathered his family together at his eldest son's house to pray for an answer. They knelt together, but when the first syllable of their prayer was uttered, the house collapsed around them, and all were killed except Job and his wife. Now pity turned to terror. Plagues had a nasty habit of spreading. Maybe curses did too.

"We are alone and forsaken," Job's wife wailed.

He didn't reply, but took himself into the desert where he sat naked in the sun, pouring ashes over his head. The next day his closest friends came from the city to console him, although cynics told it differently. Job was no longer rich. With everything gone, he was in fact wretchedly poor. He had become a stranger among the righteous. There was no obligation to a stranger, was there?

The three friends were horrified by what they saw, although it was the terrible smell that reached them first. Overnight Job had become covered in weeping sores. He sat hunched over in the barren desert, scraping ashes and pus from his skin with a shard of pottery from the smashed water jug by his side. If they hadn't been courageous and loyal, his dear friends would have fled such a monstrous sight.

They knelt in a circle around Job, extending their hands (being careful not to touch his skin) and imploring, "Let us take you home. You can't perish out here like this."

Job said nothing. The sight of sores bursting as he scraped was nauseating. Eliphaz glanced at the other two. Would God punish them if they let Job die alone after seeing his distress?

Suddenly Job spoke. His voice was a croak rising from his parched throat. "I am blameless and upright. If you believe in your hearts that I have sinned, run away. If you stay, you'll defile yourself."

"We are your friends. What should we believe?" asked Zophar.

"That I walk the path of righteousness."

"I'm certain of that," said Bildad, "but forgive me. Isn't our God a just God?"

Job raised his head and looked at his friend with pain in his eyes. "God brings all things. He brings good and evil."

Perhaps this made Job's friends afraid, because they started to weep and tear at their clothes; they threw dust on their heads as if grieving for the dead. They prayed for God to release Job, and yet the next day the friends returned with Job's wife. She almost fainted when she set eyes on her husband.

"Tell him," Eliphaz said.

"I can't weep forever," Job's wife said. "Be done with it. Curse God and die." Job knew where her words came from. She wanted to be free to remarry a man who wasn't hated by God.

"I should curse you instead, for being so foolish," Job replied, and his wife departed.

His friends stayed behind, keeping watch. The sun rose and fell over the desert. They put up a tent to protect themselves from the elements and had water brought from the city well. Job sat in the sun, hardly moving. His bones poked out beneath his peeling flesh, but he didn't die. Only, he started to speak and wouldn't stop. He cursed the day he was born. He cursed all joy from this world and called upon those who could summon dreadful monsters. He cursed the happy news that a woman would bear a son. His cursing was endless; it frayed his friends' nerves, and they came out to reason with him.

At that moment he was cursing the stars to return to darkness, but he paused when they approached.

Eliphaz spoke first. "I mean no offense, but your groans pour out like water. Where is the man who taught us so much, whose strength held us up? You should show more patience. A few nights ago I shivered in my sleep, and my hair stood on end. A spirit passed over me and whispered in my ear, 'Who can be blameless before God? The Lord doesn't trust even those who are nearest to him. Were not the angels cursed by God when they disobeyed? How much worse are men who plow the earth and sow it with iniquity'."

Job hoarsely whispered, "So what would you have me do, friend?"

"Make your peace with God. He performs all wonders. He brings rain to the fields. He causes sickness, but has a healing hand. Repent and accept your destruction in peace. You will be taken away, at one with the stones of the earth and the beasts of the field," said Eliphaz.

Job's voice rose to a wail. "If only you could see how heavy my calamity weighs. I am rash because the arrows of the Almighty are in me. But believe me, I would rejoice in endless pain if only God would release me. I'm not made of stone or bronze. Don't counsel patience. My strength is gone. I cry out like a wounded animal."

He turned a burning gaze on Eliphaz. "Hear me. A friend who withholds kindness has betrayed God."

But I'm not the one he cursed, am I? Eliphaz thought to himself, keeping quiet. The others were shocked, and they became restless.

Job held them with his accusing eyes. "Can one of you tell me where I've sinned? Have I spoken anything but the truth?"

When he was rich, Job had never been embarrassed to fall to his knees in the middle of the marketplace to pray. He looked up at the sky now.

"God, watcher of men. What have I done to you? Why do you take such care of your children and yet make the night so long and dark? Without you a man will not awake with the dawn. Show me my sin."

Bildad spoke up, more impudently than the first friend. "This wind from your mouth, how long is it going to blow? God doesn't pervert justice. You said so, more often than anyone wants to count. Now you forget everything our fathers taught us. If you are upright and righteous, as we took you to be, your days will end in greatness. I see it now. Your mouth will be filled with laughter; your enemies will walk in shame. That's what you'd tell me if I were in your place."

These stinging words had their effect. Job's reply was muted. "Do you think I'm at war with God's judgment? He is wise; he knows all. If I argued against him, I might make one point when he makes a thousand."

Just as bitterly as he had cursed creation, Job lifted his face to praise it. "God moves mountains when no one sees it. He spreads out the heavens and makes the earth tremble. When he commands the sun, it must obey. He can hide the stars from sight and trample the waves of the sea. He performs marvels without number; he does great things beyond understanding." A pause. "God brings calamity to everyone. He destroys the blameless and the sinner alike. Is he mocking us? I am blameless, but I don't ask for myself. I loathe my life. I only want to understand this one thing."

"Then let me help you," said Zophar, the last friend. "You babble on as if words can save you. You say that you're pure and clean in God's eyes. But look at you. You writhe in filth. So you beseech God to tell you his innermost secrets, to open up the truth about your calamities. It's ridiculous. You can't fathom his wisdom, which is without limits. He passes by and knows the worthless man."

A smile came to Zophar's lips. "I don't care if you cringe at my words. I said I could help you. Put away your iniquity, however deep it is hidden. Stretch your hands out to God. Once he touches you, you will forget your misery. It will vanish like water dried up by the sun."

Job's reply was even more bitter than before. "In someone who enjoys his ease there is contempt for the misfortune of another. I see that I'm a laughingstock to my friends. But I'm not beneath you. Robbers sleep soundly at night in their caves, even as they provoke God. He turns judges into fools. He makes nations great and then smashes them into dust. How have you helped me understand any of this? Birds and beasts are born with the wisdom you think you are teaching. All creatures know that God made them and has power over them. My eye has seen all this, and I understand, better than you three. Man who is born of woman is given only a few days, and they are full of trouble."

To which Eliphaz replied coolly, "If you understand so much, then you already know why you are lost to the Lord."

"Don't ask us," added Bildad.

Or drag us down with you, thought Zophar, but he didn't speak, since he was the most superstitious and feared that Job might, somehow, rise again.

The group around Job thought that they were alone, but a voice behind them said, "You are all wrong."

Heads turned. No one had noticed an insignificant boy, brought along to carry the water jugs. During their discussion he had sat cross-legged a few yards away, waiting in case one of the friends signaled that he was thirsty. The boy, who was no more than sixteen, stood up.

"I'm young, and out of respect I would never speak up," he said.

"Then hold your tongue," Eliphaz snapped. "Who are you?"

"My name is Elihu, and I have no right to interfere. I know that you will send me to be whipped when we get home. But the Lord can speak through dumb animals, can't he?"

"Apparently," snapped Zophar.

Elihu ignored him. "He speaks through anyone who is touched by the spirit. So I bow to all of you, but I say you are wrong."

The youth gestured at Job's friends. "First, you three. You are wrong because you blame Job, and yet when he challenged you to find fault with him, you couldn't. That didn't stop you from judging him anyway. You see sin in his heart but none in your own, which makes you hypocrites."

The friends would have drawn their weapons and leapt upon the boy, but his voice sounded eerie, as if it didn't belong to him. They didn't want to stab him and release a demon, not when they were alone and defenseless in the desert.

Elihu turned to Job. "And you, you protest that you are blameless. You have obeyed the law and made burnt offerings to cleanse yourself and your sons. But even a blameless man doesn't dare to question God. The Lord has no need to justify his ways to men. He created us; we are his. The Lord's gaze extends to the end of eternity. He sees into you as you cannot see into yourself. In your arrogance you would hold God to your petty conception of good and evil, as if he is bound by his own laws. Yet there is only one thing you can know, as he has told us out of his own mouth: 'I am the Lord thy God.' There is no answer to that, and no question either."

Job's friends were shaken, not just by the rebuke they had received, but by the change in Job, who had stopped trembling. His stooped body was beginning to straighten. Tears flowed down his cheeks, and where a tear touched one of his seeping wounds, the pus turned to clear liquid.

While the trance was on Elihu—for it was clear that this simple youth, hardly better than a slave, was filled with the holy spirit—he began to unfold a strange tale. He could see into the next world, and he beheld God hurling into hell the disobedient angels. But even as they fell, God kept close beside him a counsel of evil. This Adversary, or Satan as he was named, spoke only evil, and therefore he had a kind of twisted wisdom about humans. He whispered their misdeeds and sins in God's ear. The transgressions of men were so numerous that the Adversary began to boast that he was the true ruler of the world.

God grew impatient and said, "Go and seek out my servant Job. He is upright and blameless. As long as there is one such as him, you will never prevail."

Satan gave a knowing smile. "There is no one who is perfectly devoted to you, or they would not have been born of woman," he said.

Then Satan flew over the face of the earth until he found Job, and just the act of setting eyes on him caused his crops to wither. The Adversary returned to heaven.

"Let me test this Job," he said.

A kind of wager was struck. God gave Satan a free hand to bring any calamity upon Job and inflict any pain, with one exception. He could not cause Job to die. God said, "The son of man might curse the day he was born, but he will never curse me."

"And so it befell you," murmured Elihu. "Your afflictions have been a test, not a sign of wickedness."

At that instant he blinked twice and looked around in confusion. The holy spirit had left him as suddenly as it had taken him. Job said nothing, but stared straight ahead. His breathing was steady now, and it seemed from his bewildered stare as if he were waking up from a dream. The three friends scrambled to their feet and scattered, resentful and bewildered. As much as they had accused him, one truth was undeniable. In all the words that had poured from Job's mouth, he had never once cursed God.

"I have not sinned," he murmured, turning his eyes on Elihu. "I had only forgotten."

"Forgotten what?" asked the youth, grateful not to be beaten. Returning to himself, he barely knew what he had been saying.

"I had forgotten the most important thing. God blesses his people."

The words were hard to make out, because Job had started to weep uncontrollably. His father had trusted the Lord more than he ever had. Then Job knew that Satan's greatest power was not that he could inflict evil. His greatest power was to make the sons of God forget who they were.

Afterward Job returned home, taking Elihu as his personal servant, and what had been blighted turned into a miracle. Job's wife bore him more sons and daughters. His gold was restored, his granary filled to overflowing. Yet as he became richer, Job became more reclusive. He rarely left his house, and when he did, he wore a prayer shawl and kept his face to the ground. People began to use him as a kind of walking moral: never question God, or you will be made to answer. Others took the opposite moral: keep faith with God, and he will reward you with glory and splendor.

What no one guessed was that Job had become a seeker. He had once believed in the wisdom passed down from Moses and the fathers. Now he believed in nothing and everything. The Lord had stopped his mouth, the better that he could open his eyes. What did Job see? A mystery. Something that flew before the wind and answered every question with an echo.

Revealing the Vision

In the evolution of God, the beginnings are ancestral. That's not the same as primitive. God is already advanced by the time we encounter Job, because every aspect of life in ancient Israel was centered on God. As long as there are laws, customs, and a shared identity, which are complicated things, God will be just as complicated.

The book of Job dramatizes God's voice with great intensity and high drama. It isn't a story you can read and walk away from. To use a modern phrase, the story is about bad things happening to good people. The virtuous Job suffers on a mythic scale, like Prometheus chained to a rock while an eagle plucks at his innards, but he also suffers in a very human way. The calamities are breathtaking and swift. Job's crops wither. His granaries become infested. His wife despairs as their precious sons die, Job contracts a grotesque disease, and his friends run away from the sight of him. If these afflictions visited a modern person, he would cry out, in the middle of the night, "Why me?" Job is about the human yearning to know why.

As we suffer alongside Job, we question alongside him. Even the oldest records give evidence that God was doubted. Various answers come from three friends, speaking one after another in ritualistic fashion. One answer: Job, you aren't as good as you pretend. You may have hidden your sins from the world, but you couldn't hide them from God, and now he's punishing you for it. Another answer: Job, you're good, but you're too proud. You think you have total control over your life, but now God is showing you that disaster can strike anywhere, anytime. Explaining why we suffer is a thread that runs throughout the Hebrew Bible, and it's why I couldn't begin with a prettier story about some loving God who smiles down upon our lives.

Whoever wrote the Hebrew Bible spent precious few pages on Eden. Paradise was lost almost before the paint dried. There is a beautiful passage about God walking in the Garden in the cool of the evening. Later on in the Old Testament love reappears, but it is mainly the love between men and women, as in the luxurious eroticism of the Song of Solomon:

> The song of songs, which is Solomon's.
> Let him kiss me with the kisses of his mouth:
>   for thy love is better than wine.
> Because of the savor of thy good ointments
>   thy name is as ointment poured forth,
>   therefore do the virgins love thee. (1:1–3)

Almost every culture has stories of beautiful gods that romp through the world as lovers, gleaming youths like Lord Krishna, who is amorous with hundreds of shepherd girls, or the more lascivious Zeus, who seduces in the shape of a bull, a shower of gold, and many other guises. In the West, the story is bleaker and more existential. Affliction and disaster are never far away, nor is God's harsh judgment.

Job's friends are a mystical three in number, like the three Fates and the three witches in *Macbeth*, because they speak from the unconscious. Or, to use another modern phrase, they speak from the shadow, the dark realm of the psyche where sin and punishment, shame and guilt, fear and vengeance are secreted away. Sometimes the shadow erupts, and then any kind of misery can ensue. The writers of the book of Job, who seem to be various, lived hundreds of years before Christ. The exact time isn't known, although scholars tend to agree that this is one of the latest books, perhaps the very last addition to the Hebrew Bible. Something very modern is going on, however, because life continues to erupt with inexplicable catastrophes, and guilt hovers even when events are external, random, and beyond our control.

The human mind can tolerate anything but meaninglessness, and nowhere in Job's tale, whether we are listening to his perspec-

tive ("I'm innocent") or his friends' ("No, you're not"), is affliction
ever considered random: "This is about you. Somehow you made
these terrible things happen."

Human life is balanced between believing these words and not
believing them. If you believe them, you will be driven to uncover
what you did that was wrong. A desperate cancer patient who is
haunted by the possibility that she "did this to herself" winds up
in Job's predicament. In later centuries, as God evolved in human
awareness, an escape was offered from the torment of self-accusation.
"I did this to myself" or "God must hate me" leads to healing, forgiveness, and proof of God's love.

But no such escape exists for Job. God speaks in adamant, absolute terms: "I am the Lord thy God." Job's virtue counts for
nothing if God wills it so. Divine punishment needs no reason.
After the fall of Adam and Eve in the Garden of Eden, life was
ordained to contain suffering. The Hebrew Bible ends with the
same fatalism with which it begins. In Genesis 3:14 Yahweh says:

> Cursed are you above all livestock
>   and all wild animals!
> You will crawl on your belly
>   and you will eat dust
>   all the days of your life.

Such a God wants to be feared. We deserve no better, and for
the rest of the Old Testament the mixture of good and evil in
human life is thoroughly examined, leaving out nothing: murder,
rape, incest, greed, pillage, lust, jealousy, the corruption of power.
Ever and always, life is perilously close to falling apart. To keep
the shadow in check, law enters the picture; rules organize every
moment of existence, not just with Ten Commandments, but
through the hundreds of daily duties outlined in Leviticus. Virtue
was a necessity if you wanted to keep a wrathful God at bay.

Until the book of Job. It dares to question this entire setup by veering into the unthinkable: virtue is no protection at all. The tale is framed by a wager between God and the Devil, in which the Devil boasts that he can lead any man·into renouncing God, and God accepts the wager by offering up the most virtuous person on earth. In and of itself, this cruel game is enough to destroy faith. Why would anyone pray to a God who offers no protection, but instead throws you to the Devil on a whim? At the very least Satan is made God's equal, since he has more than even odds that Job will fail. Which means that religion itself would fail, and thus the covenant between God and humankind—a contract guaranteeing that virtue is rewarded—would be rendered null and void.

Hindsight tells us this daring step was necessary. For God to evolve, he couldn't remain a punishing force to be continually feared, just as the psyche couldn't be a sinkhole of remorseless guilt. The book of Job breaks the eggs before the omelet can be made, because it turns obedience on its head. Job obeyed all of God's laws, yet his life blows up as if a bomb went off underneath it.

At a subtler level, Job's story explores how the good things in life might be connected to the bad things. One of the most profound truths in the world's spiritual traditions holds that the good in life cannot be meaningful unless the bad is also. Both teach us who we are, and with complete knowledge we can transcend the temptations of good and evil. The temptation of good is also known as the path of pleasure. That is, a person tries to seek as much pleasure as possible, since pleasure is good, while avoiding life's pain, which is bad.

The path of pleasure comes naturally, and yet the Old Testament is rife with disapproval of pleasure. Its excesses lead to the corruptions of Sodom and Gomorrah, the cities of the plain that were such dens of iniquity that God wiped them off the face of the earth. King David is the closest we come in the Bible to a hero, a poet, and an Adonis too, but he was fatally corrupted by pleasure, sending Bathsheba's husband to death on the battlefield so that he could enjoy her.

Dire warnings against the seduction of worldly pleasure are still with us, of course, but they don't amount to wisdom. The spiritual argument against the path of pleasure is blunt and unswerving: life can never be total pleasure. Pain is always mixed in, and if you want to solve the negative aspects of life—everything that is shoved away to fester in the darkness of the shadow—you must go beyond pleasure also.

Job's story doesn't enter that territory, however. It focuses on the temptations of Satan, who wants us to give in and let the worst side of human nature run free. In Hebrew the name Satan means "the Adversary," and in Job's story the arguments mounted against virtue are adversarial. Being good gets you nowhere. Whatever you are rewarded with can be snatched away in the blink of an eye. You can try being good to please God, but he couldn't care less. The world's wisdom traditions encompass the temptations of both good and evil in order to answer the Adversary. And the answer is that adversaries no longer exist when good stops warring against evil. The essence of God is eternal peace.

Here I am looking down the road. The theme of self-awareness, which is a connecting thread in the evolution of God, begins darkly, but lets in more light as time passes. The experience of bliss can be the purest one of all and therefore the closest to God. God hasn't evolved this far in the book of Job. He is recognizably a tough customer, watching and judging us all the time, prone to fickle whims and answerable to nobody except himself. At the very end an innocent youth named Elihu suddenly appears to resolve the argument between Job and his three friends. We reach a very unconvincing denouement. Having posed questions that threaten to sever the bond between the human and the divine, the story cuts off the debate with pat answers. The three friends are nailed for being hypocrites. Job is nailed for pride, as if God has to answer to him.

Elihu is basically returning the whole situation to square one: God does what God does, period. The framing device returns, as God speaks in his own voice to reassure us that Job passed the test. His virtue regains its rich rewards, with a bonus to compensate for all the trouble he went through. Satan is routed; the status quo is justified once more. In an age of faith, when the ultimate goal was always to make God right, no matter how horrible his behavior, this ending would have been more satisfying. To the child in all of us, there is a fairy-tale quality about it, a reassurance that good always prevails in the end just before we are tucked under our warm blankets to go to sleep.

From a modern perspective, it's much easier to skip the pat ending and read the book of Job for its existential realism. In doing that, we turn the writers' original intent on its head. Instead of being about God's authority, the story teaches us that suffering is both random and universal. Chaos nibbles at the edges of everyday existence. The shadow can erupt at any moment, bringing untold misery. More devastating than all of this, God is dismantled through doubt. Who can worship a deity of caprice? He's the same as chaos and randomness, but wearing a human mask as our eternal Father.

In reply, I would say, "There's more to come. We're not at the end yet." Still, a willful, punishing deity hasn't disappeared; every kind of God survives somewhere, taking root in our psyche. Religious fundamentalism, whether Christian, Islamic, or Hindu, depends on the same archaic elements, in which fear and sin dominate. But infinity cannot be circled and fenced in. Countless forms of the divine pour forth, and always will. Beyond the wrath of Yahweh, humans keep delving deeper to find the essence of love and to heal fear, which requires the clarity of self-knowledge.

There is a positive lesson in the book of Job, a reason to move forward. God challenges Job by saying, "Where were you when I created the world?" He is calling for surrender, and surrender is necessary on the path. The sin of pride is about the ego thinking that it has all the answers. Job learns that God is not answerable. God isn't a puzzle that can be cleverly figured out or a supersize human being sitting on a throne in the sky. Where God is, the ego cannot be. Everything that Job loses—wealth, social status, possessions, and a secure family—are irrelevant to the soul's journey. They are not wrong or bad, as we see when God restores them. By the end, Job sees that he is connected to God in a pure way, without having to gain or lose.

A long road unfolds beyond Job's story. He is a station along the way, and every station must be experienced before the traveler can move on. Otherwise, we are fated to repeat Job's predicament rather than solve it.

2

SOCRATES

"Know Thyself"

"What if I killed a man, Socrates, right now? Just supposing."

"Even a barbarian like you has limits."

"You think I'm joking. But what would happen to me? Look around us. Nobody's watching."

Two Athenians stood on the brow of a stony hill. Or should we call it a stone hill, because there were ten rocks for every stunted scrap of vegetation? The taller man, Alcibiades, was lean and restless. He shaded his eyes from the withering noon glare.

The shorter one, Socrates, crouched on his haunches to rest his legs. "You've made a mistake. Someone is always watching."

"Who, the gods? That's a joke."

"I do what I can to amuse you," said Socrates mildly.

"No one as ugly as you could be amusing." Alcibiades licked his dry lips and took a swig from a waterskin. "I'm not being callous. You always taught me to tell the truth, didn't you?"

The trek from Athens into the hills had been long. The two set out at dawn, but so far they had bagged only a rabbit, which Alcibiades had shot with his sling. He carried the flea-bitten desert rabbit in a bag flung over his shoulder. Socrates waved his hand when the waterskin was passed to him.

"I worry about you," he muttered.

Socrates had a gnarled, sun-baked body with a flat, snub-nosed face, like that of a satyr painted on the side of a vase. He was much older than his lean, tall friend, who could have been his son. "Do you know why?" he asked.

"Why what?"

"I worry about you."

Alcibiades wasn't listening. Down below, a trail wended its way through a narrow ravine. The dirt track barely squeezed between high walls of nubbly limestone worn into a cleft by an ancient stream that once flowed there. It didn't flow anymore. Phoebus Apollo had drunk it dry, or if you traffic in impiety, the sun had dried it up. When travelers wanted to pass through the cleft, their shoulders touched the walls on either side.

Alcibiades became animated. "If I was a bandit, that's where I'd hide. The perfect ambush." He pointed to a narrow ledge where two men could lie in wait. It was visible from above, but hidden from the sight of unsuspecting traders and farmers going to market down below.

"You *are* a bandit," said Socrates. "A proven stealer of hearts. You're ruthless."

Alcibiades smirked. "I have a right to my spoils. I'm a soldier for the state. Anyway, you've never given your heart to anyone, much less had it stolen. You pretend to love, but it's just a game."

"You play at your own game," said Socrates. "You act like you're immortal, and that game is fatal."

They bantered easily and quietly, in such a way that you knew after a while they couldn't be father and son. The younger one was too casual in his insolence, the older one too fond in his gruffness, the way that even a lenient father wouldn't be. Neither one had had a lenient father when they were boys, which may explain why they drew together. That or something more mysterious and probably unsavory. Malicious tongues in the city voiced their opinion on that score, but we will get to lechery later.

Suddenly Alcibiades took a running start down the hill, as if he had spotted some prey. "Forget all that. Follow me," he shouted.

The two men scrambled down the slope, heading for the narrow ledge. Alcibiades couldn't be argued out of it or distracted by banter. His blood was up. They would crouch in their hiding place as long as it took before a victim passed beneath them. Then Alcibiades would pounce. At that moment and only then would Socrates know if his companion was in a sporting mood or meant to do violence.

The going was steep and slippery. Dry twigs and scree scattered under their sandals. Their faces were matted with dust and sweat. Alcibiades, a trained runner, didn't look back to see if Socrates needed help. Wasn't the old man famous for his toughness? In his soldiering days, during the battle at Potidaea in the north, Socrates stood guard on a cold midnight wearing only a light cloak, yet without a shiver. He was already almost forty. On campaigns where every free male was expected to carry a shield, it was reported that he could stand in place all night, never once stamping his feet or rubbing his arms against the chill. Rabbits mistook him for a tree and nibbled the grass around his feet.

When he was younger and even more impudent, Alcibiades had asked him his secret. "Do you have thicker skin than the rest of us? Like a boar's hide?"

"I didn't move because I was thinking," Socrates replied.

"I think too," laughed the youth. "I think I'd be smart enough to keep warm."

"So I'm told. You mostly keep warm under a blanket with a girl whose name you only learn in the morning."

Which was true. Athens was filled at night with the shrill sound of the *aulos*, the twin pipes that wandering girls played as they went through the streets, signaling that they were available. Alcibiades was known to open his father's doors and let an *aulos* girl come in from the cold. Socrates, who was notoriously virtuous, regarded this behavior tolerantly.

He had fallen in the habit of fondness early on. People whispered about the old man and the headstrong boy, but Alcibiades was proud to be the prize that every glance ran after. At banquets the guests lay on couches that held three bodies side by side. Alcibiades mocked Socrates for always being in the middle, with the handsomest youths on his left and right.

"How can you blame me?" Socrates would protest mildly. "Isn't one of them pushed off the couch when you appear? Usually stinking drunk."

To have the gift of beauty is like being absurdly rich. You can afford to be careless about how you affect others. Alcibiades was careless about those who loved him. He was careless in most things, actually, and reckless in the rest. The one exception, the thing he took seriously, was the army. When his choleric father beat him with a stick, the boy bent his back, covering his head to protect himself. He told himself that it was good training if he was ever captured someday and tortured by Spartans. *Hate, but keep silent.* At fifteen, he already knew how.

When they got to the shady ledge a veil of coolness fell over them. The narrow waist of the ravine was just below them; the place was silent except for nesting wrens who fussed at the two intruders. A brown mother wren circled their heads, her wings clipping the air in sharp, swift bursts.

"Feel," said Socrates, who was the first to crouch down.

Alcibiades touched the loose dirt around his feet. "It's damp." He pointed to whitened streaks on the rock face behind them where water trickled silently in a pale glistening ribbon.

Socrates shook his head. "Someone's been here first." His voice had turned sober.

"How do you know?" Alcibiades felt his ankle being grabbed by Socrates's darting hand.

"Don't move. You'll crush it," whispered Socrates.

Did he mean a snake? Prized for healing, small snakes sought the cool at noon, especially in this place dripping with water.

Socrates loosened his grip. It was taking a moment for the younger man's sight to clear after staring so long into the sun. He glanced around.

"What?"

"This."

Socrates brushed his fingers over a sprig growing out of a crack in the ledge. A sacred myrtle, its leaves shiny and pale. One touch was enough to release its luscious scent. Alcibiades had been close enough to girls who wore it; myrtle fragrance made you favored by Aphrodite. Alcibiades liked such girls, for more than being sacred.

"You said you could think," Socrates grumbled, pulling him from his daydream. "Try, now."

At twenty-five, Alcibiades had grown past the age of being Socrates's pupil, and there had never been a real school, with a roof and wax writing tablets. But he recognized a schoolmaster's barked command. Looking closer, however, he saw nothing out of the ordinary.

Socrates was disappointed, but he didn't say so. Love made him foolish. He would be stung if Alcibiades grew cross with him, seriously angry rather than playing at it, and nothing riled the handsome soldier more than wounded vanity. In a level voice Socrates explained. "Myrtle can't grow in the shade. It would wither and die. Someone has made it grow in the dark."

"How?"

"Magic. How else?"

Alcibiades shrugged, and Socrates said, "How else? That's a serious question. If you don't believe in magic, how did this sprig grow here? Perhaps the gods wanted it to. If so, they may have left it for us as a sign."

"What kind of sign?"

"An omen."

Socrates casually plucked the sprouting myrtle out by the root and tucked it behind his ear. "Your charade is dangerous. Travelers are on the lookout for bandits. The tough ones fight back."

Alcibiades frowned. Like most soldiers, he kept his courage intact by imagining that he would never be hurt. "I don't heed omens."

"Why? Because you're never afraid? You should be. Life is a walk to the edge of a cliff. Every day we get a step nearer, and what lies over the brink, no one can tell."

This turn in the conversation was making Alcibiades irritated. He drew his knife and began to sharpen it with scraping swipes against the stone wall. He might as well gut and skin the rabbit while they waited, to make sure it didn't spoil in the heat.

Socrates went on. "I was taught to read omens. I had the greatest teacher, back when I was so ignorant that I am still ashamed of it. But I don't speak of her."

"Her?"

"She was called Diotima, and if the gods didn't leave this omen, she did."

Alcibiades couldn't hide his amazement. "So you think this Diotima knew that I might be hurt today?"

"Or worse. Would you like to read omens? It's not hard once you learn to see."

Alcibiades had forgotten the rabbit by now. He squinted his eyes narrowly. "No one can understand you. Half the time you say the opposite of what you know is the truth. You're tricky, and you're proud. But you pretend to be ordinary," he said.

"That's because I am ordinary. I believe in the gods, like all ordinary people. "

"See? That's what I mean about saying the opposite of the truth."

If Alcibiades had forgotten about the ungutted animal in his sack, Socrates hadn't. He pulled it out. In death the creature looked like a limp gray rag.

"Is this the truth?" said Socrates. "Are we like rabbits? We bleed. We can be struck down. So why not call us animals and kill us for sport?"

"Because we're human."

"What does that mean?"

"I'm sure you'll tell me."

The peculiar thing about Socrates was that banter always led this way, into deep waters. "What makes us human," he said, "is that we think about the gods and they think about us. You laugh, but that is what Diotima taught me. The gods are here."

"Right this minute?"

"Yes."

"You're right, you are ordinary," Alcibiades mocked. "If the gods are here, I want to see Aphrodite's breasts."

Socrates ignored his jibe. "What do you see when you look around? The world as it is. Rocks, a narrow trail, a dead rabbit. But such a world is without purpose. Life and death dance with each other, gripped tightly together. Neither is willing to let go, and so the dance never stops. Animals accept this reality. Humans fight against it."

"Am I allowed to say something?" asked Alcibiades. "Rocks are hard. The trail is dusty. The rabbit will never feed its tender young again. I'm glad I see the world as it is, not as it should be."

"So you don't mind being an animal?" asked Socrates.

"Not if I'm the one that survives."

Socrates looked grave. "The omen is darker than I told you. If I read it right, it says that you will die violently. Not today, but one day. Your widow will bend her face to the ground with tears, but half of Athens will rejoice that you are gone. "

The contours of the young man's face sagged. "Why are you saying such horrible things to me? You should spare a friend, the way a doctor spares a patient who doesn't know he's dying."

Socrates gave his young companion a sharp look. "We are all patients who want to be told that we aren't dying. The truth is different."

Their talk had been so intense that neither heard the sound of horses' hooves until it was directly below them. Suddenly the noise caught their attention. Alcibiades's body tensed. Getting on hands and knees, he peered over the ledge. A rickety wagon was passing beneath, loaded with straw baskets. The air was heavy with the oily smell of olives. The wagon's driver didn't look up.

"Here's your sport. Go ahead, jump," whispered Socrates in Alcibiades's ear.

"It's just a boy."

"All the better. You'll probably win."

Crouching there, they could see that the wagon driver was no more than twelve, a farm boy in a wide-brimmed straw hat. It was all he could do to handle the old mare pulling the wagon, who was spooked by the narrow passage and the ringing of her own hoofbeats. After a moment they were through the waist of the ravine and the noise faded away.

"I restrained myself," said Alcibiades sourly. "The way you provoked me, I could have done something stupid just then."

"Really? Do you enjoy deluding yourself?" asked Socrates. "You've killed Spartans in battle, and one time you went mad. You let your hatred consume you and hacked off their limbs. In your bloodlust you condemned the enemy to go to the afterlife defiled. Now their shades want revenge."

"To hell with your omens. I fought for Athens. I killed as an act of honor." Alcibiades's temper gave way to worry. "How will I know which shades to appease?" he asked.

"Wait and ask them. They'll be lined up after you die."

Alcibiades bit his lip as he shoved his knife back into the sheath he wore at his waist. He looked overhead, squinting. The sun was past the zenith, showing like a brilliant bead against the rim of the rock slope. For today, the game was spoiled. Socrates was already inching upslope, retracing the way they had come. Alcibiades grunted and tossed the dead rabbit into the ravine for spite before following. They arrived back in Athens after sunset. Socrates had started to whistle. Alcibiades remained downcast. It wasn't dark, but the *aulos* girls were already piping. The shrill sound scraped against his nerves, but it aroused him too. He licked his lips to say something when Socrates interrupted.

"I could never teach you to read omens. You care too much about staying alive. I'm going home."

On the way back to town Alcibiades had felt his blood subside, but now it sprang up again, the way a dead-looking coal in the ashes, when poked, comes back to life.

"That's right, go home. You probably still have enough teeth to eat your dinner." There was a mirror in his mind, in which Alcibiades could see how ridiculous the squat old man looked beside his own dazzling Apollo-like figure. "Terrify me and then run away," he muttered under his breath.

Socrates peered over his shoulder. "Forget today. I will come back to you when you're calm," he said as the shadows swallowed him up.

The next morning Socrates wandered through the agora, the town marketplace, pinching an apple at one stall, sniffing the freshly slaughtered lamb hanging at another. He would talk to anyone, rich or poor. Nobody could predict what would come out of his mouth, but a band of youths were in the habit of following him, including Alcibiades, the wildest of them. They were eager to see whose unwary ego he would puncture. If Socrates ran into somebody of importance, that person did well to turn his back. It was dangerous even to say hello. Limping away from an argument, which always began as an innocent conversation, his opponents smarted. They had been bitten by words like horseflies that could make the skin bleed.

But none of them knew who Socrates really was. He often felt that he himself barely knew. He was forever watching himself from the inside, whereas everyone else only saw him from the outside, a strangely cheerful, curious, squat, penniless, henpecked curiosity. Some called this curiosity harmless, but others kept a sharper eye out and considered him a threat.

"You are a teacher of misery," said Antiphon, a rival teacher, a few months ago, publicly accusing Socrates. "You set yourself up as wise, but look at you. You don't work. God knows how you get any food. You wear the same cloak summer and winter. I've never seen you in a new pair of sandals or a decent tunic."

Antiphon had cornered Socrates near a temple on the Acropolis, speaking in a loud voice to attract attention. A small crowd of townsfolk lingered, wondering how Socrates would reply.

"Go on, Antiphon," murmured Socrates. "You describe me very well. If I can't be admired, at least I can be noticed, and by someone as esteemed as you."

"Am I esteemed?" asked Antiphon suspiciously, cutting him off.

"Of course. Ask anyone here. Ask yourself."

Some bystanders chuckled, but Antiphon refused to be distracted. He said, "Where does your mockery lead, but to more misery? Your pupils have learned to sneer at convention. They are lazy and impudent, and because they imitate their teacher, they will turn out just like you, mired in poverty. Do you deny that money makes life easier? It is far better than starving. In the end your followers will wake up to their miserable existence, but by then it will be too late."

"Well argued," said Socrates, who never raised his voice. "But unfortunately, you have proved the opposite of the case you were trying to make. I would show you, but since you claim to teach wisdom, I would be like a cobbler stealing a shoe from another cobbler. With one shoe each, neither of us would profit."

The tips of Antiphon's ears turned scarlet. He was one of a new class of wandering teachers known as Sophists, who did claim to teach wisdom, as Socrates said. Athens was divided about believing this claim.

"Not a cobbler, Socrates. You're more like a crab," Antiphon snapped. "A crab scuttles sideways to escape, just as you're trying to do now."

Socrates shrugged. "I only wanted to protect your reputation, dear Antiphon, but you are that strange thing, a defendant in court who insists upon being found guilty after the jury has just pronounced him innocent."

"Show me my guilt," said the Sophist aggressively.

Socrates paused a moment. "First, you are guilty of bad faith. You have no interest in what I teach. You've accosted me to make a public spectacle, in the hope that you can attract some of my pupils to yourself after they see me humiliated.

"Second, you are guilty of false reasoning. It's true that I am poor, that my food is meager, and I wear the same cloak every season. But I am happy, or at least that is what everyone tells me. Where does my happiness come from? Not from pleasure, because by your own accusation I lack the money by which men run after pleasure. Therefore, my pupils will see that money has nothing to do with happiness. So which example should they follow? Yours, which dwells on superficialities, or mine, which may lead them to the secret source of the truth?"

Antiphon abruptly turned on his heels, followed by the crowd's jeers. That was a typical encounter, of the kind that sharply divided Athens between champions of Socrates and those who wished him harm. But on this particular day he came very early to the agora and talked to no one. He was troubled by what had happened with Alcibiades. Like a cat to milk, the handsome soldier would be back, but it would turn out the same way it always did. He would be ashamed for his wildness and his lack of self-control. He would even shed tears. Yet within a few days he would go back to being Alcibiades.

And the dark omen? Socrates genuinely believed that the gods had caused the myrtle sprig to appear, or else that Diotima had left it there. He put nothing past her. Watching the farmers set up their stalls, Socrates saw her once again as he had first seen her twenty years ago, with a wild tangle of black hair and heavy eye-brows. She wore a ragged shift and no sandals. She looked like a child raised by wolves. Very little about Diotima was becoming, and this had appealed to Socrates, because very little about him was becoming either.

He was a young man working the family trade. "Can you carve me a statue?" asked Diotima, blurting out the words without introducing herself. "Or are you a statue yourself? In which case I apologize for bothering you."

Socrates faced her, covered in white marble dust. He blended in with the stone he cut. "I'm a mason, like my father," he said. "But I carve statues too. What kind do you want?"

"What kind do you make?" she asked.

"Only what you see," replied Socrates, turning away. He was surrounded by small gods and goddesses to be sold in the shops all around the base of the Acropolis.

"That's a shame. I wanted the invisible kind," said Diotima.

"Invisible? They're the easiest to make. You can do it yourself."

It was a hot day, and Socrates, bare-chested except for his thick leather mason's apron, was ready to take a break in the shade. He threw down his chisel and wiped his brow with a rag.

Diotima shook her head. "You're wrong. Invisible statues are the hardest to make," she said.

"And why is that?"

Diotima took up a small statue, a crude image of Athena with helmet and shield, turning it in her hand. "The point of all these statues is to show the likeness of divinity," she said. "Otherwise they would just be ordinary mortals. How can the divine be carved? Divinity is invisible, so any true statue of the gods must also be invisible."

Socrates didn't know how to respond. What the wild woman said made sense, and yet it confused him at the same time.

"You look bewildered," she remarked. "Good. There's a chance I may outwit your ignorance."

Socrates had a rough scrap of bread, some salt, and olive oil, which he had brought for his lunch. He sat under a tree and broke the bread, offering to share it with Diotima. Anyone could see that she hadn't eaten recently.

"Can you teach me to carve a god's likeness, then?" Socrates asked, not that he took her seriously, but his curiosity was aroused.

"I'm not a carver," said Diotima. "But I can teach you to see the invisible, and then you can decide on your own what to do." She looked at him out of deep, knowing eyes. "Beware, though. Once you see what I have to show you, you'll throw away your chisels and hammers."

Socrates laughed. "Why?"

"Because the outer form of the gods is worthless, once you've viewed their reality." Diotima gave a wry smile. "I really should warn your wife."

"So the wisdom you teach destroys marriages," said Socrates. "Mine is hobbled already. My wife and I are so lame that neither of us can make it out the door to leave." Socrates was a butt of jokes for marrying Xanthippe, a notorious shrew.

Diotima said, "Ah, you are clever, and ugly too. No wonder your wife complains."

Homely as she was, Diotima was a seducer of souls. They returned to the stonemason's site, and as Socrates chipped away, she sat in the shade talking. Her hair never grew tame; she didn't appear to have a change of clothes. At first he felt sorry for her, but it was obvious that he couldn't bring her home. The best he could do was to take two pieces of bread instead of one and tell Xanthippe it must be rats stealing into the larder.

A typical lesson from Diotima minced no words. "You are no more blind and ignorant than other men," she would begin. "You are ruled by appetite. You envy those who get more pleasure than you can get. But there are moments when you catch yourself, and then you are ashamed of your lusts."

"Is that what puts me above my cat, shame? Then it must be better to be a cat, which doesn't have enough imagination to inflict suffering on itself."

Diotima laughed briefly. "Don't try and compete with me. Just listen. Ours is the shame of a rational creature who can look at its own image and wish to be better."

"But drunks wake up with remorse in the morning and skulk back to the taverns when night falls."

So it went between them, the stonemason and the wandering lost woman. Each day Diotima dropped another hint about the mystery that hid behind veils. People eavesdropped on these lessons; people also gossiped. It was said by a neighbor that Xanthippe met Socrates at the door with a heavy stick—or anything that made a handy weapon—gripped in her fist. Yet for all the misery she inflicted, Socrates found himself growing happier, and at unpredictable moments he was strangely ecstatic.

Even so, these moods came and went. He found it hard to let go of his fatalism. "When the gods gave us reason, they forgot to make us perfect. It's all their fault. A potter chooses to make the best pot he can, because everyone knows that a leaky pot is worthless. But every human has a leaky soul. I'll rail at Zeus about this when I run into him."

"Don't play at blasphemy," snapped Diotima. "It's worse than turning into a Sophist, if that's possible." This was one of the few times Socrates ever saw her genuinely angry.

She cooled down as quickly as she had flared up, and a new humor overtook her—sorrow. "Most men are condemned, as you can see. But it's a strange prison that holds them, because each inmate has been handed the key to his cell. We get the key when we're born, and we could escape anytime we chose."

"Then why don't we?"

"Because our jailer is the mind, and a fiercer one never existed. Even if the cell door were flung wide open tomorrow, the prisoner would consider it some kind of trick and remain slumped on the floor of his cell, bemoaning cruel fate."

Diotima gave a faint smile. After making provocative statements she always fell silent, leaving the mystery hanging in midair. It was part of her seduction, because she knew, as every tease does, to unveil her treasure slowly. She might disappear for a day or two, yet when she returned, her argument picked up at the exact point where it left off.

"Fate is not cruel, however. It seems merciless only when you allow it to catch you, like a shepherd who refuses to run from a wolf and winds up between its jaws. If men weren't so ignorant, they would see that the gods want only our happiness. That is why humans began to worship in the first place, out of gratitude."

"Or fear," Socrates interrupted.

She shook her head. "Fear isn't worship. Fear arises when you believe that the gods are gone. An absent god can be malicious or vengeful. He could be the hidden reason your crops failed or your house burned down. Anything is possible when humans are no longer connected to the gods."

Socrates replied, "I could argue the opposite. The gods are amused by our ruin. They watch us murder and go to war, but do nothing to stop us. How can you claim that they want our happiness? Where's the proof?"

By this point Socrates would be so immersed in conversation with Diotima that his tools were lying useless on the ground. He didn't notice the glances of passersby, who had already begun to whisper that Socrates was forgetting how to work.

"It can't be proven that the gods want us to be happy," said Diotima.

"But you just said—"

She seized his hand to make him stop talking. Her clasp was warm and weathered, like the hand of someone destined never to live under a roof. "Listen closely. The gods are here, walking beside us. Our ancestors saw them. Pallas Athena rode in the same chariot with Achilles at Troy. They were blessed, our ancestors, but we are more blessed. The gods no longer cradle us like nursemaids with a drooling infant. They have freed us, so that we can know ourselves. Without that knowledge, life is meaningless."

How could anyone not be seduced by such talk? Socrates felt giddy, as if her words were strong wine. Diotima noticed. "You're trembling like a baby, but I won't hold you to my breast. It's a rather withered breast, as you can see. Take hope. There's more to say."

She got up and went away. Only then did Socrates notice how late the hour was. The last light was fading, and he had no new statues to sell. That meant no money to take home, which meant that Xanthippe would be in a foul mood. These things mattered, and yet in some part of him they didn't amount to anything.

Although at the end of their last meeting Socrates had promised to catch up with Alcibiades when his friend was calmer, he didn't get the chance. Hotheaded, always running after lovers, after glory or after shame, Alcibiades was rarely calm. But that wasn't the reason. Socrates didn't come to Alcibiades, because Alcibiades came to him first. He pounded on the door of his house, which stood in the worst quarter of the city, where the springs had become foul and the women had to trudge a long way to fill their clay jugs. Alcibiades knocked again. He was fearless, but he hoped that Xanthippe wouldn't answer it, or if she did, he hoped she would not be holding anything she could swing.

Still there was no sound of anyone answering the door. Alcibiades raised his hand to knock again, then thought better of it.

"Did a secret voice tell you not to?"

He whirled around to face Socrates, who had quietly come up behind him. "I have a voice like that. It tells me when I am about to do wrong." He was dangling the thread of an innocent conversation, but Alcibiades didn't take the bait.

"There's a war. You haven't heard?"

Socrates didn't reply. He looked away toward the sea, even though the sea was out of sight.

"I have to sail on the first tide," said Alcibiades. "But I wanted to ask you. Is this when I die? You said it would be violent. Will I never see Athens again?"

"How should I know?"

"What about your voice—won't it tell you?"

Socrates held out his hands like a thief giving proof that he hasn't snatched gold trinkets from a stall. "It decides when to come, not me."

Alcibiades stared at the ground, not wanting to show that hope was deserting him.

"Stay home," said Socrates mildly. "There's always a reason."

"I can't stay. My debts, my women. I just thought that you—" Alcibiades stopped short. "Never mind. I'm not myself. Come, let's get drunk."

He pointed toward the closest tavern, but when Socrates didn't follow, he turned around. "If you love me, old man, allow me an hour. Use your philosophy and make me forget this damned war."

"All right, but we have to go where I want to."

Alcibiades nodded. Socrates led the way uphill, toward the Acropolis. They walked in silence, sharing the same thought. They both knew the real reason why Alcibiades loved Socrates. The gossip about lechery was wrong, yet a pact of love was sealed between them. There had been a day, seven years before, when Alcibiades burned to prove himself a warrior. He was an aristocrat, which bought him an officer's cloak.

The fighting in this battle broke out near the city of Potidaea, one of a string of battles that had no end in sight. The delusion of empire inflamed Athens, and the price was constant war with rebel cities. No longer a beardless youth, Alcibiades had reached his full height; he was strong enough to stand in front of a phalanx of hoplites, citizen-soldiers armed with spear and shield.

That day morale ran high. Athens was thirsty for victory, and the enemy had been starved by a long blockade from the coast. But Alcibiades couldn't stand to wait, and when he saw the first sign of the enemy, mere specks on a clear horizon, he broke ranks and ran at them furiously, not looking to see how many of his men followed. No one followed. The lowest plebe knew how green he was.

Ignoring this, Alcibiades closed fast on the enemy, and if he sensed that he was alone, he didn't flinch. *Hate, but keep silent.* When he was close enough, he cocked his arm and flung his spear at a startled foot soldier among the enemy, who couldn't believe that a lone officer was dashing toward him across open ground. The spear soared and came to earth, hitting the ground twenty feet short. It quivered as it stuck in the dirt. The enemy soldier was almost amused.

"Take your spear back home," he shouted. "Your father wants to teach you to shave."

Alcibiades could have retreated with honor after this futile gesture, but instead he drew a short sword and swung it around his head, shouting for blood as he charged.

There were two of the enemy in front of him, but they weren't armed to fight. They were advance scouts sent to count the number of Athenians arrayed over the hill. Both drew their small knives, looking at each other nervously. A madman was charging at them, but at least they outnumbered him, and the first clash of weapons would draw some of their comrades, who were crouching over the rise behind them.

A scrawny copse of trees stood to the left, and all at once a man strode out of it, an older Athenian. The enemy scouts stopped in their tracks, startled, and Alcibiades, who wasn't as crazed as he acted, slowed down.

"Go back," the older Athenian said gruffly. His voice was low and steady. The enemy hesitated. It wasn't clear who the intruder was addressing.

The older Athenian brandished his sword. "I am the only one here who has fought hand to hand. This youth"—he nodded at Alcibiades—"thinks that blood is a medicine for fear. It isn't. So take my advice. Return to your ranks." He looked directly at the enemy scouts, who, when seen up close, were no older than Alcibiades. "Tell your comrades you're lucky to be alive. You met one Athenian who isn't afraid to die and another who wishes he wasn't."

Something in the man's presence convinced them. The two scouts saluted with a bow, as if they had just had a conversation about crops or women, and retreated without shouting for support.

The whole thing had the potential for comedy, but Alcibiades was trembling with rage.

"You had no right!" he shouted.

"To save you? I apologize," said Socrates. "I fight for life. In your eyes that must be a crime."

"Cowardice is a crime. That much I know." Alcibiades gestured over his shoulder. "My men are watching. What will they say?"

Socrates began to walk back toward the Athenian line. "It won't matter. They were never your men." He turned and gazed at Alcibiades. "Do something to make them yours. That's what I just did."

This pact is what made Alcibiades his. The battle went to Athens that day, and Alcibiades proved himself a reckless killer. The troops cheered. And why not? They had witnessed the ridiculous valor of Alcibiades. Instead of laughing, it was better to respect him. During the victory celebrations, Socrates pulled Alcibiades aside before he was too drunk to listen.

He said, "You owe me nothing, except to think about this day. You've tried to become an animal, and for that you will be called great. But I am ashamed of you."

Now, as they reached the top of the Acropolis, Socrates found a block of rough-hewn marble to sit on. He liked being reminded of his old profession.

"It doesn't matter if you march off and die in battle," he said. Alcibiades could have protested that it mattered to him, but he didn't. He was gloomy enough to seize any consolation. Socrates went on.

"War doesn't simply break out today or tomorrow. Being divided, humans are constantly at war inside. Even the most contented and calm-looking are pretending, or else they are deluding themselves. Fear and anger, hopelessness and despair are the enemies in the mind. What is to be done? This war inside is a sickness. The cure is obvious even though few seek it. End the division that creates joy one day and sorrow the next."

If this was a tactic to calm Alcibiades down, it worked. He fell into a musing mood.

"Maybe we were created to be at war," he said. "Death is my fate. If you can't live with dying, you are not really living." Like many people who ask for comfort, he argued to defend his own misery.

Socrates replied, "You are saying that you cannot cure yourself, any more than a man who has passed out with fever can prescribe his own medicine. But that's not the reality."

Against his will, Alcibiades heard bones crunch, the sickening sound when a sword penetrates the enemy's chest. "Don't tell me that suffering isn't real. You can trick me with words, but not about that."

Socrates shook his head. "Reality doesn't trick anyone. Illusion does nothing else." He paused. "We may never meet again, and you are afraid."

"It doesn't help to tell me," growled Alcibiades.

"We may never meet again," Socrates repeated, "so listen. I have seen who you really are, as no one else in the world has. Who you really are is shy, like a maiden afraid to leave her father's house. I can't show her to you directly. She can only be glimpsed with a sideward glance. Unless you are fortunate, she will evade you your entire life."

He regarded his young friend. "I will never lose you even if you lose yourself. You plaster a layer of pleasure over your pain, the same way a lazy builder thinly covers a wall to hide that it's cracked and ready to fall down."

Alcibiades moaned. "Stop, just this once." He turned to go. "Now, of all moments," he murmured resentfully.

The Sophists weren't entirely wrong about how Socrates's students had become infected.

Socrates rose from the marble block with a shrug. "Let's go pray. All this banter has made me forget the gods. One must never do that. Forgetting is very dangerous."

"You go. I won't pray to our fickle gods. Sacrifice a grain of wheat or an ox, it doesn't matter. They still let us die like flies on a sticky honeycomb," grumbled Alcibiades.

Socrates pointed to a dozen temples on the rocky brow of the Acropolis. "I once thought the gods lived there, which is as futile as your thinking that they don't. To be divine, a god must be everywhere. Which means that the gods are here, right beside us. When you know that, they will never desert you."

"How did you learn all this?" asked Alcibiades. It was hard to tell whether he was humbled or just resigned. His debts, his women. He had no choice but to go to war, where Socrates didn't matter a fig.

"What I tell you comes from my lips, but not from me," replied Socrates quietly. "I say what my *daemon* would have me say." This was Socrates's name for his inner voice.

"So you are possessed," said Alcibiades wryly.

"Yes, like the madwoman who misled me."

They didn't linger long on the holy mount. Alcibiades embraced his teacher and whispered in his ear, "Don't hate me. You've shown me the image of wisdom. I would rather die than forget it."

They both knew he only half meant it. Alcibiades galloped down the hill, not looking back at Socrates or the Acropolis. A soldier knows what to do the night before he sails. Debauchery can be as good as philosophy. Not everyone is blessed to be ugly and a nobody.

Much evil news would follow, but Socrates ignored it. As tenderly as he loved Alcibiades, he loved the mystery more. He continued to try and outwit ignorance with words. It was the only way to give a glimpse, in a fleeting second, of the divine.

Everyone knows how Athens repaid Socrates. He was tried on a charge of promoting false gods and corrupting the city's youth. Five hundred jurors sat for the trial, and the verdict was "guilty" by four or five votes. After his sentence was handed down, the condemned man sat up all night with a cup of hemlock by his side, chatting cheerfully with his friends, even though death was at his elbow. They wept. They begged him to escape; a boat was ready for him in the harbor. But Socrates was completely indifferent. It was as if he wasn't going to die, or never could. Once he drank the poison cup, he was ready to solve the last riddle.

What about glamorous Alcibiades? The peculiar thing about omens is that they never do any good, but they never wear off either. Alcibiades threw himself into everything. He spoke at the assembly, and listeners compared his silver tongue to that of Pericles. He led military expeditions and killed more Spartans, and when an expedition to Sicily turned into a fiasco, he took a ship by dead of night and joined the Spartans. He tried the same double game with the Persians, and whether it was beauty, courage, recklessness, or cunning that kept him alive, Alcibiades proved something. Omens can be beaten. Doom loses to the fastest runner.

Until the day it happened. He stayed among the Persians, who were masters of luxury beyond anything dreamed of in Greece. One afternoon Alcibiades strolled out of his house to walk off a hangover; even with his temples throbbing, he could hardly remember the air smelling sweeter. He closed his eyes to inhale more deeply and thus missed his attackers. They sprang on him with knives, and five minutes later he was a corpse from which flowed a surprising amount of blood. The dry ground thirstily drank it up. When his body was returned to Athens for burial, the widow of Alcibiades followed it in long veils with her face to the ground, hardly able to see her feet for the tears in her eyes, while half of Athens rejoiced that he was gone.

Revealing the Vision

Ancient Greece seems irrelevant, with its many gods and goddesses, if you accept that monotheism stands for progress. Socrates lived at least five hundred years after the book of Job was written. From a Judeo-Christian perspective, anything that he has to say reveals much about philosophy, but almost nothing about religion.

But no one could be more relevant than Socrates if you change the lens. If God is about our own awareness, then "Know thyself" has huge religious implications. In Athens during the life of Socrates, despotism was a constant threat, and since despots tend to be reactionaries, religion was used to keep people in line. Obedience, superstition, and fear are powerful political tools. In that regard, we are the children of Socrates, but also of his enemies. This sounds impossible, since it's like sympathizing with the executioner *and* his victim. But consider what each side stood for.

When they condemned Socrates to death, the reactionary forces in Athens wanted to defend the gods and keep young people from being corrupted—in this case, "corruption" is a code word for having opinions that challenge the status quo. Socrates stood for the opposite, questioning all received opinions and authority (hence the label that most people remember when they think about Socrates, a gadfly).

What remains so astonishing about the trial of Socrates, nearly twenty-five hundred years later, is that anyone cared. When was the last time a philosopher endangered the public welfare? Or when the definition of truth was a matter of life and death? Reading the dialogues set down by Plato, in which Socrates is always the best, wisest thinker and the most fascinating character, nobody sits on the sidelines. Soldiers, gadabouts, solid citizens, professional philosophers, and privileged youth all have their say about truth. A special case is the charismatic, but treacherous Alcibiades; we'll get to him later.

It doesn't matter whether Socrates spoke of God or the gods. He was interested in the divine. Why? Because he believed that creation had a divine origin, and therefore so did humans. But there was a journey to take before a person could experience this truth personally. If you think of Socrates as only the brave martyr who drank a cup of hemlock, you are missing the big questions we cannot escape: Who am I? What is the purpose of life? Is there supreme truth? To these questions Socrates gave answers that mystify people, then and now, because "Know thyself" is short-changed, turning into mild advice from a psychologist rather than a life-and-death command to transform ourselves. Socrates didn't mean know that you have a hot temper, like to eat too much, or want to get ahead in the world. The "self" in "Know thyself" was not the everyday ego personality with its hopes, fears, drives, and desires. Socrates refused to neatly define the self he had in mind, just as Buddha refused to use a word like "God."

Their reasons were the same: it defeats truth to use words, since words imply that you know what you are looking for. Instead, truth is an experience. It cannot be anticipated, any more than one can anticipate, at age five, what it will feel like to go to college, get married, and have children. Experience is fresh and new (or should be); thus truth is fresh and new. From there, it's a small step to demanding that God be fresh and new. More than anything else, such an open-ended approach to the truth showed Socrates the way to his trial and execution.

The authorities were right to be afraid of him. As a teacher, Socrates taught his pupils to question everything, but that by itself wasn't treasonous. Intellectual freedom, as we would dub it, was a small part of the Socratic method. To grasp how truly dangerous Socrates was, you have to go back to Diotima and a revolution in the unfolding of God (in translation, we find Socrates speaking of God and the gods fairly equally). Every society co-opts God to bolster the status quo. Good people go to church (or make sacrifices at the temple of Athena), obey the rules, fear divine punishment, worry about the afterlife, feel patriotic, and go to war to defend their country. God supports these activities, and so did the Greek gods.

Diotima, who gets credit from Socrates for being his teacher and much wiser than he, stands for a different perspective, one that is far more radical. She saw the entire world as a mystery, and delving into the mystery meant overturning the very notion of truth. What is true? In Athens during the fifth century BCE, the truth was a set of ideas that could be taught, and the better you mastered these ideas, the wiser you were. A school of teachers known as Sophists (taking their name from *sophia*, the Greek word for "wisdom") collected the best ideas and passed them on.

It was insulting to them when Socrates exposed their methods as empty and misguided; as a class, the Sophists are portrayed as self-deluded, if not vain, fools. Plato is our source for everything we know about Socrates, essentially, and his low opinion of them serves as a foil for the total integrity of Socrates, who feared nothing, either as a soldier when he fought for Athens or in the face of death, when he refused all offers to help him run away after the court's guilty verdict.

Socrates was a kind of archseducer. He aimed to make truth so seductive that it overtook the mind, purified it of all false beliefs, and ignited a lifelong hunger for a higher reality. For Socrates, truth and reality were the same. They were like a brilliant light compared to ordinary reality, which was like watching shadows playing on the walls of a cave. If you face one way, you are captivated by the shadow play; if you turn around, you are dazzled by the light.

This position is known as idealism, and we are the children of it, just as we are the children of the practical, hardheaded realism that Socrates was accused of subverting. Ideals, also known as Platonic forms, are the essence of everyday experience. The ideal of beauty is perfect and transcendent; because it exists, we see flowers, children, and our lovers as beautiful. The ideal filters down into the ordinary world, where we see it in diluted form. The same holds for the ideals of truth, justice, and all other higher aspirations. We are seeking the ideal, starting with everyday experience but rising higher and higher—if we are true philosophers, lovers of wisdom—until the pure ideal is revealed. This is the soul journey Socrates outlined.

It's easy to condemn those who put him to death. And yet, being honest with ourselves, we probably want the same thing they defended: a stable society without inflammatory radicals who incite discontent. To many good Athenian citizens, Socrates was a disruptive force. Those who turn over the applecart must die before they become martyrs and heroes; in their lifetime, they are seen as serious troublemakers.

In reality, Socrates worshipped the same gods as every other devout person, and he disapproved of youth run riot. Dissipation wasn't part of his teaching, any more than blasphemy was. Yet in a deeper way Diotima taught blasphemy to her pupil, because "Know thyself" is extremely subversive in the end. To take it seriously means that you will go on a search for God that enters the inner world and places a lower value on the outer world. It means that you will be in the world but not of it, that you will become the light of the world rather than hiding your light under a bushel basket. I can use phrases associated with Jesus because the link to Platonism is quite strong.

In fact, some scholars believe that the Gospel of John in the New Testament was written by someone well versed in Plato's thought and the Greek ideals. The Christian tradition is most people's direct link to Socrates. John's Gospel contains no miracles and no Christmas story. It begins with the most abstract approach to God in the Bible: "In the beginning was the Word, and the Word was with God, and the Word was God." The word (logos, in Greek) took on a deep meaning for early Christians. It described who Jesus was and where he came from. John is quite explicit about this:

The Word became flesh and made his dwelling among us.
We have seen his glory, the glory of the One and Only, who
came from the Father, full of grace and truth. (1:14)

But why should Jesus need Socrates and vice versa? One reason
is that when Jesus was crucified, his disciples were left behind expecting, quite literally, that the Messiah's purpose had been to
overthrow the Roman Empire, free the Jews from bondage, and
reign supreme over the earth. Only then would the Old Testament prophets like Isaiah be justified and fulfilled.

When that didn't happen, the disciples felt bereft and defeated.
John is seen as the rescuer of Jesus's mission. He says, in simplest
form, "The Messiah did what he was supposed to do. The Jesus
who walked among us was divine as a word, an ideal, a spirit.
Mortal eyes are fooled into seeing him as mortal too. Seen with
the eyes of the soul, Jesus was an incarnation of spirit, as are all of
us when we come to God."

What else is John's message but "Know thyself" restated in
Christian terms? And yet no teaching is harder to follow. One
despairs that Socrates and Jesus were both persecuted for telling
the truth, yet it's not unexpected.

If you want to see how challenging "Know thyself" really is, try
to live it for a week. Once a person spends any amount of time
looking inward, what is revealed is conflict, confusion, and a completely disorganized world "in here." Fear and anger roam at will
through the psyche. The shadow, which we touched upon in the
story of Job, rules over a hidden realm of guilt and shame. Atavis-
tic impulses like jealousy, lust, and revenge war with reason. Even
if the inner world doesn't reveal turmoil, the alternative may be a
humdrum conventionality that becomes more depressing the
closer you examine it. "Know thyself" makes for a rough week and
a challenging lifetime.

The status quo depends on conformity, not just the dronelike conformity of bees in a hive, but a shared agreement not to look too deeply into human nature. Unable to rid ourselves of mindless drives like lust, greed, and aggression, human beings bought civilization at a price. We gave up complete authenticity in order to stay safe and sane.

Socrates taught the opposite, as did Jesus. He taught that if you go deep enough, there is supreme light beyond the confusion and chaos, the id and the ego, sex and the lust for power. Only the light is real. In various guises, we will encounter this claim over and over as human beings ponder who God actually is. Diotima apparently passed the idea on to Socrates, and he took it to the streets. The Sophists were deluded to assume that the truth could be doled out in neatly wrapped packages. But Socrates may have been deluded to assume that the way to the truth can be taught at all.

The raucous, brilliant, rebellious, treacherous Alcibiades raises grave doubts on that score. He led disastrous military adventures abroad, the worst being an infamous war to conquer Greece. Then he abruptly turned on his heels and betrayed Athens by selling his services to the Persians, who made what use of him they could before killing him. Socrates taught a high-born, gifted pupil who wound up making no use of his teaching whatever. When Alcibiades drunkenly breaks into a banquet, he insists on lying on the couch closest to his old teacher, and when the company takes to praising Socrates (this is in Plato's *Symposium*), Alcibiades's voice is the loudest. But he was not a good man. In our day, preachers would frown and call him godless.

Yet every morality tale needs a prodigal son, which is what Alcibiades turned into. The difference is that he wasn't redeemed. That concept, which requires grace to descend from God to touch a person's soul, has yet to arrive on the scene. Reflecting on Socrates, a skeptic may ask how much good wisdom has done anyone. Isn't God about faith in the end? Not necessarily. In India there is a saying about the spiritual path: "One spark is enough to burn down the whole forest."

Which is to say, once you've glimpsed the light, eventually the darkness will be conquered. Socrates brought the light of the mind. He wasn't so much a gadfly as a spark (he used a homelier term, calling himself a midwife to the truth), but whether the truth needs to be born like a fragile infant or revealed by burning down the forest of ignorance, the end result is the same. Reality is the light, and the light can only be found in ourselves. In the words "Know thyself" is buried a new belief, that human nature is capable of reaching God without dogma, authority, and fear. The inner journey is afoot, and God has become the highest goal: complete self-knowledge. To quote another Indian saying, "This is wisdom you cannot learn; you must become it."

3

ST. PAUL

"I Am the Light of the World"

The Roman Empire is law. It is peace and efficiency. But above all, the empire is power, enforced by its legions, who spread terror everywhere at a flick of the emperor's wrist. It would be insane to laugh at these things. That is, unless God told you that empires are like straw in the wind and crumble like dust in the hands of the Lord.

One man who had such thoughts wasn't undone by them. They taught him how to survive. At this very moment he was parched and panting with exhaustion. He looked sickly and underfed. His limbs were like sticks with knobs where elbows and knees should be. No one would have given him much of a chance, if he had been sentenced to the galleys. But he hadn't been, luckily. The judge was indifferent to religious fanatics, so to this one, who appeared on Rome's records as Saul, he handed down a light sentence.

"Thirty days on the road gangs. And make sure he doesn't get near any other Jews. They're stirred up already." As far as keeping order went, for the legions putting down a food riot was half the trouble of a God riot.

As Saul slaved on the road gang, sweat dripped into the scrawny prisoner's mouth; it tasted salty and dirty. A light wind had risen over the desert, which was a mixed blessing, since it stirred up a choking dust even as it cooled your skin.

The prisoner next to Saul, a fat Cappadocian who stole a loaf of bread but didn't run far enough before he started to devour it, poked him in the ribs.

"You, pick up the pace. That guard is watching, and he looks like he could eat nails."

Saul nodded and passed a limestone block down the line. He never fought back when he wound up in prison, except with his tongue. You didn't know who might be concealing a dagger, even after the Romans did their morning search. Would God want one of his chosen to carry a weapon in self-defense? No. Of that Saul was sure.

Under Roman justice he was named Saul, and he didn't say different. Jewish names sometimes went down well, especially near Antioch, where the judges were mostly Jewish. Otherwise, he'd offer his Latin name, Paulus or Paul. There was always a chance of leniency for someone like him, born a Roman citizen. Leniency was nothing more than being given bread without green mold on the crust and water without black specks in it—good enough. If you could look in his heart, though, Saul was dead. He perished the instant Paul was born.

The watchful guard glowered at the sun overhead. He uttered an oath and turned his face away, so the pace slowed down again. The Cappadocian was bored enough to make conversation.

"What were you done for?"

"I scare people, some of them," said Paul.

"How?"

"I tell them that God loves them."

The conversation ended there. Paul smiled to himself. He was almost fifty, and so far what had he suffered for Jesus? He had been lifting rocks since dawn, and to keep his mind off the pain in his back, he counted up in his mind. Publicly whipped? Five times. Thirty-nine lashes minus one, given by the Jews, his own people. Clubbed over the head until he was senseless? Three times. Stoned? Only once, thank God. Already several brothers had died from stoning. Stephen was the first, a horrible way to be taken into God's embrace.

Paul's mind skipped ahead to avoid dwelling on the thought. Shipwrecked? Three times, including that one night he spent in the water, praying until dawn came and the survivors were pulled from the sea. Most of his prayers had been about sea monsters.

After surviving such torments, he wasn't proud of his courage. Pride was a sin. The closest Paul came to being proud was this: among all the brethren, he toiled the hardest, walked the farthest, and bore affliction with utmost silence. He loved scaring people with God's love. The poor Jews he met expected to fear and obey the Lord. Paul showed them a blinding love instead. No wonder so many ran away.

Did he feel loved at that moment, trapped in this killing heat with the guards testing their short whips on their thighs, just for practice? Yes, he did. In fact, that moment was a supreme example of God's love, because pain was a reminder to look for grace, which was everywhere.

For Paul there were only two kinds of men in this world, those Paul had converted and those he might convert. Nothing else mattered. Even under the lash he never missed a moment to practice his skills at debate, running over his opponent's argument in his head.

If God is love, why do we suffer?

To remind us that we are children of Adam and Eve, who brought sin into the world.

But you say that your Messiah died for our sins.

Absolutely.

Then why are the Romans, who don't believe in the Messiah, lording it over you and punishing you?

Because they do not realize that they are damned.

Damned? Look at them. They eat grapes and sit in the shade while you suffer under them like a dog. So what good is your salvation?

"My kingdom is not of this world," said my master. I am promised a banquet in heaven at God's table. The faint sound that will reach my ear is the screaming of pagans in the fiery pit.

Just to imagine such a debate filled Paul's heart with a sense of victory. God had delivered him so many times that he might do it again, at any moment. The shackles and chains around his feet could turn to flowers. The guards could fall to the ground with shaking fits. Musing on this, he fumbled the next rock and almost dropped it.

Up the line a Greek Cypriot with half an ear missing and filed teeth growled, "Keep it moving. This is my last day. I'm not letting you screw it up."

"It could be your last day on earth," Paul said.

"What?"

"God may hurl you into the furnace, where there will be wailing and gnashing of teeth. Mind the Lord, my friend. He is watching."

The Greek Cypriot would have struck him except for the rock he had to pass along. "You're saying the gods want to kill me?"

"No. I'm saying that death comes to all. Have you considered how you will be judged? You should. You don't look like a man who lives carefully." Paul indicated the missing piece of ear. Usually he didn't preach in the middle of hard labor. But you never knew the right moment, until the Lord showed it.

On a mission to Philippi Paul had been jailed with another missionary, Silas. They were marched into a deep dungeon where half the prisoners were insane or paralyzed from the isolation and darkness.

Paul could feel Silas trembling as they lay back-to-back for protection, wrapped in filthy rags.

"Be strong, brother," Paul whispered. "God sees us." He had a premonition.

Just before dawn the ground began to shake. Paul woke Silas and motioned toward the door. The second tremor would come in a few seconds, and Paul knew without thinking that it would be much stronger. The dungeon would erupt in terrified cries and a crush to smash down the door. God's timing had to be precise if his two missionaries were to survive. The second tremor came like thunder from the earth; the prison walls started to crack—they were like eggshells to the Lord—and glimpses of dawn could be seen among the falling debris. Silas sat up with a start, staring in confusion.

"Come, brother," said Paul, pulling him to his feet before Silas was awake enough to be terrified.

The prisoners panicked, as Paul foresaw, but he and Silas were now nearest the door when it fell off its hinges. They made it to the stairs as the earth roared. Thick dust stifled the dim light, and a swarm of bodies clawing their way up the stairs pulled the two Christians apart. Silas repeated God's name as he clung to the shaking walls, groping his way upward. At ground level he spied a three-foot fissure in the outer wall and slipped through.

He bent over, coughing dust, his eyes running with tears. When he could see again, the scene filled Silas with awe. The earthquake hadn't torn the prison down, but made only the single crack that he had squeezed through. All around, the nearby buildings were still standing. The Romans in the barracks weren't even awake, until a solitary guard began to shout as escapees ran down the street, many half-naked and dragging their chains.

Silas called out Paul's name with one breath and praised God with the next, but as one prisoner after another squeezed through the crack, he couldn't spot him. There was no time to waste. The Roman garrison was alerted now; he could hear the clank of swords and tramping boots. The first soldiers on the scene made a wall of shields to push back the last stragglers coming out, and within minutes the opening was surrounded.

What choice did he have? Silas ducked into a twisting narrow alley and ran. He was still young, and he ran a long way before the burning in his lungs forced him to stop. He didn't know the town, so he couldn't find the cluster of small houses where several Christians lived. Lost and alone, Silas tried not to think of his wife back in Antioch. He slid to the ground from exhaustion, his back against a wall that was still cold from the night chill.

"Look at this. Does bread get any finer? Eat. Terror is good for the appetite."

Even before he heard the voice, Silas had felt a man's shadow pass over him. He looked up. It was Paul, a glint in his eye and a round loaf of crusty bread in his hand.

"Don't worry, I didn't steal it. It's a gift, from the jail keeper."

Silas was astonished. "Who?"

Paul sank down and broke the bread in two. He muttered a short prayer and handed the larger half to Silas.

"I converted our jailer."

Astonishment kept Silas from eating. "During the earthquake?"

"What better time? There was a miracle at hand. I couldn't just let it go to waste." Paul reached into the sack he wore at his waist. "Not leaving out olives and cheese, which our sleepy jailkeeper had set out for his breakfast. Don't look so surprised. How many miracles do jailers see? He was impressed, and he offered this bread as a token." Paul ignored Silas's astonishment. "It's good, isn't it? I should convert a few bakers."

Silas pointed to a stray dog that was sniffing at them from a distance. It whined, testing to see whether they would throw him a scrap or kick him away. "You'd convert him if you could, wouldn't you?" said Silas.

Paul gave his companion a sidelong glance before deciding that this was a joke.

"Yes," he said curtly. "He looks ready."

Raising the next bite to his mouth, he noticed that his hand was trembling slightly. Paul felt immensely calm inside, but apparently his mortal body was stirred by the earthquake and God's intervention.

Paul considered this incident with the converted jailer a great victory. He reported it to the church at Antioch, where the strongest believers lived. Strong or not, they would falter if he didn't regularly reinforce their faith with good news. Faraway Jerusalem was harder to persuade. There the Christians were as suspicious of Paul as an old rabbi in the provinces. Mistrust grew, no matter how many miracles he reported. Called before the assembled faithful in Jerusalem, Paul had to defend himself. His persecution of Christians as Saul was well remembered. For now, the Romans were lax about letting Christians assemble, and when Paul appeared, the torch-lit hall was full.

The elders, some of them styled as apostles, sat on a raised platform. Paul was reminded too clearly of judges' benches. If he was inclined to be nervous, he rose in a fit of anger.

"I am not here to be looked down upon," he began. "Judge me as you wish. I have a calling no one here can challenge. If you speak against me, you speak against the mission I was given by Jesus."

This was a brazen claim, and it caused such an uproar that he couldn't continue.

"You never met Jesus!" a voice shouted. Half a dozen others took up the cry.

Paul raised his hands to quiet their outrage. "I met Jesus in spirit. If you truly knew him, you would understand."

The outcry against him doubled. His impudence was shocking. The leaders in Jerusalem had claimed sole authority since the crucifixion. Chiefly they were two, Peter, the preeminent disciple, and Jesus's own brother, James. Both were seated in the company, but neither showed any reaction.

Paul raised his voice over the din. "How can you deny me? If you say that only you who were with the Master are the true church, it will die when you die. Is that what you want?"

He didn't wait for a reply. "I know how you distrust me. I am a Roman citizen by birth, and the Romans hate us. I persecuted you myself, because your beliefs were beyond reason. Back in Rome they don't understand a king who is not of this world. Neither did I. But you also know what happened to me when I saw the light."

"What you *say* happened," an angry voice shouted.

"So that's it?" Paul shouted back. "The Lord calls me, but you have the right to sit over him? If I don't win your love, then God's love is cancelled?"

The murmuring quieted. Paul felt the slightest wave of sympathy; he had to play on it.

"When he was teaching, anyone could set eyes upon Jesus," he said, "including the foolish eye, the ignorant eye, the lustful, vain, proud eye. I don't demean what you saw. You have a blessed eye, because you saw the Lord incarnate. At the same time, don't demean what I saw."

The disgruntled had quieted down completely; he was beginning to win them over. But Paul knew that very few of them had the courage to think for themselves; they looked at Simon Peter to find out what he thought.

With a faint gesture that brought total silence, Peter had something to say. "The Lord's blessing falls on everyone, like the rain. Didn't our Master say so? Then how would you separate the worthy from the unworthy?"

It was an ambiguous utterance, and Paul faced it head-on. "The man I once was, Saul of Tarsus, would be unworthy if he were standing here. By the grace of the Lord he is dead. I had a second birth."

Grumbling arose; he had gone a step too far. The brothers were tired of hearing about Paul's miracle story. How Saul the zealous persecutor of Christians had been struck from his horse while riding from Jerusalem to Damascus. How the light of Christ blinded him for three days, until it was restored by a gentle brother, Ananias. Paul repeated it in every sermon before Jews and gentiles. Some might call that vanity.

Now an old man, Cleopas slowly elbowed his way to the front; the company respectfully gave way. He nodded at Simon Peter, who said, "Bear witness." The room became quiet again.

"I was too afraid to walk with the Master that terrible last day," said Cleopas. "I didn't pick up his cross when he stumbled. From a distance I beheld the three crosses being raised on Golgotha, and I ran away." Cleopas gestured toward Paul. "Is not my unbelief greater than his?"

Someone vigorously shouted, "No!"

Cleopas ignored him. "Our brother Paul preaches that even the worst may be saved through faith. He is stronger than me in that too. Let me tell you why."

The old man unfolded a story. He and another disciple were walking away from Jerusalem after the Romans executed Jesus. It was better to leave the city quickly, for their own safety. The Pharisees might convince Pilate to crucify Jesus's disciples next.

On the road Cleopas said little, lost in his guilty thoughts, until his companion began to weep. He rejected Cleopas's attempts to comfort him. "We'll never see him again. Our devotion was a waste," the companion cried. "We followed a false messiah. Don't you see that?"

His companion's rashness upset Cleopas, who was naturally gentle, but he had to speak out now. "I've seen him heal the sick with my own eyes. So have you. And what of the three women, and the angels?"

Three women of Galilee, including Mary Magdalene, had followed Jesus and his disciples as they wandered. These same three had gone to the tomb of Jesus that morning and found it empty. Suddenly, as they stood in confusion, angels appeared to them announcing that Jesus was alive. Death was nothing to God, and he had lifted his son from the grave. When the women ran back to the disciples with this news, an uproar occurred; one faction rejoiced while the other angrily denounced the thieves who had stolen Jesus's body during the night.

"I saw you rejoice with the women," Cleopas reminded his companion, who would have replied sharply, but they were interrupted by a stranger approaching on the road. Instead of nodding and passing on his way, the stranger gave them a penetrating look.

"What were you just talking about?" he asked, speaking in Aramaic.

The two disciples shrugged nervously, unwilling to give hints about themselves. The stranger was a fellow Jew, but that didn't make him safe.

"You are walking from Jerusalem. Has something happened there?" the stranger demanded. He never took his eyes off Cleopas, who felt his heart burning with grief.

"You don't know? The city has erupted," his companion told the stranger, and he recounted Jesus's trial and his betrayal by the priests of the Temple.

"So the Jews are squabbling over the Messiah again," said the stranger.

"Of course, what else?"

"Messiah fever ends with sticks and stones," the stranger mused.

But the fever had not broken. Under Herod the Romans had recently redoubled their persecutions. More than ever, the Jews needed a mighty leader to drive the invaders from the holy land.

"You are a Jew," said Cleopas, overcoming his wariness. "You must feel the same need as we do."

"So, the Messiah will come when our people are most in need?"

the stranger asked. "Then why hasn't he? We're desperate enough."

"We thought he did come," the companion replied in dejection.

"Did he arm you? I don't see weapons unless you are hiding them under your cloaks," the stranger remarked.

"Jesus was a man of peace," Cleopas interjected.

"Then you must expect two messiahs. One to defeat Caesar, the other to calm the waters."

The stranger's talk was challenging, and the three became absorbed. He took them back to Moses and visited everything that scripture said about the Messiah, that he would be persecuted and misunderstood, that the learned would not understand, but only the simple of heart. He would be a man of sorrows on this earth, but a king in heaven.

"Our Master *is* in heaven," cried Cleopas.

He was shaken by the anger that flared up in the stranger's voice. "Your master has fools for followers if he shows them miracles and still they do not believe." This was his only outburst, and it subsided quickly.

When they reached the village of Emmaus, Cleopas knew a place friendly to disciples, and he invited the stranger, who was about to continue on, to have supper with them there. Seeing the darkening sky, he agreed.

At this point in his tale Cleopas had a hard time suppressing his emotion, which happens with old men, but he was not ashamed of it as many old men are.

"We sat down at table, the bread was brought. The stranger bent his head to bless it, and when he broke bread, our eyes were opened. It was Jesus! God had blinded us to test our faith. Even as I rejoiced to see our Master again, I trembled inside. For three days I had doubted him. How could I believe in a Messiah that the Romans could kill at their whim?"

The old man pointed to Paul, raising his voice, which no longer quavered. "If I can be blessed to see our Master alive, so can he."

It was a stunning moment, and Paul had to force himself not to follow it up with more rhetoric. He embraced Cleopas and waited while he slowly hobbled back to his seat. Did Peter, leaning back in his rough wooden chair, betray suspicion in his eyes or approval? Paul, who had to read men well in order to survive, didn't care. He showed a careless disregard as he looked away. The spirit had anointed him. It didn't matter a straw what Peter, the great Simon Peter, thought about it. If Jesus wasn't a king of this world, didn't it follow that his true disciples were not of this world either?

The atmosphere had relaxed by now. From his throne Peter nodded without comment. He would relent that far, at least. If winning were enough, this was the end of it. But who said that winning was enough for Paul?

To the crowd he said, "I sense that you have given me your approval. But not everyone with his full heart. I don't care, because I love you all fiercely, as souls baptized in the name of the Holy Spirit.

"I see you as ghosts compared to unbelievers. Your flesh is a mirage. You are really the light of God. I say this to you, and I would say the same to Caesar before he killed me, or to the next gentile as he is about to spit on me."

Paul intended these words to create a stir, and they did. Jerusalem buzzed like a hornets' nest all week. Jerusalem was happy to see his back as Paul went on the road. Let him go and be as reckless as he wanted, people said. The Lord would protect him— or not.

The miracles never ceased. Paul converted the masses, one person at a time. Many were so fervent in their belief that they witnessed the risen Christ with their own eyes. Rome became nervous. These Christians believed in the impossible, and yet the impossible kept spreading without check, infecting one town after another. Local officials kept reassuring Rome that everything was under control. In fact, they could hardly tell Jews from Christians. Why even bother? Both had grandiose fantasies about a Messiah who would overthrow Caesar. The only difference was that the Christians had had their Messiah, and now he was dead.

When miracles are abroad, people want more, and this left room for magicians. Paul was set against their kind: magus or sorcerer, whatever title they fancied, they were blasphemers and sons of the Devil. But it wasn't yet the Lord's will for Paul to fight them. He bided his time, converting two thieves in one jail. Sometime later, when he had returned a third time to the faithful in Antioch, God's hand moved over Paul. He was guided to Cyprus; the sea looked dark as he made the passage over.

"Do you see anything there, brother?" he asked Barnabas, the disciple whom God had picked for his companion. Puzzled, Barnabas gazed into the waters, which were unusually still; he shook his head.

"Fish?" he said.

Paul smiled. The calm sea, glassy and still, was like a mirror. Not one to see yourself in, but one to see through. Just as the face hides the soul, a reflection in a mirror hides what lies behind it. Infinite love was veiled by a woman's eyebrow that needed plucking, a rouged cheek, the first wrinkles of a preening lover gazing at himself when his mistress wasn't looking. Vanity makes us love the reflection, which is why God must send hints and omens, to stop our self-love and force us to see the truth.

They landed in Cyprus, and Paul immediately had an inspiration. "We must find the God-fearing," he told Barnabas. This was a special term among Christians. It had become fashionable to shop for a god. Pagans had become disgruntled seekers, and a few knocked on the door of the synagogues. The Jews inside felt afraid, but some argued that isolation only made them more hated. Let the pagans see for themselves what a holy place was like.

Cautiously the doors were opened to these seekers, who became known as God-fearers, because they reverenced God even though they had no religion. Even high-born Romans looked in. They sometimes heard the rabbi preach against the Christians, and this made them curious. On Cyprus there was one of these curious Romans, Sergius Paulus by name, who presided over the city of Paphos as proconsul. The local Christians pounced on Paul and Barnabas with great news. This powerful man might want to be baptized. One more sermon, a powerful one, and his spirit would surely cross over.

"I'd be ashamed not to convert a man named Paul, but what sort is he?" asked Paul.

"He's a man of reason, a sensible man," the local brothers said.

The worst kind, Paul thought, but kept it to himself.

His premonition was justified. Sergius Paulus was found in his house reclining on cushions with a tolerant smile on his face and a beaker of wine, half empty, in his hand. At his feet sat—what else?—a magician making cotton balls appear and disappear under a red velvet cap. He wore an even wider smile and was drinking from an even bigger wine beaker.

"Elymas, get up," the proconsul ordered, wiping his mouth with a napkin. "Your God is waiting for you to defend him, and put down that wine. Yahweh isn't Bacchus. He wants you sober." So this Elymas was a Jew who had insinuated himself with the Romans.

Elymas turned to Paul without extending his hand. "I've heard of your prophet. The one who rose from the dead. I won't perform that trick today. I respect you as one mind to another."

"A magician with a mind would be refreshing," Paul replied.

Elymas laughed with civilized tolerance. Paul was rankled, but he knew better than to be goaded. The two of them, the Roman and the magician, had probably concocted this little opening scene.

Boldly Paul addressed the proconsul. "I am of no use to a reasonable man, and you are of no use to me. My message is faith. Five hundred brothers and sisters have already witnessed the risen Christ. I am one of them."

Sergius Paulus frowned. "More politeness might serve you better."

"When a man's house is on fire, who does him more good, the servant who is too polite to wake his master or the one who pounds on his door?" asked Paul.

Elymas interrupted. "I can produce fire if you want," he said smoothly, "but nobody here is asleep."

"All are asleep who mock the risen Christ," said Paul sharply and turned back to the Roman. "I am not disparaging your understanding, but it takes no mind to see the sun. Reason is great; faith is greater. With his paltry sorcery this magician may persuade you of anything. Falseness is his trade. But I bring you a matter of life and death. Don't fritter it away because you are amused by illusions."

Sergius Paulus saw an opening for a contest. "Will you take this lying down?" he asked Elymas.

"I am not offended. Jesus was a great magus. His followers call him the Holy Spirit. But I am master of spirits, and they speak when I command." Elymas bowed to Paul with mock respect. "Even if your sincerity is undoubted."

"Are you entertained by your own blasphemy?" Paul asked.

"As entertained as you are by your own rhetoric," said Elymas. "Why do you think the Romans are masters over us Jews? They use reason; they laugh at superstition. I suspect you rail against me, because you know that you have already lost before you began."

The proconsul was enjoying himself, and Paul allowed the magician his oily arguments. He had to, until the Lord told him what to do. All at once, he did.

Paul turned fiercely on Elymas. "Unrighteous sinner, you shame yourself in the eyes of God. He knows you, and he is angry."

Paul raised his hand. The gesture looked so much like a magician's that Elymas smiled.

"The Holy Spirit commands!" Paul shouted.

Suddenly Elymas groped at the air. Then with a moan he collapsed on the ground.

"Do you see it, proconsul? I do, and so does this wretch," Paul declared.

The Roman, who had jumped to his feet, looked bewildered. "See it? What do you mean?"

"The Lord has surrounded him with a dark mist. Now he's clawing the empty air. For a season this blasphemer will be blind."

"Elymas, take my hand," Sergius Paulus commanded. He held his outstretched hand a foot from the magician's face, but Elymas only made pitiful noises as he reached toward emptiness.

The proconsul was shaken, but only for a moment. Magi visited every day. The new one knew higher magic. "Stay. Teach me," he said, searching in his toga for some gold coins.

Paul shook his head. "All you care about is power."

"Which I will share with you. Come." The proconsul had found some gold and waved it in the air.

Paul pointed to the blind magus. "Here is power beyond your understanding. It was not my mind that did it, and your mind is equally useless before God."

He started to leave, and the Roman almost called for soldiers to block his way. His hand was halfway to the bell cord. But Paul stopped of his own accord, returning and kneeling by Elymas, who was no longer making a sound.

Paul spoke to him. "This Roman has no more use for you. In an hour you will be wandering the streets helplessly, begging to be healed. Nothing will help. But in a few months the blindness will lift of its own accord. The Holy Spirit has done this thing."

Elymas clutched at Paul's arm. "Take me with you."

"You would suffer more than you do now."

"No!" Sheer panic was in the magus's voice.

The spirit shifted in Paul from anger to gentleness. "Jesus preached, 'I am the light of the world.' He did not call himself the light of Jerusalem or the light of the Jews."

"But he is the Messiah," Elymas murmured. "He must be for the Jews."

"Which means you own him, as a Jew owns a cow or a prayer shawl?" Paul leaned closer and reduced his voice to a whisper. "Hear me, sorcerer. *He owns you.* That is all you need to think on. There is no debate worth having."

He was ready to leave now, and he shot the Roman a hard glance, making his hand fall from the bell cord.

"So you won't help him? You know very well that I'm going to have him dragged into the street," said Sergius Paulus.

Paul shook his head and walked away.

Later, Paul related the incident to Barnabas, who related it to the brothers in Cyprus.

Soon it spread throughout the Christian world. Skeptics in Jerusalem said nothing. They kept their counsel, suspicious of the man who rode to Damascus and no less suspicious of the man who was riding to grace. Paul didn't care. He saw every convert he had made standing behind him, every possible convert waiting up ahead. It was only a matter of time before they lined the whole road as far as God's eye could see.

Revealing the Vision

If you were to meet someone from the golden age of Athens on the street today, you might look down on their belief in gods sitting atop Mount Olympus, enjoying a never-ending party at human expense as they roiled the seas, inflicted famine, and destroyed individuals at will. But those fifth-century Athenians might look down on you for believing that God is a matter of faith. In the Christian era the divine light moved from the mind to the soul. God rose above the natural world. He no longer roiled the seas or bothered with thunderbolts. He became more wondrous and mysterious. He kept one of his old ways, however, that of forcing his devotees into peril.

Two peculiar phenomena dominate the early Christian church: miracles and martyrdom. They account for why the new religion spread like wildfire. Early Christians were on the receiving end of persecution, but also the gift of visible miracles. In the first generation after the crucifixion, all of Jesus's closest followers died for their beliefs, and when a rabid mob stoned Stephen, the first martyr, only a year or two after the crucifixion, they were goaded on by a hater of the new faith, Saul of Tarsus.

How this persecutor named Saul turned into Paul and became the greatest single shaper of Christianity is one of the crucial conversions in human history. Paul's experience on the road to Damascus has become the prototype for all dramatic conversion stories. Being blinded by the light, which is what happened to Saul on his journey to inflict more pain on Christians, defines the essence of experiencing God in a sudden epiphany. But there's a larger question to ask. Why should the threat of a violent death cause a religion to spread? Persecution is usually quite effective, for a short or a long time, at keeping the powerless downtrodden.

Christianity had a secret weapon. Martyrdom opened the way to miracles. This connection was made from the very beginning. The crucifixion was an act of utmost violence, but it led to the resurrection, an event of supreme miraculousness. St. Paul played a central role in cementing this connection. He insisted that a true Christian must believe in the literal fact of the resurrection. Soon, to die for Jesus became a sacrifice that ensured a passage to heaven. The fact that the same belief exists in Islam derives directly from Christianity; both are "religions of the Book" that promise salvation in the afterlife, placing the physical world so far below heaven that inviting death in God's name is a righteous act.

Paul also states that five hundred converts had personally witnessed the risen Christ. If that is so, then the early church was the focus of the greatest mass mystical event in history. Paul's writings survive in the form of a sheaf of letters sent to congregations in Ephesus, Corinth, and other areas from Israel to Asia Minor. Scholars believe that these letters could be the earliest genuine record of Christianity, predating even the writing of the four Gospels.

Be that as it may, the force of Paul's mind prevailed. If only the first letter to the Corinthians had survived, his words would be indelible, since they are written with such passion and confidence:

> Love is patient and kind; love is not jealous or boastful; it is
> not arrogant or rude. Love does not insist on its own way; it
> is not irritable or resentful; it does not rejoice at wrong, but
> rejoices in the right. (13:4–6)

These words echo Jesus, of course, but they are all the more reassuring because they come from a flawed mortal who had been transformed. In another voice Paul can chide and correct the newly formed believers. In yet another he sets down in plain language what it means to enter the miraculous world opened by Christ:

> When I was a child, I spoke like a child, I thought like a
> child, I reasoned like a child; when I became a man, I gave

up childish ways. For now we see in a mirror dimly, but then face to face. Now I know in part; then I shall understand fully, even as I have been fully understood. (13:11–12)

The poetic writing is breathtaking. The mind behind it had to work against unseen opponents, however, to win the day. We don't know if Paul was a rival to Peter, Jesus's most favored disciple, or James, the brother of Jesus, who had the strongest hereditary claim to lead the new faith. I portray them in conflict because the picture of early Christianity has been turned on its head in the past fifty years. It was once accepted that after the crucifixion there was a uniform religion led by Peter and the other apostles, but this picture depended on the absence of contrary scripture like the Gnostic gospels. When they came to light, very late in the game, these documents revealed a contentious, fermenting situation full of power struggles. Some very diverse beliefs were held by various groups for centuries until they were branded as heresy.

I've placed Paul at the center of this turbulence and portrayed him as a spiritual warrior. We cannot say which of the early church leaders was the most charismatic, but it is undeniable that the volatile mixture of mysticism and violence needed Paul to stabilize it. Without him, the Christian God would be even more confusing and contradictory than he is already.

Words like "confusing" and "contradictory" are not used by devout Christians, but the New Testament is full of peace juxtaposed with punishment, forgiveness with vengeance. Christ predicted universal peace on earth, yet he is also quoted saying, "I have come not to bring peace, but a sword" (Matt. 10:34). I've already touched on the fact that the shock of the crucifixion left the early followers of Jesus feeling left behind. They couldn't help but cry out, "What should we believe? What should we do?"

Some answers were radical. The Gnostic gospels, as an alternative to the four canonical Gospels, are a late discovery; they were found in 1945 by accident when two Egyptian farmers wandered into a cave near the town of Nag Hammadi and found a jar full of ancient manuscripts. Their discovery, now called the Nag Hammadi Library, contains dozens of diverse documents. In the theological hubbub that arose after they came to light, the official picture of the early church was strongly challenged. Here were believers a hundred years after Jesus's death who held that God is both mother and father, that Mary Magdalene was Jesus's favored disciple, and that a congregation should gain nearness to Christ through direct revelation rather than written gospels. One document tells us that the crucifixion itself was an illusion. As the mob watches Jesus's agony on the cross, he appears in the flesh to Peter to tell him that only the ignorant believe in such spectacles, because they cannot see true spirit. In the modern era, these are fascinating possibilities, even though the Gnostic gospels are not part of any recognized faith.

We can't escape the fact that Paul's brand of Christianity crushed all opposition, and some of his harsher prejudices have cast a shadow over "Paulianity," a term that is both admired and denigrated. The bad side of Paulianity is that it is authoritarian, chauvinist, and puritanical. Sex, like all temptations of the flesh, stands against spirit, and only marriage makes it palatable in the Christian scheme. Faith must be absolute; church authority stands in for God's authority. If an ordinary person receives a message from God, it is mistrusted until tested and approved by the church leaders (in contrast, the Gnostics, whose name comes from the Greek word *gnosis*, which literally means "knowledge," accepted messages received directly from God—perhaps the Shakers, with their ecstatic epiphanies, are an analogy).

History is written by the victors, which is never more true than in the history of the early church. Leaving ancient arguments aside, the God portrayed by Paul is remarkable as an evolution from the past. To begin with, this is no longer a bargaining God, offering rewards for good behavior and punishment for bad.

Divine love is now offered freely, as grace. It doesn't have to be deserved. In taking this step, Paul solved the problem of the fall, when Adam and Eve were driven out of paradise. As long as the taint of their sin existed in every person, a lifetime's struggle against it was necessary and probably wouldn't work anyway. Sinners were always bound to backslide; such was the power of temptation and the weakness built into human nature.

But Paul offered redemption and salvation, wiping the slate clean. No longer frowning down upon his errant children, God sent his son with a message of transformation. Jesus is the perfectly transformed human being, the new Adam. He is all goodness, and he dispenses all grace. This would be inspiring enough, but the same transformation is also held out to true believers. Jesus tells his disciples that they are the "light of the world" and will perform even greater miracles than his own.

Paul portrayed a world full of the miraculous. Thanks to Jesus's sacrifice, an ordinary person could "die unto death," transcending the ultimate fear. The spectacle of early Christians singing hymns as they were devoured by wild beasts in the Colosseum proved that the spirit was more real than the flesh. This is the secret that binds miracles and martyrs. Miracles reach down, via divine love, in the midst of agony.

One searches for passages in the Old Testament where God is primarily to be loved rather than feared. The New Testament is full of them. To theologians the term *agape*, one of several Greek words for "love," defines God's bond with humanity, and the touchstone is John 3:16, still one of the most moving verses in its simplicity: "For God so loved the world, that he gave his only begotten Son, that whosoever believeth in him should not perish, but have everlasting life."

It cannot be verified if these words were written before Paul's letters or after, nor do we know if Paul read them anywhere else. Surely both writers knew that the new message resonated with an old one: "By faith we understand that the universe was created by the word of God, so that what is seen was not made out of things that are visible." Thus the New Testament echoes the mystical creation of the world in Genesis—the visible world came into being through divine words: "Let there be light."

Did John intentionally echo the Old Testament? That again we cannot know. Much is lost; much is legend. But Paul drummed one formula into his readers: believe and you will be saved. It's not a universal formula. In the East, religions like Buddhism and Hinduism have no murdered saints, no emphasis on faith in supernatural events, no resurrection from the dead. Instead, the common thread in the East is consciousness. A religious person seeks to escape pain and suffering by finding a higher reality that leaves pain and suffering behind, rendering them irrelevant. The entire journey is done within, and therefore Gnosticism, or direct contact with the divine mind, finds in the East a refuge where it isn't a heresy.

This isn't to say that religion as it flowered in Asia lacks divine love and miracles. In popular Buddhism the young Prince Siddhartha was carried over the walls of his father's palace, where he lived a life of suffocating luxury, on a magical white horse held aloft by angels. A devout Hindu sees the beautiful god Krishna as an exemplar of love. But Christianity isn't a religion based on higher consciousness; it is based on salvation, the ultimate personal miracle.

To atheists, all miracles are primitive and childlike, a form of wish fulfillment not far removed from fairy tales. In a recent book for young adults, the British evolutionary biologist Richard Dawkins, who has become the outspoken voice of modern atheism, looks into miracles from a rational point of view. He concludes that they are fakery spread by charlatans, including the miracles reported in the New Testament. Science knows how reality works, Dawkins assures us. We need to get past myths and wish fulfillment, since they promote unreality. It's a powerful, persuasive attack, if you insist that only the physical world is real and only the rational mind can deliver the truth.

But the argument loses its potency once you realize that spirituality is based on the irrational, not by being feeble and childish, but by celebrating the inner world. There are levels of the mind where rationalism cannot go. Here we find the source of imagination, art, beauty, truth, faith, hope, love, trust, compassion, and most of the other things that make life worth living. To an atheist this sounds like a sentimental justification for believing in the unreal. However, if you look deeply, Christianity cannot help but be about consciousness, despite itself.

To enter the miraculous world, where ordinary people can be transformed, where God's presence is felt and death loses its sting, there is no physical journey. As Kabir, one of the most inspired of India's mystical poets, says, you can read all the holy books and bathe in all the holy waters without finding your soul. The soul is an experience, not a thing. All experiences take place in consciousness. This is undeniable even for so-called supernatural experiences of the kind that atheists scorn.

Whether he is loved or hated, Paul was a teacher of higher consciousness, demanding that the early church accept the resurrection, which meant accepting a world no longer imprisoned by natural laws. We think of Christianity as being about the life to come, when souls join their Father in heaven. But Paul changed forever how this world looks. He led a revolution of the mind by saying that coming back from the dead was not just real, but the most real thing that ever happened. His stubborn insistence that God dispenses grace to the whole world was the same as creating a new world. In my own mind, miracles don't cause distress. As Einstein said, either nothing is a miracle or everything is. That may seem like one person's belief system competing with countless others. Yet Paul added another argument for all the mystics to come. Miraculous worlds only await the touch of awareness.

4

SHANKARA

"Life Is a Dream"

Five old men, the village elders, had come to listen to the young stranger. But only one was actually listening. Two others nodded off in the sun, another was counting his money, and the fourth had smoked too much ganja that morning and was no longer present on earth. They were squatting in the courtyard of the local Shiva temple, but no priests had emerged.

"You come from the south?" asked the head elder, the one who was paying attention. "They have temples there. Respectable ones," he added.

"I wasn't driven out," said the stranger. He waited for a question that wasn't pointless. His accent already told that he was from the south. He wore the saffron robes of a monk and the marks of a Brahmin—those with the highest spiritual knowledge.

The elder who was counting his money stopped for a moment. "We grow our own beggars here. We don't need anymore."

The elder stupefied on ganja found his tongue. "Don't tell him where I live." His chin fell back on his chest.

The stranger sighed. Monks fell under the law of hospitality, which was sacred. But people whined about it, except in the backwaters, where superstition lingered stronger than in the towns. In both places an unwelcome monk could be kicked from the door.

"I won't trouble anyone for food," he murmured.

He didn't absolutely need the approval of the five elders, known as the *panchayat*, but he believed in showing respect. Besides, he would be stirring up trouble soon enough. There were always five elders in every village he came to, just as there was always a grove of five trees on the outskirts of town. Five is a holy number. Every child was taught that; no one questioned it.

Shankara felt the time crawl by. "I've been on the road for four days. I survived a bandit attack to get here. I only want to speak to your priests, and then I'll be gone."

"Bandit attack? Why didn't they kill you?" asked the head elder.

"They seemed interested in God, so we wound up talking." The monk gave a brief answer, not mentioning that the bandits had bowed to him and touched his feet before they let him go.

The head elder rocked on his heels. It was the hottest part of the day, and for awhile the monkeys quit squabbling with the parrots overhead in the trees. The air was sultry and heavy, but the clouds on the horizon meant it would take weeks before a proper monsoon moved in for the season. The wandering monk wore his begging bowl on his shaved head as protection from the sun.

"Your father blessed this pilgrimage of yours?" asked the money-counting elder.

"My father is dead. But my mother blessed me before I left. She had to," said the stranger. Again he didn't expand his answer. In fact, a tale circulated around his leaving. When he was bathing in the pool near his house in the village of Kaladi, a crocodile had seized him by the foot. The other Brahmin boys screamed and jumped out of the water. His mother ran to the bank of the pool, expecting her son to already be dead, but instead he was calmly waiting for her, the crocodile still attached.

"I must die to this life," he told her. "I know what my new life should be, and even this savage creature knows. If you bless me,

he will let me go." The boy, who was only seven, spoke very pre-
cociously.

After that, his mother had no choice. The wandering monk
was eight when he turned his back on Kaladi and took to the
roads, which was astonishing, even in a land where highway robbers were interested in God. If he hadn't found refuge with gurus
on the way, the boy could easily have been snatched and killed.

Years passed. It was impossible to guess his age now. Fifteen,
sixteen? He looked young, but his name was well traveled. Stories
about the young Shankara had reached everyone in India.

"I really do need to talk to a priest," Shankara repeated.

The truth was known but unspoken. The *panchayat* had assembled to greet him the moment he set foot in the village. The local
priests hoped he would be bored to death by some old men. With
any luck he would move on and not confront the priests. In eight
years of wandering, in all parts of India, the stories were that
Shankara had a devastating effect in debates. Wherever he went,
God toppled, the god that paid priests' salaries, that is.

The last village he had stopped in was like all the rest. The
chief priest, born to a specific sect in the worship of Devi, the Divine
Mother, sat down to argue with supreme confidence. He had
ruled village life for decades and begun to believe in his own in-
vincibility. Novel ideas didn't frighten him, any more than a new
summer crop of mosquitoes. He had tufts of gray hair on his
head, with smaller patches on his chin and sprouting from his
ears.

"You say that the world is an illusion?" he asked.

"It doesn't matter that I say it. The sacred Vedas declare it,"
Shankara replied.

"But you claim direct knowledge. You came here to dispel illusions, didn't you? So make the world disappear."

"All right," Shankara nodded. "Wait until this evening when
you fall asleep. The world will disappear, as it does every night."

The invincible priest didn't smile, although he had to admit it was a clever answer. He said, "Something harder. You declare that all things, big and small, exist as in a dream."

"Yes. Just as a man wakes up from a dream to see the light of day, so he should wake up from the dream of this existence if he wants to see the light of God." They were both comfortable using the word "God," since it was understood, after many centuries, that each of the many images worshipped in thousands of temples all wore a face of the same divine presence.

"In dreams, anything can happen," remarked the invincible priest. "So if this life is a dream, you must grant that anything can happen here."

"I do. Nothing is impossible for one who knows God," Shankara replied.

"Ah. The maharajah has a palace so huge that a horse would collapse before galloping from one end to the other. In my dreams I can have such a palace. Can I have one when I'm awake?"

"I can exceed your wish. Strip off your clothes on the coldest night of the year. Stand naked outdoors for an hour. When you run back into your warm house, it will be better than any maharajah's palace."

The priest allowed himself a smile, which was important. Shankara could always crush his opponents and wander to the next village down the Ganges, but he was determined to leave goodwill behind him. He didn't want his opponents to resent it when they lost the debate. Far better if the priests became pillars of a new belief.

The invincible priest wasn't there yet. "I can call on a servant to run into the jungle and bring back a cobra. If I laid a poisonous snake in your lap, would that be an illusion too?"

"I bow to you," Shankara replied. "You know the scriptures well. For isn't it written thus: 'To believe in this world is like a man who stumbles in the dark upon a coiled rope. Unable to see clearly, he cries "Snake! Snake!" until the whole village is aroused.

Now everyone runs around in fear until one man brings a torch and says, "See here, it is only a rope." That is how Maya, the goddess of illusion, works'."

"But it doesn't prove that cobras aren't real, unless every snake is the same as a rope," said the invincible priest, certain that he was pouncing on a point.

Shankara replied, "I was proving that only the man who brings a light knows what is real and what isn't." He smiled. "Anyone who reads the scriptures grasps the point, doesn't he?"

The invincible priest squirmed. The wanderer had perfected the technique of making his opponent accept the truth by citing texts that every Brahmin supposedly knew by heart. Isn't that how they kept control over simple devotees, with holy words no one else could read? As he flattered the Brahmins, Shankara subtly turned the same words around. They discovered that, like a cobra's sting, the sting of his mind was fatal.

It seems ordained that those who bring light into the world become shrouded with legends. Shankara was walking through a village one day when a gang of boys started running after him throwing marigolds in his path. He asked them why.

"We want you to step on one," an older boy replied, although even he was quite shy.

"Step on one?"

"You are a *sidha*, a master of supernatural powers. If you step on a flower, we can sell it to heal the sick."

"Who told you such a thing?" Shankara demanded.

The boys were confused and intimidated, but between them they told a tale they had heard about the *sidha* standing before them.

Shankara had taken a master by the name of Govinda, who lived in a cave by the sacred river Narmada. As was the custom, the disciple waited on the master, acting as his personal servant. Every morning Shankara would leave food before the mouth of the cave for his master's breakfast. One day, however, the river overflowed its banks, threatening Govinda's cave and the surrounding countryside.

Shankara prayed for guidance, after which he rushed to the cave and placed his small clay water pot in front. Immediately the pot swallowed up the flood, until God ordered the Narmada to return to its banks, for the flood had actually been a test of the young *sidha*'s powers.

The boys' eyes were shining as they retold the tale. Instead of scolding them, he obligingly stepped on a few marigolds, reminding himself to return when the boys had grown into men, so that he could give them something more useful than legends—although it isn't recorded that he ever contradicted the tale.

When he arrived in a new place, asking to debate the most learned men, the Brahmins usually made the mistake of underestimating him at first. He was thin as a reed, for one thing, and when you're peddling wisdom, it's better to be fat as well as old. If someone pointed this out, Shankara would say that he didn't win by sitting on his opponents, only by persuading them. Of what? He shrugged. The truth.

"Isn't it arrogant for a stranger to come here and claim to know the truth?" his opponents argued.

"Ignorance is more arrogant," Shankara replied. "It claims to blind all men and erase what is real from their minds." He lowered his eyes. "Not that such a thing has happened here."

On this day Shankara and the five elders had been meeting for an hour. Shankara heard his stomach rumble. The one who kept questioning him was stubborn. He never ran out of questions, and each one grew more trivial. The wandering monk couldn't hide his impatience any longer.

"How much?" he asked.

"What?"

"How much were you paid to waste my time? Before you pretend to be outraged, I'll say one thing. I'm not here to destroy your faith."

The head village elder had worn a tolerant expression up until this moment; it vanished. "They say you topple God. We can't permit that."

"I see, so God needs you to protect him? I'm impressed. I've now met someone more powerful than God himself."

The words were meant to sting, and they did. The head elder rose and gestured to the others. "I'm not so impressed," he said. "I've met someone who thinks God is deaf and blind. But you're wrong. He hears profanity, and he punishes it."

Shankara stood up and moved in on the old man. "Is that why I'm stuck talking to you, because God is punishing me?"

The old man's face reddened, but Shankara didn't wait for a spluttering reply. He raised his arms and addressed the empty courtyard. "I was told to come here. This is a marketplace, they told me. The peddlers of faith set up their stalls here. So where are you, peddlers? Come, sell me some faith if you think I have none."

From inside the temple there was no answer to his challenge, only the faint buzz of chanting. The priests were obligated to perform rituals almost without pause as long as the sun was up and several times during the night.

"Have it your way," Shankara shouted. "When I get to the next village, I will bring the news that this is the home where ignorance loves to dwell. It has made its devotees too frightened to talk to me."

A sharp ear would have detected a change in the buzzing that issued from the sacred chamber inside the temple; now it was more like wasps than prayers. After a moment a priest appeared at the door. He held the implements of ritual in his hand—smoking incense, a bowl of water, some marigolds—as if he could barely spare a moment.

"Don't scold me," Shankara addressed him. "The rumors about me are wrong. I'm not here to topple God. My words won't crack the temple walls."

"Like all words, yours will vanish into thin air," said the priest, who was twice the age of the intruder, with a brow as heavy as his scowl.

"Some words penetrate the heart," said Shankara, more mildly.

In a child's tale he would have had to slay the demons that blocked his way, but Shankara wielded a secret weapon. He charmed people, even when they thought that they should resist him. The priest's scowl didn't melt yet, much less his heart. But he didn't call a servant with a switch either.

"We are both Brahmins," said Shankara. "I come from a family that gave alms every day and performed the rites of *puja*, propitiating Shiva as you do. I respect our way of life, which was dictated by God. I respect you."

The priest gave a slight nod.

"As I look at you, I think you are the wisest man in this village," said Shankara. "If so, please sit and debate with me. If not, send the man who is considered by everyone to be wiser than you."

He knew that he had caught the priest in a trap, his own vanity.

"If you respect me as a Brahmin," the priest said, hesitating unless he stepped farther into the trap, "then you see that I am busy doing my duty right now." He brandished the ritual implements. "Why should I interrupt holy work for idle arguments?"

"Because you need to see for yourself if God speaks through me. That's what you've heard, isn't it? That my words are divine."

The priest lost his composure. "Outrageous!"

"Why?" said Shankara. "Isn't it held that the first words came from God? Are not words the agent of reason? Therefore, if I speak to you with sound reasons, aren't they from God? Otherwise, we would have to say that I speak for the demons."

"Always a possibility," interjected the head village elder. It was a lot of trouble to cleanse a holy place after a demon infested it.

Shankara smiled. "Even then, since all things are made of God, even the demons have divine nature once you pierce their disguise. So come, sit. Either you will hear the voice of God or you will have your chance to defeat a demon, and a very thin, poor one at that. He would be grateful for a chapati and a cup of fresh water."

In the eight years since he left home, Shankara had repeated this scene hundreds of times, ever since his own guru, on the banks of the sacred Narmada River, had sent him on his mission.

This priest was craftier than most. "It would take too long for me to tell you how I serve God," he said. "But there is a villager, a householder, who lives a life of perfect devotion. I taught him every lesson. Go to his house, and if his devotion crumbles before your arguments, return to me."

The priest gave a flick of the wrist, which sent a servant to fetch bread and water for the intruding stranger. Personally, the priest had no use for wandering monks: half of them were crazy and the other half criminals in disguise. But Brahmin to Brahmin, he couldn't refuse hospitality.

After the priest went back inside, the village elders relaxed, pleased with this outcome. They watched Shankara eat, which he only did after the required blessings.

"Your priest is clever," said Shankara, "which he mistakes for being wise."

"Why do you insult someone who offers you food?" exclaimed the head elder.

"Am I insulting him? I thought he insulted me, because he portrays me as someone who is willing to attack a devout man's faith. If he keeps his faith, I must walk away as the loser in the debate," replied Shankara.

The elders smiled, since they saw very well what the priest's tactics were.

"How will I find this householder of perfect devotion?" Shankara asked.

"His name is Mandana Mishra. You'll have no trouble finding where he lives. He keeps six parrots caged at the gate to his house. They argue philosophy all day and make quite a noise."

As Shankara was sent on his way, he could hear the snickers of the *panchayat* behind him. He continued down the road until he spied the caged parrots, who squawked a warning when he approached. If they had philosophical things to say, they kept them to themselves. On the porch of the house a man was performing ritual offerings. Shankara knelt beside him, bowing with his forehead to the floor. Mandana Mishra sprinkled water to the four points of the compass, muttering a prayer. It took several minutes before he acknowledged that anyone was there.

"Apologies for interrupting your devotions," murmured Shankara.

"There is no sin," replied Mandana smoothly. "A guest at the door is God. We are taught that this is more important than daily prayers."

He showed Shankara into the house and ordered his wife to bring refreshments, which she did silently. One look around told the story. Mandana Mishra surrounded himself with images of the gods. The altar for *puja* was lit with a dozen ghee lamps; the air was heavy with the mixed smell of incense, burnt butter, and ashes. When Shankara explained why he was there, Mandana beamed. He was thrilled to be offered as an example of perfect devotion.

Shankara said, "We cannot debate without a referee. We could send for the high priest, but I want the severest referee possible. Would you agree to let it be your wife?"

The couple stared at each other, startled.

Shankara went on. "In a household like this, where God means everything, the wife must be as wise as the husband. If she says that he has been defeated, no one can dispute her. The last thing a wife would want is to see her husband lose."

The couple agreed, and Shankara sat cross-legged on the floor opposite his opponent; Mandana's wife, Ubhaya, sat to one side .

"Words are empty unless something valuable is at stake," said Shankara. "What shall we wager?"

Mandana smiled. "We are both too poor to wager much. I can offer a handful of rice, but you have nothing."

"We have both given up any hope of riches," Shankara agreed. "But we own something more precious. Let's wager our path to God. If you win, I will stay here and become a householder, following your lead in every ritual and prayer. If I win, you will follow me and become *sanyasi*, a wandering monk."

Husband and wife hesitated a long moment, but in the end the wager was accepted. Shankara was courteously allowed to set the topic of the first debate; he chose faith.

"I was sent here to test your faith," he began. "But I don't need to, for I see that your faith is like a cart with no wheels. It would be pitiful to challenge it." He saw the offended look on Mandana Mishra's pious face. "I'm being kind to tell you this. A cart is only good if it can take you to market or haul in your crops. Faith is the same. It is meant to carry you to God. But if you bow down and perform empty rituals all day without finding God, you might as well bow down to a broken-down cart."

Mandana raised his hand. "The scriptures command us to show our faith through these rituals you dismiss, and the scriptures come from God. Are you saying that God can be untrue?"

"Why do the scriptures command you to pray?" asked Shankara.

"It is not for me to question that."

"Because it would show a lack of faith," said Shankara, finishing Mandana's thought for him. "This is false reasoning, for, like a dog chasing its tail, you say that one must have faith in faith. Give me a reason why."

"God is beyond reasoning," declared Mandana.

"If that were true, then any jumble of words could be called scripture. Nonsense would be divine if all that is needed is lack of reason. Madmen would be better than priests."

"This is just trickery," Mandana shot back. "Scripture cannot be denied."

"Oh, so the dog has found a second tail to chase. Now scripture is right because it is scripture. If that were true, then I could slip lies into the holy books of the Veda and they would turn true simply because of where I put them."

Mandana's wife became alarmed, sensing that her husband was on shaky ground. "Tell him from your heart why we all need faith," she urged.

Mandana nodded meekly. "You are right, my dear. A faith that doesn't come from the heart is no faith at all." He gazed benignly at Shankara. "Faith is the duty of every man, because we are put here to lead a good life in God's eyes. You can't persuade me not to be good. Faith is my bargain with God. If I obey his word, then when I die I will be liberated. The cycle of birth and rebirth will end, and with that, all suffering ends."

"So faith will make you immortal and bring you into the presence of God?" said Shankara. "It sounds ridiculous. A murderer could practice piety, and by your argument, when he dies he only has to cry, 'God, I believed in you. Liberate me, for what is one sin when I have so much faith?'"

"A murderer?" said Mandana. "You can't equate such a sin with the life of a good man."

"So being a good man means being without sin? If you are without sin, my dear opponent, don't bother with faith. You are God already," Shankara replied. "Ask yourself, why is this life full of suffering? Because men are ignorant of the truth. How does it serve God to have the faith of ignorant men? If you needed a house to be built, would you say, 'Send me only those workers who have never built a house?' It's the last thing God wants."

Mandana shook his head. "You can't equate faith with igno-rance. There are wise men who have faith. I imagine that you are one of them, or have you lost your faith by becoming so wise?"

Shankara looked pleased; he wasn't debating a dolt. "The faith of the wise is different from the faith of the ignorant," he said.

"Then grant me that mine is the faith of the wise," Mandana shot back.

"I can't."

"Why not? Can you set eyes on me and instantly see whether I am wise or not?"

"I don't need to. I will prove your ignorance to you. Let's say you met a man who is selling amalaki fruit. You pay him, but in-stead of putting your fruit in a sack, he takes a scoop of air and, pretending it's fruit, puts it into the sack. When you protest that he is handing you air, he says, 'Have faith. There is amalaki in that sack.' What would you say to that?"

"You know what I would say."

"I do. You'd say he was a cheat. So is the faith of the ignorant a cheat. They pay for it. They eat it and say that it's sweet. But what nourishment is there? None. How much suffering do they avoid? Very little. On the other hand, the faith of the wise is pure sweetness and nourishes the soul. How? By taking you where faith is meant to go. Faith is another word for hope. We have faith that God is real, because it is our dearest hope. I may hope for a child to be born to me, but until the child is born, hope flutters on the windowsill like a candle. It signals to God, but is not the same as reaching God.

"What does it take to actually reach God? Two things, knowl-edge and experience. The scriptures give us knowledge. We are told how to worship, how to perform our duties in leading a good life. More than this, we learn how to go inward to find the spark, the essence of God that is inside us. It is our source. Such knowl-edge, though, is only half the path. The other half is experience. What good does it serve you to know that a rose has a beautiful scent when you have never smelled one?

"Mandana Mishra, your house is full of hope for God, as an empty vase is full of hope for roses. Yet you can have the experience, and then your hope will be fulfilled. God wants to be felt, seen, touched. He is lonely sitting apart from us. In finding God you find your own essence. Life exists for no other reason. Know that God is your self. At that moment you will awaken to eternity."

This exchange was only the beginning. For twelve days the villagers didn't lay eyes on Mandana and his wife. They peered in at their window to see if the wandering monk had done something terrible to the most devout man in the village. All anyone could see, whether by the light of day or candles at night, were the two debaters sitting facing each other on the floor.

As dawn rose on the thirteenth day, Ubhaya began to weep. All three of them were exhausted. Mandana had run out of arguments and resorted to repeating himself, mumbling feebly with heavily lidded eyes as sleep overtook him.

"It's no use," said Ubhaya mournfully. She was ready to declare Shankara the winner, even though it meant seeing her husband leave to become a *sanyasi*.

Before she could render judgment, however, Shankara raised his hand. "There is no victory unless I defeat your husband, but according to scripture, the wife is half of the husband. So let me debate you before you tell me I've won."

Ubhaya was astonished, but she grasped at this straw. Everything that Mandana Mishra knew about God she also knew, but she had more wits about her.

"Does God want a man to have a worse life for believing in him?" she began.

"No. God is our own nature. He can only want the best for each person," Shankara replied.

"If that's true, how is it the best for my husband to become a monk? As a householder he gives alms, while a monk begs for them. A householder keeps the sacred fire burning; a monk shivers in the rain. On the road Mandana would face all kinds of dangers. You barely escaped death yourself, or so you say," declared Ubhaya.

"You speak of danger to his body. It's not the body that finds God or loses him," said Shankara.

"I know my husband. He is meek. He will crawl from village to village in fear. Who can find God when he is constantly afraid?"

"Fear can be an incentive too. When you realize that fear is born of duality, you long to go where fear is banished," said Shankara. He was reciting a holy verse that Ubhaya would know. "You are a devout woman; your husband is humble before God. Yet look inside. Aren't you afraid that you may take one wrong step and then God will crush you?"

"Are you deliberately frightening me?" she asked.

"No. It isn't by being more afraid that anyone conquers fear," said Shankara.

When Ubhaya looked away without reply, Shankara went on. "The world is divided because we are divided inside. In everyone the same thing is happening. Good wars against evil, light against dark. How can anyone find peace in such a state?"

"I was at peace before you came to our door," said Ubhaya.

"It was the peace of one who is sleeping. A prisoner who is about to be beheaded in the morning can find the same peace if he manages to fall asleep."

"But if the world is created out of good and evil, that can't be called an illusion," argued Ubhaya. "It's the will of God, who made the world that way."

"You are speaking what most people believe," Shankara conceded. "But reality is slippery. A baby cries with rage if his mother takes away her breast. That is his idea of evil. A little boy playing in the fields will hate another little boy who throws a rock at him. That is his idea of evil. A Buddhist monk will wait by the side of the road holding out his begging bowl, and a passing Hindu will spit on him. That is his idea of evil."

"Yet for all of them, evil is real," said Ubhaya.

"Are you so sure? Experience whirls around our heads like a swarm of flies. But there can be flies in a dream too. They are just as pesky; if they bite, it hurts and we see blood. But when you wake from the dream, your skin is untouched, and you know that the swarm of flies was an illusion. It took place in your mind."

Shankara swatted at the air, which always had a fly or two buzzing around because of the sweet smell of offered fruit. "What makes these flies real? Your senses, because you see them and hear them buzzing. But they would be like flies in a dream if you woke up. That's the only difference. You know how to wake up from your dreams at night, but you haven't learned yet how to wake up from this world. You asked me if God wants the best for us. He does, and the best is to wake up completely."

Ubhaya, who was genuinely devout, felt moved. But her panic over losing her husband was stronger.

"If Mandana follows you, will you become his guru?" she asked. Shankara nodded.

"And a guru knows everything necessary to remove darkness?" Shankara nodded again.

"But you are sorely lacking," said Ubhaya, raising her voice, "because you know nothing of how men and women live together."

It was the first time Shankara was taken aback. "I know they love one another, and God has shown me infinite love."

"Men and women also lie together. What do you know of that? If you want to steal Mandana from my bed, how do you know that you haven't deprived him of great bliss? And for what, a promise that you can lead the way to a higher world? You think it's higher because a woman has never shown you any differently."

It was a brazen speech. Shankara blushed and lowered his eyes. "I swore to be celibate. Whatever you are offering, it's impossible for me to accept."

Ubhaya laughed softly. "You say that it takes experience to

realize God. Yet when this experience comes near, you run away. If you are so easily routed, why should my husband trust his life to you?" Ubhaya was an honest woman, but she could barely keep herself from stroking Shankara's cheek if it meant that she might win.

He backed away, saying, "God wouldn't deny me anything, and if this experience is missing, the fault is mine. Give me eight days."

Ubhaya's heart leapt with hope. "You intend to learn the art of loving a woman in eight days? All right, but if you experience bliss, you must admit defeat." She stopped, knowing that Shankara had set a trap for himself. If he slept with a woman, he would be breaking his vows as a monk. It would be a sin for Mandana to follow him, no matter how clever his arguments were.

Instead of getting up to leave, Shankara said, "I will sit here and not move. No matter what happens, see to the welfare of my body. Keep it warm. Protect it from harm, and pour water into my mouth when it gets dry."

Although they were startled, Mandana and his wife agreed. For the next eight days Shankara sat with his eyes closed. He didn't respond to sounds, and when his mouth was opened to pour water into it, he remained as motionless as a corpse. Finally, on the eighth day, he stirred.

"I am ready," he said, opening his eyes.

"For what?" asked Ubhaya, suspecting a trick. "If you imagined the delights of the bed, that is more of an illusion than anything."

He shook his head. "I begged God to experience the love between a man and a woman without breaking my vows. You saw my body in this room, but I wasn't here. I was taken to the palace where the maharajah enjoys his many wives. For eight days I was inside his body. He is a vigorous lover, and his wives are skilled in every art. I have returned with all the experience you mocked me for not having."

Ubhaya felt the ground give beneath her. "If that's true, then you experienced tender, all-consuming bliss. In the throes of love, nothing else matters. If God wants the best for us, name something better than this."

Shankara replied, "After he made love, the maharajah was exhausted and his spirits dulled. He was listless, like a man without a mind. His bliss sharply came to an end. I won't speak of the other problems of the bed, the jealousy among his wives, the fear that he would one day lose his powers, the suspicion that women didn't really love him but put on a show. But God offers bliss that is unending. It neither comes nor goes. Where I shall take Mandana, the fruits of divine love will make him forget the bedroom forever."

Suddenly Ubhaya wailed and threw herself at Shankara's feet. "I can't bear to lose him! Why would God give my husband eternal bliss only to throw me into the greatest pain?"

Shankara replied gently. "The pain is not from losing your husband; it is from losing yourself. In this world the path of pleasure leads everyone to run after their desires. You have been fortunate. You could have been pursued by a man who wound up beating you or betraying you with another. Wisdom looks beyond today's happiness. Tomorrow Mandana's love could turn to indifference or even hate. Emotions are fickle. He could wither and fall sick; you might die in abject poverty. Knowing this, wisdom rescues us. It restores us to our true self, and with that, fear is banished. For as long as you are subject to pain, fear is your ruler."

Ubhaya bowed her head and let her husband go. They wept when they parted, and he looked back many times before she saw his figure disappear in the distance. It was the custom for a *sanyasi* to take on a new name when he renounced his old life. Mandana took the name of Suresvara. Wherever Shankara went, he followed; the years melted away and then there was a great shock. The master died at a cruelly young age, only thirty-two. They were staying in a village that barely appears on the map. Shankara felt feverish; the next morning he didn't wake up.

By this time there were many disciples, and a crowd followed the body to the ghat where it was burned to ashes. Suresvara saw to it that the ashes were scattered over the river with a hundred floating lamps surrounding them, like stars gathering to mourn the sun after it goes out. The disciples scattered to the four winds. Shankara had foreseen this. He established four great centers where wisdom would be preserved until the end of time.

When young monks were presented to Suresvara, who became eminent as a guardian of truth, they were looked upon kindly, but with a little pity. It would take a lifetime to absorb the teachings of Shankara. To keep up their courage, Suresvara told a simple story.

"I was walking with Master when we came upon a filthy man in the road, an untouchable, and I rushed ahead, shouting, 'Get out of the way! A Brahmin is coming.' Not for anything would I have Master's body be tainted by contact with an untouchable.

"But Master raised his hand and said, 'Who is supposed to step aside? If it is this man's body, you know that the body is unreal. If it is his true self, which is infinite, how can he move anywhere? He already fills all of creation.' And with that, Master fell to the ground and bowed before the untouchable."

Suresvara recounted this incident, because he remembered how he wept when it happened and how shocked he was at the same time, as shocked as the newcomers were when they heard the story. Untouchables were still despised; that was a rigid custom, the way society was set up. Wisdom would have to wait.

When Suresvara grew old, he lay on his deathbed and regretted only one thing, the fate of his wife, Ubhaya. His own life had reached eternal bliss; he had no fear of not being liberated. Yet this one hurt pinched at his soul. He breathed his last. The room where he lay vanished, the four walls melting like smoke. He found himself in the high Himalayas, alone, with snowflakes pelting his face.

In the distance a small speck appeared, and after awhile Suresvara saw that it was someone on foot, walking in his direction. In a few moments a hooded traveler approached him. He removed his hood, but it wasn't a man. It was Ubhaya, looking exactly as she did the day they were married.

Suresvara quaked and sobbed, "Can you forgive me?"

"What was best was best," she replied.

"But not for you," cried Suresvara.

"Shall I throw off my cloak and show you what I was reduced to?" she asked. He nodded, afraid to see her ravaged body and the rags she must be wearing.

In the driving storm Ubhaya dropped her coarse wool cloak, but she wasn't dressed in rags. Her body was pure light, more blinding than the white snow that swirled around her. She was revealed as no mortal woman, but the goddess Saraswati. Suresvara reached to touch her hem, and at that instant they both disappeared. Bliss melted into bliss. He had used his life for the one thing that matters most. The high peaks looked on and rejoiced.

Revealing the Vision

In the East, God didn't evolve as he did in the West. There is no punishing Yahweh, no biblical prophets, no redeeming Christ. Without those three ingredients, God's nature could follow entirely different lines. It is only by accident that the Father, Son, and Holy Ghost are three, and so is the Indian conception of Brahma, Vishnu, and Shiva. But the fact that three gods are responsible for creating, maintaining, and destroying the universe scandalized Westerners when they first encountered India, for the same reason that they were scandalized in China, Japan, and other parts of Asia. "The gods" meant paganism; the benighted souls of Asia needed to be converted to "God," the one and only.

The charge of paganism is still leveled at the East, but with a twist. With enough force, you can conquer a country and make conversion to God mandatory, upon penalty of death. But in Asia people shrugged off the difference between God and the gods. They had been taught that material life was *maya*, an illusion of the senses. It hardly mattered if the illusion contained one God or many gods. When the scales fell away from their eyes, people would see the luminous reality that lies behind the veil of appearances. As their life mission, the great sages of India, China, and Japan gave directions for how to escape the bondage of illusion, which brought pain and suffering with it. If Christ taught that this vale of tears ended in heaven, Shankara taught that suffering ended with enlightenment. Since both paths eventually lead into the light, would Jesus and Shankara have seriously disagreed if they had faced each other in a debate?

That would have been a purely hypothetical question for Westerners arriving in India three hundred years ago. Most paid no attention to Eastern spirituality, since it was all dismissed as paganism. But when it was examined, the teaching that life is a dream seemed like dubious metaphysics or else poetic license taken to extremes. There are times when all of us feel as if we are walking through a dream. Some of these are happy times—as for a bride on her wedding day—others are tragic—as for survivors in the aftermath of an earthquake. A trancelike moment could easily be a slipup in the brain or a lapse of focus. But twelve centuries ago, Shankara declared that our entire life is spent not understanding reality. What we take to be real is a walking dream, one from which we must awake.

Shankara was not trying to make people feel that their lives were worthless, though. He held that once awake, having freed ourselves from illusion, we could master reality. His arguments were so powerful that he conquered all comers in debates that ranged the entire length and breadth of India.

This is a topic that shouldn't be restricted to antique debating contests or the sometimes bloody religious conflicts between East and West. Practical things are at stake—life and death, in fact. In one place Shankara writes, "People grow old and die, because they see other people grow old and die." Outrageous? Not if life is created from awareness like a dream, for when you encounter any bad event in a dream, it vanishes as soon as you wake up. In a dream, if you contract cancer, you could be just as frightened as if you were awake. But if it comes naturally to dismiss dream cancer as an illusion, why are we trapped in waking cancer?

The modern-day South Indian guru Nisargadatta Maharaj was confronted with this dilemma once when a student asked him how to overcome the fear of death. This student was in great fear of mortality and urgently wanted an answer.

"Your problem," Nisargadatta replied, "is that you think you were born. Whatever is born must die, and this knowledge gives rise to fear. But why do you accept that you were born? Because your parents told you so, and you believed them, just as they believed their parents. Look inside. Try to imagine nonexistence. You cannot, hard as you try. That's because reality lies beyond birth and death. Realize this truth, and your fear of death will be no more."

The logic is impeccable and suspicious at the same time. What makes it suspicious can be stated quite simply. If you spend a day at the beach, soaking up the sun, idly watching other people, and occasionally cooling off in the sea, everything seems real; the hours pass and events occur. If you did the same thing in a dream, a day at the beach might take only a few moments as measured by brain activity. Once you woke up, you would realize that your day at the beach was an illusion because it all happened inside your consciousness.

Shankara is saying that your "real" day at the beach also takes place in consciousness. Physically, this fact is undeniable. All experience is mediated by the brain. You cannot see, smell, hear, touch, or taste anything without the appropriate brain activity. If you view a rainbow, your visual cortex is at work whether the rainbow is seemingly "in here" as part of a dream or "out there" as part of the real world. We cannot prove that the rainbow "out there" exists on its own. Shankara says that it doesn't. To him, all external things are experiences in consciousness, and the ultimate consciousness, the beginning and end of everything, is a universal, absolute consciousness we can call God.

It might seem that Shankara is reducing everything to the subjective. Actually, he is raising awareness above crude facts. Experience is far richer than the data that science uses to explain things. In a court of law you cannot objectively prove that chocolate is delicious or why you feel that the woman you love is the most beautiful in the world. Yet that hardly matters. Only consciousness can explain consciousness. What we experience is real for us, uniquely and mysteriously. To someone with agoraphobia, a fear of open spaces, it doesn't matter that open spaces are harmless or that going outside is a pleasure for most people. To the phobic person, anxiety is anxiety. Shankara is saying that consciousness is self-sufficient. It creates the world, as a sleeper creates a dream. The problem is that we have forgotten that we are such powerful creators. Shankara invites us to remember again.

We could veer into a long discussion about science here, because science depends entirely upon objective facts. Subjectivity is considered unreliable, wayward, and far too personal. But after all the arguing, we only wind up in Shankara's clutches, because modern science has deposed the physical world entirely, which is his main point. Quantum physics has reduced the physical world to an illusion. Atoms, the building blocks of the material universe, are not solid, tiny objects. They are a whirl of energy that is invisible and has no physical properties like weight or solidity. In turn, this energy winks in and out of existence, returning to the void that is the origin of the cosmos thousands of times a second. In the void there is no time or space, no matter or energy. There is only the potential for those things—so what is potential?

To Shankara, along with the ancient Vedic sages in his spiritual tradition, the creative potential that gives rise to everything in creation can't be physical. This includes the creative potential in everyday life. Let's say that you discover that your four-year-old child is a musical prodigy or an extraordinary math whiz. As the days go by, his or her potential unfolds step-by-step, and you witness the flowering of a talent that began as a mysterious, invisible seed. When potential unfolds, it's not like a bag of sugar that you steadily empty. The more sugar in the bag, the more you can pour out. But there is nothing physical stored somewhere giving rise to more and more creativity. Instead, an invisible potential (such as musicality or a knack for numbers) finds a way to emerge into the physical world.

God has done the same thing. According to Shankara, the only God that could exist is not a person, even a vast, superhuman person, but something invisible and yet alive, a kind of infinite potential that can create, govern, control, and bring to fruition everything that exists. This God cannot be limited; therefore, he cannot be described. Not that "he" or "she" or even "it" is correct. No single quality can define God, who like the air we breathe is mixed into every cell without being detectable. Imagine that you hand a yellow tulip to someone who has no knowledge of genet-ics, and you say, "What makes this flower yellow isn't yellow. What makes it soft, shiny, and pliable has none of those qualities. It doesn't sprout in spring or grow from a bulb." The claim sounds preposterous until you understand the path that leads from a gene to a flower. In Shankara's world, all paths lead from God, and all are in consciousness.

To name this all-pervasive source, the Indian spiritual tradition uses several suggestive labels. *Brahman* is the most all-inclusive, since it means "all that exists," derived from the root word for "big." To get at the impersonal mystery of God, the term *tat*, or "that," is used. When someone becomes enlightened, three great realizations, or awakenings, are involved, like three stages of waking up in the morning. The first is "I am that." I am not a self bound by a body and trapped in the brief space between birth and death. I am made of the same essence as God. What is that essence? It can't be put into words. It is "that." This is a highly personal experience, as all epiphanies are. But Shankara isn't both-ered by the subjectivity of such an astonishing revelation. To stub your toe on a rock is just as personal, just as subjective, and just as much a product of consciousness.

The second awakening occurs when the divine is seen in some-one else. "I am that" expands into "You are that." This widening continues until the whole world is consumed, leading to the third awakening, "All of this is that." Once the entire world is experi-enced as divine, one enters the state of unity consciousness. There is nothing that is not yourself, in its pure essence.

Shankara was established in unity consciousness; that is his claim to enlightenment. Can such a state be faked? Are there judges who can validate that it exists? Skeptics pose such ques-tions because they don't accept the first premise of the Indian spiritual tradition, which is that consciousness is all. By accepting materialism instead—the doctrine that all things and events have physical causes—we can agree on all kinds of things. Rocks are solid. Fire burns. Pleasure is different from pain. You and I have a stake in such a world, so we don't question it. Shankara declares that you must stop having a stake in the world, and when you do, you will be set free. Rid of fear and worry, totally at home in the world, you become a child of the universe, liberated into a state of complete openness with whatever comes your way.

But what if you are the martyred Giordano Bruno, the Italian friar killed by civil authorities in 1600 after the Roman Inquisition found him guilty of heresy, and what comes your way is seven years of torture before you are burned at the stake? Dreams can turn into nightmares, after all. What is the true way to escape? Bruno could not, for all his brilliance and insight. There are two answers to this predicament. You can either wake up from this dream called life or you can master it. Here we touch on the human face of God. God forces nothing and expects nothing. Captivated by maya, or illusion, people have devised an angry, punishing, judgmental deity. You can devote a lifetime—or countless centuries—to pleasing such a God and end up empty-handed. You can spend the same lifetime defying God and still not escape life's pain.

But if God is pure potential, things change radically. Potential is infinitely flexible. A God of potentiality doesn't need to be obeyed, feared, or placated. He exists to unfold anything and everything. Our agonies arise because we do not realize the divine potential in ourselves, which can alter our fate. If you realize this fact, you may seek only to wake up from the horrors of the dream. In that case, your goal will be to return to the light, where total peace and complete absence of pain exist.

Or you could decide to fulfill your divine potential here and now. In that case, God becomes much more human. He embodies all love, all creativity, all the good possibilities in life. With this realization, you don't seek to return to the light. Instead, you master the dream, a poetic way of saying that you expand your consciousness. Expansion is how false boundaries are dissolved.

Psychologists recognize a kind of ultrarealistic dream state, known as lucid dreaming, that cannot be distinguished from being awake. While having a lucid dream, you are there, fully, with all five senses operating. Then comes the first hint of waking up. Perhaps you are immersed in a jungle adventure running from a tiger. You feel its hot breath on your neck when suddenly the faintest notion occurs: this is just a dream. At the same time, you know that no one made the dream but yourself, which is why it holds no danger.

Shankara describes a permanent state that is very similar, in which you fully participate in the world, but you faintly know that you are dreaming. This state of so-called witnessing is the Vedic version of what Jesus names as being in the world, but not of it. It's a very desirable state, because you become creative in-stead of passive. Poised on that edge before you wake up from your jungle adventure, you know that the dream belongs to you. Suddenly you are an author. Some lucid dreamers can even reen-ter their dream, willing themselves not to wake up. They can do this because they are, after all, the authors of their dream.

In the same way, you are the author of your life. It may seem that all kinds of outside factors hem you in and deny your author-ship: disease, aging, the forces of nature, social rules and stric-tures, and ultimately death. But Shankara asks a simple question that explodes these external limitations: Has anything that ever happened in a dream actually hurt you? When you wake up, the whole dream is gone. Tigers, angels, demons, pursuing enemies, and voluptuous lovers. All share the same unreality.

Mastering the dream is good news and bad news at the same time. The good news is that you are the true author of your life, with the capacity to make anything happen. To arrive at mastery takes time. There are cautionary tales, like the reckless, unfortu-nate Giordano Bruno, who saw the light, but did not escape the dream. Shankara outlines how to undergo the process of mastery, using all the tools of Yoga. These tools are all about consciousness. They teach you how to use your mind instead of allowing your mind to use you.

The bad news? It's not the prospect of failure. Once the process of awakening begins, it is unstoppable, even if you have to cross into new lifetimes to reach your goal. The bad news is that mastering the dream isn't like being Midas. You won't turn everything you touch into gold. The lure of riches, endless pleasure, power, and even saintliness starts to fade once you know that it's all a dream. Unity consciousness is the ultimate mastery known to the world's spiritual traditions, but it cannot be described in worldly terms. When the two domains of reality, "in here" and "out there," finally merge, a new existence dawns. It is indescribable before you reach it, which is why there's another saying that Shankara's tradition insists upon: "Those who know It speak of it not; those who speak of It know it not."

Making God disappear from the physical world is either a sign of progress, because it removes the self-centered belief that the deity must look and act like a human being, or it is a scandal, just as it was to the first Westerners, because you can't just wipe God away like that. He will notice, and his reaction won't be pleasant. What is liberation in the East remains heresy to many in the West. The only certainty is that God has more faces to show. Matters are not settled yet by any means.

5

RUMI

"Come with Me, My Beloved"

Defendants. Why don't they know when to quit?

"I didn't beat my wife, Your Honor."

"How did she get those bruises, then?"

"I was holding a stick and she ran into it."

Silence is blessed to a man of virtue. The Prophet, peace be upon him, was famous for his silence. When the men sat around the fire to sing and recite poems in the desert, he sat tongue-tied in the dark, hoping not to be noticed. Then Allah sent an angel to speak through him. Gabriel touched his soul, and with one word—" Recite!"—the Prophet was filled with God's truth. He surrendered to the miracle, even when the voice of God made him quake with fear.

In court it helped to think about miracles. The room stank of guilt and desperation. The next defendant would be like the first, armed with a tongue of brass.

"Your brother came in on you sleeping with his wife."

"It was the coldest night of the year. If I didn't lie on top of her, she would have frozen to death."

The court had no choice but to find the lot of them guilty. Not that the plaintiffs were satisfied. The next town over had twice as many thieves with their hands cut off. It was ages since anyone could remember a public execution.

"Am I interrupting, Your Honor?"

The *qadi*, or judge, blinked his eyes; he must have dozed off from boredom and the heat of the day. The air was stifling. There was no jury. The trial consisted of both parties arguing their case, without lawyers or prosecutors. But this *qadi* liked to be backed up by devout jurists who sat to advise him. They were half asleep too. The plaintiff coughed in his hand, delaying to make sure that somebody was paying attention.

"There can be no doubt about the facts," he said, raising his voice as if the courtroom was packed with awed listeners. "Abdullah al-Ibrahim ran over his wife with an oxcart. She was my daughter Aisha. Her ribs were crushed, and she died in agony three days later."

A wail arose from the hapless defendant; this one, at least, was speechless. So far he had cowered abjectly, crouching on the floor without a word. He was sixty. The dead woman was barely twenty.

One of the *qadi*'s jurists raised his hand. It was Jalal al-Din Muhammad.

"May I ask our brother a question?"

The judge nodded; the dead wife's father frowned. Convictions went through the floor when Jalal intervened. He was mild and kept to himself, a scholar. He should have stayed where he belonged, nodding over the law by candlelight.

People knew why Jalal sat at trials. So he wouldn't seem like a nobody, his enemies sneered. Strangely, everyone among his enemies had land and gold, and they spent a great part of the winter, when the fields lay fallow, bringing lawsuits.

Jalal rose and approached the cowering defendant. It was fairly outrageous how he called criminals "our brother" and placed his hand on their shoulders.

"How many fingers am I holding up?" he said. He raised four fingers, standing no more than a yard from the defendant.

Abdullah hesitated. "Three," he mumbled.

Jalal turned to face the judge. "He's innocent. Let's go home."

He spoke quietly, but his words produced an uproar from the families on both sides. In the din of voices the wife's father let fly a curse. He had been a farmer himself before he gobbled up parcels of land during droughts. Now he was vain enough to keep his best silk slippers in a cedar chest, just in case the sultan came calling.

He vented his fury at Jalal. "Ridiculous! You're claiming that someone else ran over Aisha? No one else was there."

"No," Jalal replied.

The *qadi*, who had retired from his large rug-weaving factory, where half the women in Konya worked, called for order. "Then what are you saying?"

"Look at him. Our brother has milky eyes. He ran over his wife as she was bending to sort the stalks of wheat, so that the ox cart could roll over them. He didn't mean to."

The judge leaned down from his high table. "You didn't see her?"

The defendant crossed his arms over his chest, refusing to answer. It wasn't pride. If he admitted that he couldn't see, his sons would have the right to seize his land. He'd become no better than their slave. Abdullah had been covering his eyes for months, claiming that flies bit them, when it was cataracts all along.

The "not guilty" verdict made the spectators scream, half for joy, half in fury. The *qadi* shrugged. He knew how it was with these country folk. If Abdullah's sons wanted his land badly enough, their father would be found in a ditch or simply disappear. The judge wasn't happy about Jalal, even so, who was patting the blind old farmer and trying to assure him that he was free to go. Advice and interference were two different things. Making the *qadi* look foolish was out of bounds entirely.

Jalal found himself walking home alone. This would have been his wish anyway, even if a friend had caught up with him. He wasn't fit for company. He was having impure thoughts, and it was dangerous to let them slip out. There was no helping that. Guilt loosens the tongue. It can take awhile. Impurity burrows deep and hides like a mole. But unfortunately guilt isn't blind like a mole. Jalal felt that everyone could see into his soul. If he bought a fish in the market and the old woman pressed his change into his hand to make sure no coins fell through his fingers, her touch burned. When she mumbled, "Thank you, sir," it was obvious she was crying, "Sinner!"

Jalal spent hours examining his guilt, with the precision of the Arab astronomers he admired so much when they mapped the stars. Was guilt hot or cold? Cold, like a frozen rock pressing down on your heart. Shame, on the other hand, is hot, like a fire spreading across your face. Guilt is nagging rather than stabbing, constant instead of intermittent, hard instead of soft. Jalal smiled to himself. He should have been a court physician, he knew the anatomy of his guilt so well. But court physicians are frequently executed if they don't cure the sultan. That was a sticking point. Jalal's guilt was not being cured; it was growing worse, festering like an unlanced boil.

He crept along with his head ducked and almost ran into someone. The man shouted "Hey!" before he almost ran over the absent-minded scholar with his cart. Jalal looked up and stepped aside, but the driver wasn't moving on.

"I have a question for you, sir." The man took his hands off his cart and touched his forehead with respect.

A pang struck Jalal. The question was bound to be religious. People trusted him to be wise, to give them a fatwa no one could dismiss. Now he recognized the cart driver, vaguely, from the mosque.

"Sorry, I'm on my way to—" he said.

The driver cut him off. "It is written that God forgives no great sins, like murder. I know that, but if I hate my wife and send her to live far away with a relative who starves her to death, gradually, you understand, am I a murderer?"

Jalal took a deep breath to steady his nerves. "Yes," he replied.

The man shook his head, pursing his lips. "That's what my cousin said, and he's as ignorant as dried mud. Oh well." He flicked his donkey with a light switch, nodded cheerfully, and moved on.

Jalal leaned against a wall, feeling terrible. He was thirty-seven, and for his entire life men came to his house, and before that his father's house, with these questions. He was proud of the answers he supplied. They came quickly, for he had a good head for the Quran; it was a complex document. Allah didn't always choose to make his words clear, and if he contradicted himself, that was his prerogative. The children of God aren't babies to be spoon-fed. Who could complain? However knotty the Holy Book was, to complain was a grievous sin.

Impure thoughts came relentlessly to mind, and the worst of it was that his piety masked his inner rot. There were moments when Jalal expected a student to grimace, holding his nose, and say, "Do you smell that too? Let's open a window."

Then what would the teacher say to the pupil? "That stink is just my soul. Please copy the next verse."

A flood of guilt swept over him. In the midday sun he shivered with cold and turned his steps toward the bazaar. He had nothing to buy; his wife went to market at dawn every day anyway. But when he was sure she wouldn't see him, Jalal mingled with the noisy, jostling crowds. The press of other bodies against him made him feel less lonely. Merchants shouting in his ear distracted him from the misery of his impious thoughts.

In a few minutes he got the relief he sought. In the narrow byways among the stalls all kinds of bodies rubbed shoulders and poked elbows. Since all the best produce was gone before noon, sellers had to work harder to push the dates squeezed by picky housewives and brass pots with tiny dents where they had been knocked on the ground.

"Fresh mint, there won't be any more when it gets cold! Pomegranates picked from the Prophet's orchards! Lamb fat rendered a day after they were born!"

It was all show, yet Jalal felt comforted by it, since it pulled him out of himself. He smiled at a young girl peddling silver trinkets.

"Very nice," he murmured, thinking how innocent she looked.

The girl smiled and leaned toward him. "Look into my eyes and see the world before it began."

Jalal was startled. "What?"

She raised her voice over the hubbub. "Your wife would look nice in these." She held up a pair of hoop earrings.

Jalal was certain of what he first heard, and he was about to say so when it struck him that the voice had been a man's. Some man had leaned in from behind and said those shocking words into his ear.

"Look into my eyes and see the world before it began."

Jalal whirled around to catch the man, but by now he was lost in the milling crowd. Jalal's ears burned; his heart raced. He didn't want the girl at the stall to see him like this, so he rushed away, pushing into the mob. Anger began to rise in him as he repeated the words and felt more and more offended.

Strangely for such a mild man, he was suddenly overcome with fury. He pushed a tottering old woman out of his way and blindly kicked at a stray dog.

"Why won't you look? Your eyes are small, but they can see across the universe."

There it was again, the same voice. This time Jalal was quicker. He turned around and grabbed at the cloak of the man behind him.

"What did you just say to me? How dare you!"

He had grabbed hold of a black porter, an Abyssinian with a

bale of cotton over his shoulder. The porter looked frightened and mumbled excuses in his native tongue. It was obvious he didn't know a word of Arabic. Everyone close by turned their heads. Jalal let go of the poor man, turned red, and dashed away. At his back he felt the sting of mocking voices.

He ran fast enough to sweat, although he knew very well that it was panic sweat. Allah read his impure thoughts. That went without saying. Now he was being punished, and it was only the beginning. Rebuke from God is terrible. Worse, it can be devious. Your own mind can torment you with words that could be satanic or divine, you never know which.

When the angel Gabriel first came to the Prophet, peace be upon him, there was more fear than joy. The angel said "Recite!" The holiest of holy books was being delivered as a gift—to whom? To a simple, troubled man, a merchant of Mecca, who craved to know God's will. Muhammad went to the cave often, to meditate on the sinful world and the feebleness of faith. It seemed as if every people had been given the word of God except the Arabs. They had forgotten that they were the sons of Abraham. Allah had every right to destroy them. Instead, he showered them with the blessed words of the Quran.

When a blessing arrives in a blinding light, however, the mind can become unhinged. Every Bedouin child is raised in fear of jinns and demons that can be inhaled while you sleep or tilting your head back to drink wine. The Prophet was just a man among men, and he had been raised in the desert by Bedouins. The sight of Gabriel filled him with panic. He ran outside the cave, stumbling up the mountain. When he got to the summit, his sandals torn, his feet bleeding, his only intent was to hurl himself off a cliff onto the rocks below. He was stopped only when he gazed up at the sky and saw the angel in a new form, spread out as a faint light as far as the horizon. Then Muhammad realized that Allah abides everywhere in creation. There is no escaping him, and so dying was futile.

How desperate that moment must have been! Jalal could feel it now himself, the panic of nowhere to hide. He wanted to clap his hands over his ears, shutting out the insidious voice. But reason took hold. The voice wouldn't return, not if he calmed down. Quickly Jalal left the bazaar. He found an empty square, a place he knew about where an old well had dried up. Nobody went there anymore. It was an empty place with blank walls on all sides.

Jalal arrived quickly. The square was vacant. He sat on the crumbling edge of the well, looking around several times to make sure he was alone. Gradually his heart slowed. He felt normal again, and almost safe. Strangely, his panic seemed to have driven out his guilt, because when he looked inside, there was a cool sensation of peace.

"Come with me, my beloved. There is a field beyond the reach of life and death. Let us go there."

Oh God! Jalal's heart leapt into his mouth. He didn't bother to whirl around and find the man who spoke in his ear. There wouldn't be anyone there. But instead of jumping to his feet and running away, Jalal felt himself paralyzed, his legs as limp as a baby's. His body knew that there was no escape, and, like a criminal surrendering on the day of execution, it waited.

When there is nowhere to hide, we all hide anyway. After the angel inspired him, the Prophet ran home and shut himself in his rooms. For months he didn't tell his family about the divine visitation, and it was a longer time before anyone outside the household heard the first words of the Quran. For Jalal, things began the same. He ran home and shut himself up, away from the sight of men, but then everything sped up. On a cold, bright day there was a knock at the door. Jalal's wife was out; he waited for a servant to answer it, and when one didn't, he preferred not to shout and answered the door himself.

It was a stranger, dressed from head to foot in black and leaning on a wanderer's staff.

"I've come. I hope you're better, although in your position I
wouldn't be," he said. "Let me in."

The stranger's voice, in well-accented Persian, was soft, but
compelling. He was somewhere around Jalal's age, with the same
scholar's beard. Jalal stood aside to let him in. "In my position?" he
asked haltingly.

"You're twisted into a knot. God does that. When a contradiction is tight enough, the mind gives up."

"And God wants this?" asked Jalal. He felt a tingle up his spine,
but didn't want to accept what it meant: the stranger's voice was
the one that had spoken in his ear.

"God wants you to be clear about things. Right now you
aren't." The stranger looked around, chose the largest, most comfortable cushion, and sank to the floor with a whoosh of breath.
He had walked a long way.

"Tea," he ordered, as a maidservant entered the room. With a
glance Jalal gave her permission to bring some. The stranger
threw his staff across the room with a clatter.

"If you want to be an abject sinner, go ahead. The trouble is,
you can't be abject and proud at the same time. That's why you
are confused," the stranger declared. The cushion he sat on,
cross-legged and erect rather than slouching back, was near a
window. Jalal had a clear view of the man's bright, darting eyes.
When they landed on Jalal, they seemed to laugh at him.

"We must all live with the knowledge of our sins," Jalal murmured.

"Don't evade," said the stranger roughly. "You're probably right
to be abject, only you need better reasons. You're proud because
you think you're better than the Prophet, peace be upon him. The
Prophet hid under a blanket for two days after God's voice spoke.
You intend to hide forever. Isn't that a kind of pride?"

The mention of God's voice caused Jalal to go stiff. The maid arrived with the tea, so he had to seem calm while she poured two glasses. When they were alone again, the stranger jumped in first.

"My name is Shams. I know about voices. For a long time I have prayed to Allah, asking for the companionship of one who can abide my company. He didn't take me seriously, but then one day a voice asked me, 'What are you willing to pay in return?'

"I said, 'My head.' When you despair of finding someone who understands, your life is a small wager. So the voice told me who you are and where to find you."

Shams raised his glass in a toast. "So here we are. The two most fortunate men in the world—or the two most cursed."

Shams's words shook Jalal to the core. If he had the wits to act like a lawyer, he could have peppered him with a stream of suspicious and disbelieving questions. Something stopped his tongue. He leaned back and, to his great surprise, sighed with relief. He felt like a parched wanderer in the desert who has a vision of an oasis. For days nothing lies ahead of the wanderer but the same barren sands, and then, just when he has drained the last drop from his waterskin, he stumbles over the next rise and, behold, his vision is real.

The stranger, Shams, smiled. "I was in the bazaar the other day. I saw you, in fact. Among ordinary people I pass as a traveling merchant, a weaver. That is my trade, in fact; but I am the son of an imam in Tabriz, a great man."

Jalal nodded. "The voice prepared the way, so I wouldn't turn my back on you."

"Just as the voice I heard prepared my way to you. We are both blessed. Not that I have forgotten the possibility that we are cursed."

The empire of the Seljuk sultans was vast, stretching from the Aegean Sea across many lands conquered centuries before by the Romans. To the Arabs these lands were still *Rum*, or Rome. If you met a traveler from there, you might tell your friends that you ran into a *Rumi*, a Roman. But the world would stick the tag on one

man in particular, not that Jalal knew it yet. He, our Rumi, began
to pose questions. He was less nervous, and he wanted to know
everything about this Shams-i Tabrizi who had been sent by the
will of Allah. Who were his people? Was he the fortunate eldest
son or the bereft youngest?

"Who I am is unimportant. Let's just say that I am you," said
Shams.

"And who am I?"

"An insect collector, apparently."

"Why do you say that?"

Shams looked round the room. "Your books are scattered everywhere. You pore over the Quran and the law. In my experience, weevils and worms gnaw their way into old books, and since
the words you read are useless, the only reason to hold on to your
books must be that you collect insects."

Despite, this, the stranger knew as much about the contents of
books as did Rumi. To exchange learned words delights a scholar's
heart. It bores the world, however.

Soon enough Rumi confessed his state of crisis. Once the
words started pouring out, he couldn't stop himself. Shams was a
tireless listener, but not necessarily a patient one.

"Stop saying 'God' all the time," he snapped. "It gets on my
nerves."

"But we are talking about God," Rumi objected.

"Alas."

"What do you mean? You are a seeker yourself, aren't you?"

Shams shrugged. "And you are a fruit seller who has run out of
peaches. God used to be a luscious peach, the sweetest and ripest
imaginable. He dropped like honey on the tongue. Time passed.
The sweetness dried up; the honey turned bitter. Now what are
you peddling? You cry, 'Fruit here! Luscious, desirable fruit.' But
all that you have to offer is a dried, shriveled skin."

At first Rumi resisted. God, he was certain, isn't a peach. "I
want knowledge. You give me poetry," he accused his visitor.

"Of course. If you have no roses to smell, at least their scent can be captured in a poem," said Shams.

Rumi threw up his hands. "Peaches. Roses. You're laughing at me."

"So that I won't weep."

"Meaning what?"

"I see the emptiness in your heart. You've papered it over with fine words. Moving through the world you get respectful nods from other men. But they don't love you. In fact, they hate you for your learning. They fear that you will find out their secret and expose them."

"What secret?" asked Rumi.

"That their hearts are as empty as yours."

If Shams continued to batter away at him like this, Rumi didn't know what would happen. He was exhausted after an hour. Any more and he might faint or fall sick. They sat alone in the room, surrounded by cold tea and dirty glasses, yet behind the door Rumi had a wife and two sons. After a while there was a gentle rapping from the next room. Rumi sat up, suddenly remembering that he had a life to lead.

Shams saw his eyes glance at the door. "I know," he murmured. "The world is with us, but only for a little while longer."

There was no menace in his voice, but Rumi grew alarmed. "What's going to happen? Are you hiding a knife?"

Shams refused to answer, gesturing for Rumi to go to his family. That night the visitor slept in a rough wool blanket outside the house, taking breakfast with the family, saying nothing except polite mumbles. Rumi eyed him uneasily. By the light of a new day Shams seemed eerie, like an apparition that should have vanished in the night. Once they were alone, Shams told Rumi to ignore him.

"I'm your shadow today. Act as if you don't notice me."

"Why?"

"Nothing mysterious. I only want to observe."

Rumi was certain that something mysterious had to be going on. He followed Shams's instructions, forcing himself not to look over his shoulder as the day unfolded, a typical day. He prayed and studied and told his sons what was expected of them. He went to the *madrassa*, the religious school that he had inherited from his father, where he taught twelve boys to read and write. The hardest part came after sunset, when Rumi sat by candlelight to read the Quran. Seeing Shams in the corner made him too anxious to concentrate.

Without preamble Shams spoke. "I told you about peaches and roses. Now it's time for candles and oceans."

He smiled at Rumi's reaction. He looked relieved that Shams was no longer his silent shadow, but he was baffled and a little annoyed that more riddles were being posed. Shams approached the candle that stood beside Rumi's book, which gave off good light with little smoke. It filled the room with the oily scent of beeswax.

"If God is light, is he in this candle?" Shams asked.

"Perhaps."

"Why perhaps? Is there a place that Allah is not?"

"No, but the light of God isn't the same as ordinary light. If the candle burns out, can you say that God has disappeared?"

Shams laughed. "God disappears all the time. When people lose a child or their money or all their sheep, in my experience they usually lose God. But that's not the point. Accept for a moment that this candle is God."

Rumi nodded.

"We worship the light. We call it God. But how many candles can you light, how many holy lamps or ritual fires, before you get bored? The light no longer stands for anything. It's just a smelly candle whose stub you will throw out in the morning. Do you know what that means?"

Rumi tried not to show his annoyance. "Tell me."

"It means that time is God's enemy. If something can die, snuffed out like a candle, it cannot be God, since God has no be-

ginning or end." Shams held up his hand to keep Rumi from interrupting him. "I see your impatience. Hold still for a moment.
Oceans."

"I'm listening. I've traveled and seen the ocean."

"I can read your mind when you beheld the ocean. *How vast, how
awesome! This too must be God.* You contemplated eternity. So what?"

"Isn't awe enough?"

"Enough for what, to enclose infinity? You didn't even embrace
the ocean. If you dipped a cup in it and took a bit of ocean home
with you, after a few days it would evaporate. So much for your
awe. Where is God in it?"

"Tell me. I don't want to guess," said Rumi.

"Nowhere. Space is God's enemy. The oceans are vast. You can
spend a lifetime sailing over them, beholding their expanse. But
still infinity would stretch beyond your eye. I've laid before you
two truths you cannot escape. Time is God's enemy, and so is
space. What can you do once you surrender to these truths?"

Shams hadn't changed his tone of voice, which was like a
schoolmaster's. Rumi used that tone all the time, droning flatly as
half of his students dozed off. But instead of dozing, Rumi felt his
spine tingle. Shams noticed.

"Ah, the first glimmer," he said with a note of triumph. "Think
how long you've waited to hear my words. Sit back. Enjoy being
stupefied. Bask in your ignorance."

He was mocking Rumi, but what he said was true. In a flash
Rumi saw his ignorance spread out before him. He had spent
years praying and studying. He had traveled to the far reaches of
the sultan's empire visiting holy shrines. But if God was beyond
time and space, none of it mattered.

Shams leaned close enough that Rumi felt his warm, moist
breath. "You have tried to capture the sea in a teaspoon and the
sun in a candlestick. Stop."

Rumi trembled. The room felt small and dark; he wondered if he shouldn't be afraid of Shams. Wouldn't you be afraid of inviting an assassin into your house? An assassin of the mind is more fatal. The instant this thought came to Rumi, the candle burned out, and without warning he felt Shams's arms wrap around him. Rumi flinched; his instinct was to push the stranger away. But Shams held on, squeezing him tighter.

"Love me!" he whispered fiercely.

Rumi was shocked. He tried to jump up, but Shams's embrace pressed him down in his chair.

"There's no escape," Shams whispered. "You will never go beyond time. You will never touch the hem of God, which is outside the universe. There is only one choice to make. Love me!"

Rumi had never known such panic as he felt at that moment. The darkness was suffocating. He had an overwhelming urge to cry out to Muhammad, the old servant who slept across the threshold of the house at night to protect it from burglars. Something in him, however, was not panicking. This surprised Rumi; it was enough for him to hold still in Shams's grip.

"Better," Shams murmured. His grasp loosened.

"Really?" Rumi laughed nervously. He heard his heart beating wildly and was sure that Shams heard it too.

Now Shams's arms relaxed; they were still wrapped around Rumi, but loosely, the way a father might hold his son as they sat by the river in springtime enjoying the return of warmth. In a low voice Shams began to sing.

Take me to that place where no one can go,
Where death is afraid
And swans alight to play
On the overflowing lake of love.

His singing voice was sweeter than his speaking voice, which carried an edge. Rumi kept still. He loved poetry, and even more he loved to hear it sung, with a reed flute playing somewhere in the distance. He felt a warm tear roll down his cheek.

Shams took a breath and repeated the refrain.

And swans alight to play
On the overflowing lake of love.
There the faithful gather
Ever true to their Lord.

Rumi shivered and was glad that the room was dark, because tears covered his cheeks. An assassin had entered his house and turned into an angel.

The shock of what had happened to Rumi quickly spread through the town. Konya's learned jurist had lost his way. He wandered the streets at all hours, wide-eyed, holding his hands up to heaven. He seemed delirious and fevered. He sang in a loud voice, and when people addressed him, he acted as if he didn't recognize them. This might have been forgiven, attributed to the full moon, even if some of his friends whispered darkly behind his back. Rumi was so respected that his reputation wasn't ruined in a week. It took a whole month.

"Our students are leaving. We'll be ruined!" his wife wailed. Rumi gazed at her blankly, as if he didn't know her either.

It was obvious that this distressing change had occurred after Shams arrived. People accosted him.

"You don't like who he has become?" Shams replied.

"You do? He's lost his mind. Soon he will lose all his friends. Nobody will have anything to do with him," people said.

Shams shrugged. "Sometimes a person decides to become real. If you are shocked, think how he must feel."

No one was satisfied with this cavalier explanation. Resentment against Shams grew, but Rumi rarely left his side. If Shams was in the room, he stared at him constantly, and the simplest sentence that Shams spoke caused Rumi to exclaim "Ah!" in a loud voice.

There were intervals when Rumi calmed down and could be questioned. Piecing together his words, which were rushed and fragmentary even during these calmer moments, his friends gathered what was going on with him.

"I didn't know who I was," Rumi explained. "I clothed myself in false knowledge, not just about myself but about everything. Why are we here? To find the truth. All my life I've prayed and studied. My father was a Sufi, believing that God is drawing us near. He taught me that my soul wants to join God, not after I die, but now, at this very moment."

So far, none of this was a secret. The Sufis were a sect with great influence. The common people respected them because they wandered harmlessly seeking God. They were gentle; they took their search seriously. Shams was also a Sufi, from a different sect, but, then, there were many of these, and each had its own *tariqa*, its methods and rituals for finding God. But that was no reason to lose your mind, said Rumi's friends.

Rumi's eyes would widen and his face glow with the innocence of a child. "I know, I know. But who ever finds God? The search is never-ending. If I counted up the words in all my prayers, there would be millions. I had to run away. So do you. Everyone must run away. It's our only hope."

He would become quite worked up at this point and lapse into a kind of whirling dance while singing songs that came into his head, passionate songs that most people found outrageous.

Death killed the one I was,
Now I am love itself!
If there is wheat around my grave

O, make your wine from it
And drink the elixir of life!

Strangely, the more that Rumi made a fool of himself, the more
that people began to listen to him. They followed him in his wan-
derings, waiting to hear what might burst out of him. Then small
clumps began to gather at his door. He had lost his respectability—
no, he had thrown it into the gutter with a wild laugh—and in
that moment God touched him. Always he sang about love and
what lay beyond this world.

Don't come to my grave to weep.
I have left there,
I do not sleep,
I have joined the deathless dance of lovers,
And how my spirit flies!

If they listened, people gradually understood. Love was something new in their ears. The holy books spoke much more of fearing Allah, who holds eternal punishment over the heads of sinners.
The faithful dreamed of the garden of Paradise promised by the
Prophet, where wine flowed like a river and fruit fell from the trees,
yet sin was inescapable. Children were warned to obey without
question, because next to faith God most loves obedience.

Deep down, though, they knew what Rumi was about. If you
give a poor man an acre of land around his house, he will be
pleased and stay there for life. Build a wall around that acre, however, and all he will want is to escape. Rumi had gone over the
wall, and although people held their breath, waiting for him to be
struck down, nothing happened. Months passed, and he still sang
his delirious songs, attracting anyone who heard the soft call of
the soul to be free.

Eventually Rumi noticed that he wasn't alone. Every day his
doorway was blocked by a small crowd sitting on the ground

waiting for him to emerge. Someone started to write down his words. Even when he was swinging around a post, reciting for hours in a trance, teachings came out. Risking heresy, some began to claim in private that he was reciting the Quran of the Persians.

Nothing stays private long. The clerics of Konya were greatly disturbed. They formed a delegation and came calling. Rumi received them meekly. Gazing around, his guests were surprised that his library was neat and undisturbed. Rumi knew what they were thinking.

"I didn't burn my books. Why should I? Allah cannot be touched by fire. But then, I would probably have to write them all over again."

He spoke lightly, but the head cleric in Konya, a mullah who was twice as old as Rumi, glared at him suspiciously. "You would defile the holy books, except that it's inconvenient? Is that what you are saying?"

"I am saying whatever you hear," murmured Rumi.

An argument would have broken out, but the clerics were silenced by Shams walking into the room.

"A convention of insect collectors," he said in greeting, which no one understood. The sight of him was unpleasant enough.

"You have corrupted our best teacher," the head cleric accused.

"I've liberated him," said Shams. "Now he will be a perfect teacher."

"Only the Prophet is perfect, peace be upon him," chimed in another cleric.

"Every soul is perfect, but it shines through us as if through a dirty window. Who knows how we would be once the window is cleaned?" said Shams, as impudent as you please.

He had eaten well and was picking his teeth with a brass toothpick. The clerics rustled angrily. They weren't there to debate, only to issue a warning. A vague warning, as it turned out, since none had the power to exclude Rumi from worship. If they kept him out of the mosque, he could pray privately. If they banned children from his madrassa, there would be trouble among the common people, who had begun to love him. Rumi had flung the school doors open to the whole town.

The clerics rose to leave when Shams held up his hand.

"I wagered my head to find this man who outrages you. You wince when he gazes at me with love, refusing to accept that one soul is seeing another. God willing, we will all see each other that way one day."

"God willing, that day will never come," snapped the head cleric, who had enough proof that Satan lies in wait for the unwary.

The scandal didn't evaporate; neither did Shams. His presence was intolerable to anyone who mattered. One cold winter evening Rumi and his mystical friend sat talking. A servant came in, saying that someone at the back door wanted Shams. He still did his weaving. A customer, perhaps?

Shams gestured that he would be right back. He went to the back door. He never returned. Captors may have thrown a black sack over his head and spirited him off into the night. A whim may have taken hold, and Shams simply walked away on his own. The rumor mill, seeing a satisfied look on the face of Rumi's younger son, held that he had organized an assassination. If so, Allah had exacted the price of Shams's head.

Rumi refused to believe the rumors. He was too shocked to eat or sleep, almost to breathe. When grief no longer paralyzed him, he packed a horse, took two servants, and searched for Shams everywhere he might be, as far away as Damascus. No trace was ever found.

When he wended his way home, Rumi reflected for a long time. "I know what has happened," he finally announced.

"That's good. You can live with your loss," people said.

"Never."

What grief had taught him was this: to ache for Shams was the same as aching for God. Rumi poured his ache into poems about

Shams. First there were hundreds of these, then thousands, then tens of thousands. Yearning became his obsession. Then one day, after another spring had come, Rumi was wandering in his orchards, lost in himself. He felt a light touch on his shoulder.

"Shams!"

But when he turned around, it was just the petals of the plum trees, the first to bloom in April, that had touched him. As his fingers brushed them away, Rumi stopped. How can a person feel the touch of flower petals through thick wool clothing? Suddenly he heard Shams laughing, and his words came back.

"God disappears all the time."

So that was it. This longing for Shams was the same longing we have for a God who disappears, not because he hates us, but because all of life is a search—for love, for truth, for beauty. Whatever God stands for must be elusive; otherwise, we would all feast like a lazy rich man and fall asleep from excess and dullness.

Rumi stooped and gathered a handful of white plum petals, raising them to his nose. The scent was faint—some people smell nothing and wait for the cherry trees a month later—but to Rumi it was intoxicating. From that moment on, his search for perfect love was tinged with joy, even though seeking would never end.

Hearing his poems, people were astonished; there was so much love in Rumi's words and so much pain. Some couldn't bear to listen. When they shuddered, they knew it wasn't just for him. They felt afraid for themselves. They felt unrequited passion. They felt a voice that beckoned from eternity.

Motes of dust dancing in the light—
That's our dance too.
We don't listen inside to hear the music—
No matter.
The dance goes on, and in the joy of the sun
Is hiding a God.

Revealing the Vision

If the West was troubled by making the personal God disappear, as Buddha and many sages in India had done, Rumi brought him back with a passion. In his fervor, his thirst to make God his lover, his willingness to take his search to the edge of madness, Rumi is the complete devotee. Worship becomes all-consuming. Every moment is spent in a feverish search for one thing: the bliss that comes from ecstatic union with God.

From a romantic viewpoint, this sounds marvelous, but there was a stern necessity behind it. Like Judaism, Islam follows scriptures that are about law, obedience, the peril of temptation, and fear of the Lord. Can human nature sustain such an austere, disciplined relationship to God? Perhaps, for the few. But human nature has a great talent that is the reverse of its greatest weakness. If told not to stray beyond the safe confines of virtue, we always find a way to transgress—jumping over the fence is our way to freedom and also to disaster.

Rumi knew both extremes. His biography, about a respected jurist who overnight became a free spirit, appeals to our modern taste for rebels. But his time with his beloved master, the mysterious wandering Sufi Shams-i Tabrizi, was brief, a matter of less than a year. During that time Rumi became versed in the ecstatic way, the path of increasing bliss through love of the divine. But there was a fateful side to Shams, who seems to have known that the path, for him, would end violently. He disappears from the pages of history by walking out a back door to meet an unnamed someone. After that, nothing is known, except that Rumi's grief was unbearable.

When grief is this intense, it's common for people to find surrogates to fill the void they feel inside. Parents who lose a child will preserve the child's bedroom intact, moving nothing, as if love can be frozen in time. At least remembrance can. Rumi did something like this in poems. He turned Shams into an immortal beloved, not for erotic reasons, but to regain the sense of perfect bliss that had descended upon him without warning, only to be lost just as unexpectedly.

In many of Rumi's poems you cannot tell God, the immortal beloved, and the lost teacher apart. Yet the way he writes about the search for God is so personal and passionate that it is irresistible:

> In love that is new—there must you die,
> Where the path begins on the other side.
> Melt into the sky and break free
> From the prison whose walls you must smash.
> Greet the hue of day
> Out of a fog of darkness.
> Now's the time!

Outside the isolated sphere of Persian poetry, Rumi is known in translation for short verses and pithy sayings:

> The idol of yourself is the mother of all idols.

> Fortunate is he who does not walk with envy as his companion.

> You're misled if you think the self is easy to subdue.

These make it seem that he is an effusive romantic, inspired to deliver brilliant gems that are easy to assimilate. But within his own tradition, Rumi is celebrated for monumentally long discourses on the Sufi way. The term *sufi* originated with the coarse wool cloak that wandering mystics wore, and to this day their practices are outside the rigorous boundaries of the Quran. It's a historical oddity that so many Westerners see the Sufis as appealing representatives of Islam, when to insiders they may be too unorthodox, too outside the Book. When Turkey became a republic under Mustafa Kamal Ataturk, after a three-year struggle for independence (1919–22), Sufism was outlawed along with other public displays of Islam. For a time Rumi's tomb in Konya was closed to the public, and it was decades before the whirling dervish dances that are central to the Mevlevi order were allowed to be performed. Whatever we think of Sufism, the various orders posed a threat to the secular state and reactionary belief.

When you are caught up reading the poems, none of that matters. The pure, undistracted path of the mystical lover of God is laid bare, along with its pain when the divine lover is absent. Of course, when you aren't under its spell, this kind of God-talk can seem histrionic, even hysterical. In the India of my childhood, there were respected, even revered, holy figures who acted—and perhaps were—insane; they were known as *mastram*, those who are mad for God. So Rumi's line, "You give away everything, even your mind," isn't poetic exaggeration. It is perilous to start out on a journey that could cost you your sanity, not to mention home, family, and social acceptance.

But it's a mistake, I think, to assume that the devotional path laid out by Rumi is a kind of spiritual bargain in which you trade reason for unreason, safety for risk, and ordinary happiness for bliss. The devotional path, like all profound paths, is about transformation, not bargains with an unseen God. The goal is still unity consciousness. However, instead of examining the obstacles that exist in our consciousness, which is the path of contemplation, or sorting out the real from the unreal by intellectual focus, which is the path of knowledge, devotion is an all-consuming love affair.

The romance of such a path quickly disappears, because no matter what path you take, obstacles and resistance block the way. Someone on the path of knowledge may be totally frustrated, saying, "I don't know where I'm going. My mind feels jumbled and confused. I'm exhausted thinking about God and never finding him." The devotee's frustration is emotional: "I feel numb. I can't find the bliss I once knew. God runs ahead of me like a teasing lover, never allowing me to touch him when I desperately want to." What saves both paths is that the course of the unfolding of the soul is well mapped. You may feel exhausted and empty, and in your struggle the condition feels unique. It isn't. The tradition of seekers is the longest in recorded history. For as long as we have records about God, we find seekers working their way to the divine presence.

Reading Rumi feels so persuasive because he reports everything from his own experience, no matter how humiliating. But he has a universal dimension that amplifies the personal, making it far more significant. Here he is in detached mood, speaking as if from an otherworldly perspective, a perch in eternity:

When a lover of God gets ready to dance
The earth draws back and the sky trembles
Because his feet could stomp with such wild joy
That the sun, moon, and stars might fall from heaven.

Reading about how the poems were written, one gets the impression that Rumi was always in a trance, sometimes dancing, sometimes swinging in circles from a pole. The sight of him doing those things riveted his followers and bothered respectable society. Yet the word *ecstasy* comes from the Latin meaning "to stand outside or apart." Bliss isn't a hysterical, moody, changeable state. Rather, it is an attribute of God and therefore completely stable. What causes the apparent hysteria and moodiness of Rumi's situation is loss. Feeling no bliss, running after an absent God, desperate not to be abandoned, a seeker on the devotional path isn't acting out ecstasy, but the opposite.

Which is why, I think, the respectable devotional paths found in the West, such as you'd meet in silent convents and peaceful churches, would be foreign to Rumi. Sufism is highly organized and disciplined, so we outsiders cannot speak credibly about the kind of experiences anyone has in the order. One suspects that

Rumi's kind of spontaneous awakening is rare, however. He doesn't teach a path to us Western readers. Yet as a torch held aloft at the beginning of the path, who is more inspired? There is a bright flame inside Rumi, and his hope is that he makes you see the same flame inside yourself.

I'll end with one of his most famous extended metaphors about the transformation that devotion may finally bring. A pair of lovers wake up in bed, and the woman—we imagine her tousled hair and intimate warmth—nestles into the man and asks him a question that feels vain:

> In the earliest dawn two lovers awoke
> And sipping some water she said,
> "Who do you love more,
> Me or yourself?"
> She wanted the truth.

The man gives her an answer that isn't kind to her vanity, yet speaks from the heart:

> So he replied, "I can't love myself,
> I don't exist anymore.
> I'm like a ruby held up to the sun
> Melting into one redness.
> Can you tell the gem from the world
> When a ruby gives itself to sunlight?"

Then Rumi enters to speak in his own voice, taking the man's place and raising a lovers' chat into the sublime:

> That's how holy ones can truthfully say
> *I am God.*
> So be a ruby at dawn
> And hold to your practice.

Keep up the work, digging your well
Until you strike water.
Hang a ruby in your ear
And it will become the sun.
Keep knocking at the door
And joy will look out the window
To let you in.

If the West wants an antidote to the East's habit of making God disappear, Rumi doesn't fit the bill. He offers a personal God who is approached with love and devotion, but the path of devotion makes the seeker disappear. The light that embraces him extinguishes personality. It even extinguishes the lesser love between two lovers. In the evolution of God, holding on to the image of a patriarch sitting above the clouds becomes more and more a stubborn habit. This is especially so when, as with Rumi, the divine is a feeling in the heart that expands into all-consuming bliss. Bliss has no name or face. The world's visionaries go in a different direction. Their paths mingle, but still no single picture of God emerges. A deeper transformation is taking place.

6

JULIAN OF NORWICH

"All Shall Be Well"

Heads turned when Mistress Kempe rode through town. You couldn't miss her scandalous white dress—she called it her "pompous array"—which properly belonged on a virgin. Mistress Kempe had borne fourteen children, the first of which drove her insane for a time. (She was lucky to recover from her distraction, if recover she did.) Now she wouldn't let her husband touch her anymore.

"You'll enjoy pleasure enough when you arrive in heaven, John Kempe," she told him tartly. He wasn't so sure it was a fair trade.

There was also talk about her crying in public, with big blobby tears and wailing for Jesus. You never knew when it would happen. Mistress Kempe said it came from the unbearable ecstasy of beholding God's works all around her. Was a haywagon crossing her path or an old donkey one of God's marvels? Perhaps, but the crying was so loud and strange (something between a screech owl and a squealing piglet) that it unnerved people.

"God has made me what I am, and I won't apologize for him," she replied to all complaints.

A rich retinue followed her everywhere, even when she went to buy a sack of turnips. Any new queerness to be spotted in Margery Kempe was a popular topic.

She put on a show of enjoying the attention. "Jesus is the one who speaks to me, every day. That's all I need or want. The rest is like dust on my slipper."

"Is he speaking to you right now?" people would ask, making her laugh.

"How could he? I'm the one talking right now. Are you deaf?"

She was actually worried about her holy outbursts, but in public she was brazen, as befits the daughter of a five-time mayor of Bishop's Lynn. As a member of Parliament, too, he was regularly called down to London, especially during troubled times.

"What times would those be?" asked the wags in the local taverns. "The plague, the war in France, the new taxes that have starved half the peasantry, or the rebellions that killed off the rest?"

If Margery's visions came from anywhere, they came from the feeling that the end of days might be near. By God's mercy, the whole of England saw nothing but woe even before the boy-king, Richard II, proved to be a weakling, grossly deceived by his corrupt ministers.

In a land that prayed three times a day and attended church twice on Sunday, how much more did God want? The worst troubles had come in 1381 when Margery was eight. In one year the poll tax tripled, the lion's share going to finance endless foreign wars and the rest lining the pockets of corrupt courtiers. A tax collector was attacked by an enraged mob south of London. It was a spark, and the peasants were dry tinder. Mobs assembled without warning. They marched in from the country, moving over the land like a raging monster. Pitched battles arose. A summer of violence cost the archbishop of Canterbury his life, and he wasn't alone. The peasant army even faced down the king and demanded their freedom from serfdom. Who could believe it?

Soon the rebels started marching north. If they entered a town, they sought out tax collectors for rough justice, burned down the best houses, and defiled God's places. The panic was akin to the panic that greeted the Black Death. Margery was only eight, pampered and innocent. She was packed up in the night and whisked away from their town, Bishop's Lynn. She was frightened by being wrapped up in a thick wool blanket and half suffocated in the bouncing coach. She never laid eyes on the rioting serfs. She barely knew any to begin with, being a city girl with a rich father.

But worse didn't come to worst. Before that summer was over the peasants were routed. They were armed with sticks and knives, no match for arrows, lances, and armor. Everyone ran to the center of Bishop's Lynn to see the most notorious leaders hanged, drawn, and quartered. Margery was torn between curiosity and fear. She couldn't resist, however, and decided to slip a groat into her maid's hand to sneak off to the executions. It would be gruesome, no doubt, but she wanted to see something special.

"My child, what could you dare to see?" her horrified maid asked.

"Just before they tear the body apart," said Margery soberly. "I hear that the hangman cuts out the man's heart and shows it to him so that he can repent and find God's mercy. That's something I'd like to see for myself."

Her maid balked, and in the end she got the groat anyway for promising not to tell Margery's father about such a wicked desire. Looking back, Mistress Kempe didn't consider it wicked, but God must have disagreed. A stony repentance would take up her whole life.

The first crisis came when she was twenty, still a bride and the mother of her first baby. The delivery was difficult. Margery became feverish, and soon she fell gravely ill. No herbs or prayers could break the fever. Her body was wracked with pain. It was so severe that she became delusional; she saw demons swirling around her, clawing at her with shrieks and laughter. Darkness blotted her mind, and when her husband came into the room, Margery turned her face away.

"No visitor can do me good now except death," she said.

Hope was defeated. A priest entered the house for her final confession. He was hesitant, though. "I will hear your confession, daughter," he told Margery, "but let's also pray for your recovery. I will remain as long as God needs me." This was more than optimism and certainly not charity. Her family could afford to pay a sizable piece of silver for a constant vigil.

"No, I must die after what I will tell you," said Margery weakly. "God will have none of me then."

The priest had heard every possible sin in the confessional. He reassured her that she could be forgiven, no matter what.

"Don't say that until you hear my great secret," Margery replied.

No one found out what she whispered in his ear, but the priest rushed from the room, horrified. He refused to give absolution. He wouldn't even finish the confession. John Kempe watched in bewilderment as the priest fled the house. When he entered his wife's room, she was raving, her eyes rolled back. He had no choice but to clap her up in the storeroom until the demons that tormented her mind finally claimed her life.

Months passed, and Margery woke up shaking every day, certain of her damnation. She wasted away as she pined. Since everyone accepted the same truth—her soul was lost to Satan—there was no reason to take extreme measures to keep her alive. So it was a little upsetting when the family entered the storeroom, ready to wrap a corpse in a winding sheet, only to find her sitting up and claiming that Jesus had appeared to her.

It was a miraculous visitation. Jesus stood by her bed, looking down at her with melting eyes. "Why have you forsaken me, and forsaken even yourself?" he asked.

"I did forsake him," she admitted. "But no more. He stretched out his hand, and what was damned in me is now blessed. The rest of my life belongs to God alone."

Her family was perplexed and skeptical. Margery wandered

around for days in a kind of ecstasy—the loud, strange crying started then. No one could deny that she had miraculously regained her strength; and her speech, when she could draw breath to make sense, was sane. But having her around posed problems. A young wife beset with an abundance of religious feeling should do the right thing and enter a convent; that had happened often enough. The family got Margery into the cloister, almost. The day came when her solitary bag was packed with the bare necessities for travel. She was found sitting on the floor, surrounded by her many fine dresses, weeping into a rich brocaded handkerchief. She waved it at her family.

"My beautiful things. I can't leave them behind."

And she didn't. The wagon was sent away, and Margery resumed her pompous array.

She wasn't proud of being proud. She just knew that a nun's life would be too barren. Life with John Kempe was far from barren, one baby following hard on another, until he died suddenly after she bore him his fourteenth offspring. The rich widow started dressing herself in white and amplified the scandal by insisting that Jesus was coming to her again, quite often as it turns out. She could be seen every day around Bishop's Lynn silently moving her lips, and everyone knew who she must be talking to. Everyone who believed her, that is.

Did she believe it herself? That was a vexing question. She had no way of proving that her visitations were divine. They could be demonic; she had had one experience of demons already. The only way to settle her dilemma was to find someone who spoke to God without a trace of doubt. A saint would be convenient. Second best was the blessed old lady who lived on the other side of the forest.

Providence bestows all things. When it came to the city of Norwich, Providence bestowed three things: wood, churches, and dead bodies. The blessed old lady, called Julian, was a witness to all of them. The supply of lumber that made the town rich seemed endless. Only the plague years stopped the carts trundling in long lines from the forest (carts that came in handy for stacking up corpses like cordwood during plague time). English oak was famous everywhere, so the streets of Norwich were full of foreigners who had sailed from strange places to buy wood. When Margery Kempe came to town, she took notice.

"It was like Babel. I heard a Dane, a Russian, and a Spaniard on my way here," she remarked.

"You speak those tongues?" asked Julian.

"No, but I travel. God's body is scattered everywhere. I follow the pieces. Last week I was holding the skull of John the Baptist. Quite marvelous." It was a peculiar way of saying that the Widow Kempe had enough gold to go on holy pilgrimages for most of the year, anywhere in Europe she hoped to find peace—and answers.

"Where is the skull of John the Baptist?" Julian asked.

"Here and there, it seems. France, Germany. I've seen several, sometimes just the jaw. It was set in gold in the middle of a great salver on the high altar."

The blessed old lady wasn't a relic yet. She was a recluse, dwelling in a bare hut beyond the edge of town. There was a jug of elderflower wine on the table that stood between them. Widow Kempe poured half a cup for herself and diluted it with water.

"Call me Margery," she said, sipping her wine.

Everyone knew Julian's name, although her birth name somehow had been forgotten during the long years when almost no one saw her except for the serving maids, and they came and went. People got used to seeing a silent devotee kneeling in the dimmest corner of the church of St. Julian, and that turned into the name they gave her, Dame Julian.

"So the wood trade has paid for all these churches," Margery said. "I wonder if anyone can fill them."

She knew about Norwich and the boons of Providence. Norwich boasted that it had more churches than any city in Europe north of the Alps. "And the churches collect money to keep the dead bodies away."

Julian frowned. "The last time the plague came was twenty-five years before you were born. I was only six, but I remember. Everyone does, if they survived."

Looking back, Julian was happy that she hadn't been older. Older people still woke up with nightmares about the plague. Margery had never personally seen the Black Death, only heard gruesome tales. A town's populace could be mown down as if by one sweep of the scythe. Those who rushed to bury the dead would often be buried the next day. The stench of littered corpses made strong men faint. Most of these stories were kept alive from the pulpit when priests warned about God's wrath. Nothing worked quite as well as a plague to squeeze tithes from the poor.

"Does my white dress offend you?" Margery asked. She was reluctant to speak about her real purpose for visiting. "Our reverend bishop hates it. More than our bishop, actually. All the ones I've met so far."

"Do you meet many bishops?" Julian asked.

"I'm forced to."

Which was a terse way of saying that Margery had been put to tests of faith many times, as you'd expect when someone makes a public spectacle of piety. None of her stern examiners, however, ever caught Margery in heresy. None ever said her visions were real either.

"They haven't led me to the stake or noose, not yet," she boasted.

In truth her worries had turned to anxiety and now to dread. Her pilgrimages had become more frequent, because Margery was fleeing. She had enough riches to pay off a priest who might condemn her. No mobs had forced her to escape imprisonment. But it was herself she was trying to flee. In dreams the demons were clawing at her again, just as before. Only now it took days and much wailing to get Jesus to appear to her. The trail was exhausting and lonely. No one supported her holiness anymore, no matter how much gold she offered.

Julian was a last refuge. She was revered without being feared. The poor had no qualms about calling her a saint, and superstition swirled around her. Her existence was meager and stubborn. She wore plain brown homespun clothes and ate only enough to sustain two medium-size stewing fowls. Her spirit was as untouchable as a unicorn or phoenix. She spent hours praying, and the only time guests were allowed was when God told her to open her door. So that grubby coins wouldn't touch her, someone accepted alms before you went inside the dark chamber where Julian sat.

Or more likely knelt. Julian hated surrendering a moment to anyone but God. Praying made her glow, even though she rarely saw the light of day.

Margery was sure the old lady knew her purpose for being there, so she decided to get in the first word. "I've come to find certainty about my visions," she said after a moment's silence. "How can I tell?"

"If the bishops don't know, how can I? They are in authority over poor souls like us," said Julian, who had suffered through her own examinations when she was young. These were stern and harsh. If you failed, you sometimes didn't leave the room again.

"The bishops are protecting themselves," said Margery.

"Then perhaps you should ask Christ the next time he talks to you."

Margery laughed. She could tell that she wasn't being mocked. She was being understood, and this made her relax.

Suddenly Julian seemed to notice the white dress. "You aren't a virgin?" she asked.

"No. I wear white because I want to be pure again. "

"It's surprisingly hard to become a virgin again," Julian mused.

"I meant my soul."

"So did I."

Julian gave her an enigmatic look. "God speaks to you, and you want my advice? That could get both of us in trouble. What kind of answer would satisfy you?"

"An answer I can believe in. Sin has weighed down my life. I admit it. Half my fortune has been spent trying to remove the spots from my blackened soul."

"My dear, you know the answers you were taught. When Our Lord rises again, all the dead will return. Then and only then will we be perfectly pure."

Margery twisted her mouth. "I'm not one for waiting."

"You won't be waiting. You'll be dead."

Julian saw the look of disappointment on her guest's face. What was she expected to say? Behind her worldliness, Widow Kempe was suffering. Julian drew a deep breath. "Our task is to believe in the teachings of the Church, not to create new ones. All new ideas have the same thing in common. They are heresies."

Margery replied, "But what if the true teachings are kept from us? I mean deliberately, by the very ones who are supposed to tend our souls?"

She was stepping on dangerous ground now, and she expected Julian, like everyone else who feared the Church, to choose her words carefully. But she didn't.

Julian's voice grew sharp. "God doesn't have to speak through priests. A cracked jug can carry only a little water."

"Sometimes none," Margery added.

"Sometimes none."

A passing cloud turned the room dark as it blocked the sunlight coming through the one window in the hut. The two women couldn't help but notice, and if they were the kind to read omens, this might have been a sign from above—and not a good sign either.

Yet the veil of darkness seemed to draw them together. Margery heard a small clicking sound, which she knew well. The whole time they were chatting, Julian had been saying the rosary, her flicking fingers hidden under a lap shawl.

"Priests believe that everyone is about to tumble into hell," said the old lady calmly. "That's what frightens you. You might be in peril of damnation, if you listen to them. I don't believe it. Is it possible that God should love his children and yet see them damned?"

A sense of relief swept over Margery. "So there's a way out?"

Julian's eyes were small shining dots in the darkness. "Of course." She paused to gather her words while never ceasing the quiet click of her rosary beads.

"I'm going to tell you the absolute truth. As with most things absolute, you won't believe me."

"Go on."

"Close your eyes and listen. These are not just words to reassure you. They will be your salvation."

The power in Julian's voice made Margery feel comforted and uneasy at the same time, a strange mixture. She closed her eyes. The tiny window in the hut afforded no light. She saw only blackness, and she waited. A gift from a saint might be at hand.

What makes a saint? The world speaks in a way the rest of us cannot hear. Normal life deserts them. If Julian's life was shaken by the plague when she was a girl, Margery's was undermined by the peasant rebellion. God works on the soul in mysterious ways. Margery never got to see the hangman hold a villain's heart before his eyes so that he might repent. But she passed burned-out skeletons of houses in town, with black holes where windows should be. Every time her maid passed the fresh graves of victims murdered by the mob, the same warning was repeated. "That could have been your father." Close friends of his—merchants, magistrates, landowners—disappeared overnight.

Fear colored Margery's memories, but so did other feelings, all sinful. Hatred of priests inflamed the peasants, and hatred is slow to die. When the rebels confronted King Richard, their leaders complained bitterly about priests who owned vast lands and paid for their own private armies. The clergy were supposed to live in poverty and act like men of peace. What excuse did they have for outrageously flouting their vows?

These bitter questions didn't get answered. There was no need once the rebel leaders had been executed. The mob scattered to the four winds, every man disclaiming in a loud voice that he had sympathized with the revolt. Miraculously, no one had ever been the king's enemy.

Hatred stayed close to home, keeping quiet. One of the executed leaders, a renegade preacher named John Ball, was never forgotten. He'd had the courage to deliver sermons in the open air, like Our Lord himself. Crowds gathered on the commons of south London. Ball read out loud from an English Bible, which was close to treason, almost as bad as preaching about God under the open sky. As for the rich, high-born priests, Ball said a sentence that lingered long after he was killed by the crown's henchmen. It was a cry for the common folk against the aristocracy: "When Adam dug and Eve spun, who were the gentlemen then?"

Those words reached Margery's ears and burned into her conscience. She ran to her father, the mayor.

"Did God give Adam and Eve the whole earth to tend?" she asked.

Her father smiled. "Well, Adam."

"And did Adam work the soil?"

Her father nodded.

"So it was God's wish that whoever works the land should own it?" said Margery.

Her father reminded her with a frown that she was eight. Margery repeated the question.

"God's first wish doesn't matter now," her father replied.

"He changed his mind?"

"Yes."

"But if God is perfect, he's always right. He wouldn't need to change his mind."

Her father frowned again. He didn't think about demons, not that early on, but he was disturbed to have a child showing signs of stubbornness and peculiarity.

"Have no fear; God is perfect. He doesn't need to explain himself to young girls." One comfort to the mayor was that his daughter would never learn to read and write. There is no better protector of faith than ignorance.

Which put an end to it. But questions have a way of burying themselves in the ground, like seven-year locusts. When they emerge again, it surprises people that there are so many more than anyone ever remembered. Margery's conscience gave her no peace, as much as she prayed. Her father owned several farms in the country. He assumed she enjoyed sitting beside him when he visited his lands, and sometimes when he drove the horses himself, he let her hold the reins.

Margery secretly began to fear these outings. The serfs lined the narrow dirt track that led from the farmhouse to the fields. The men tipped their caps, the women curtsied as if none of them had taken part in the mass rage against their owners. But they were owned as surely as slaves. None of them ever earned enough money to buy their own land, and most wore out their bodies before they were thirty.

Why had God made life so difficult for almost everyone, allowing comfort and ease for the few? Guilt crept its way into Margery's mind. She knew what the Bible said. After their disobedience Adam and Eve were punished sorely. God said,

Cursed are you above all livestock
   and all wild animals!
You will crawl on your belly
   and you will eat dust
   all the days of your life. (Gen. 3:14)

Margery didn't see the rich eating dust. At her father's table they ate venison and goose, and on holidays they feasted on roast peacock decorated in its shining plumage, just like the king at Westminster. Being rich meant that God loved you better than anyone else; but then a horrible thought occurred to her. If God's love brings such comforts, he must hate almost everyone. On her rides to the farm Margery had seen old women so tired and bent over that they actually were eating dust as they planted the spring seed.

For years she kept her doubts to herself. They festered, and when she went through the agony of her first childbirth, she had to have the boil on her soul lanced. Her great secret must be told to the priest. Lying in pools of sweat in a room that sweltered with the shutters sealed, Margery felt the cool relief of absolution even before it was delivered, never suspecting the trap she had set for herself.

"I think God hates us. In fact, I'm sure of it," she said in the priest's ear. "My life hasn't been spent closed up in my father's house. I've seen witches burned for believing that they consorted with the Devil, and two confessed that they bore his child, which had a tail that had to be hidden in swaddling clothes. They drowned Satan's child, and for that alone they were damned."

"My child!" protested the priest, wanting her to stop while there was still time. If she kept going, forgiveness would vanish.

A wave of pain struck Margery, making her groan aloud. "No, I must."

The priest waited nervously while she regained the strength to speak. Her skin was ashen, and he was as sure that she would die as Margery was.

"God must hate us to give us corrupt bishops who condemn the innocent just so they can seize another parcel of land for themselves. I've gone with midwives and seen babies born in squalor, looking like raw-skinned animals before they died a few hours later. God gives us no mercy. We sicken and grow old. We stew in our sins, knowing that divine punishment is certain while divine love never arrives."

Now the priest was greatly alarmed. "You asked me for confession, but these words are proud and sinful."

Ill and wan as she was, Margery turned her head toward him with burning eyes. "I don't believe in you, priest, so you can't frighten me," she said. "Your salvation is as toothless as your punishments. Life here on earth is already hell enough."

The priest felt a surge of outrage that swept away any compassion he had for the dying young mother. "God's mercy will be to take you now. If you survive, you will know what it means to be charged with witchcraft and blasphemy." He held his voice steady, despite his anger, wanting to present the stony face of authority.

Margery uttered a laugh that came out as a croak from her parched throat. "If you stand for God at this moment, prove it. Does Our Lord forgive me or hate me? I need a sign. If you can't summon one, I might as well consult an ass about God as talk to you."

This outrage is what sent the priest flying out of the room in a black humor. Margery looked back on the incident with a heart full of strangeness. Perhaps she spoke out of delirium. Perhaps her words were what drew the demons to dance around her bed, because within hours she saw them. Or did her blasphemy draw Jesus to her bedside? Was it necessary to swear against God's mercy in order to make him hear her? The only thing she was certain about is that Jesus did come, and her heart was flooded with mercy when he said, "Why have you forsaken me, and even forsaken yourself?"

Her recovery and her visitation from Jesus became common

knowledge. The priest who could have destroyed her decided not to. He wasn't showing mercy. The mistress he kept on the side talked him out of taking rash action that would provoke retaliation from Margery's powerful family. Better to let an uneasy peace prevail, and peace was always uneasy in the years following the revolt.

Devotion soothed Margery for a long time. Jesus reassured her of his mercy by telling her so every day, and when she went on her pilgrimages, she couldn't help but fall weeping at the foot of each and every holy relic.

"I feel that God is here before me," she said to the sacristan who had unveiled a piece of the holy shroud in Italy.

He smiled graciously, and Margery didn't notice that he was holding out his palm expectantly. But she knew a little Italian, and when her back was turned, she heard him mutter to a lackey, "*Stupida!* Did she pay at the door? Show me."

One cynical remark isn't enough to shatter faith. Margery's was worn away by slow degrees, the way pilgrims slowly wear down the steps of a cathedral. Her travels showed Margery unspeakable poverty, far worse than what she saw on her father's lands. The heads of prisoners were stuck on pikes lining London Bridge after the hangman was done with them. Margery couldn't help wondering how many had been guilty only of irritating the king's mistress when they refused to be her lover. A monarch can kill a few rivals on a whim; God killed everyone in the end. Was he indulging a whim?

Margery's faith was ravaged and torn by the time she came to Julian. When she was asked to close her eyes, she felt a soreness around her heart and realized that she was powerless to heal it. What could Julian do to relieve her pain?

Margery shivered as the old lady repeated her insistent words.

"I am not going to comfort you. I am going to give you the same salvation that God gave to me. *All shall be well, and all shall be well, and all manner of things shall be well,*" she murmured and stopped.

There was nothing more? Margery squeezed her eyes tight, awaiting a thunderclap or some other sign.

"Do you understand?" asked Julian, speaking in quite a normal voice.

Margery heard the clink of cups and then a splash. She opened her eyes and perceived, dim as the room was, that Julian was pouring more wine, this time for both of them. She was wreathed in smiles.

"Marvelous, isn't it?" she said. "Oh, wait. I can see that you don't understand. I'm so sorry." The look of disappointment in Margery's face was unmistakable. Instead of reproving her, Julian laughed. "What did you expect, dear woman? I can't shoot lightning out of my breasts."

"I expected—"

Margery stopped there and meekly accepted the cup of wine being held out to her.

Julian sat back in her chair. "I knew that your visions were genuine the moment you stepped in. You weep from ecstasy, even though it embarrasses you and makes you a spectacle. You spend your money on holy pilgrimages and give to charity. All of this speaks of your love for Jesus, and he comes to those who love him with a full heart. How can I not believe this? He came to me."

This was the most that Julian had said since Margery arrived, and her frailty made it difficult. But she wanted to keep on. "I wasn't concerned about your visions, but about your sin."

Margery cringed. "You think I'm horrible."

Julian tilted her head back and laughed. "My child, no one is horrible. Sin is not the sign of our evil. It is something no one imagines. I would not have imagined it if Our Lord had not told me himself."

Margery couldn't speak. She had spent years fearing that she would be declared a danger to the Church. Now she was sitting politely over wine with someone who could shake the Church to its core, if the common people rallied around her visions. The doctrine of sin had kept them as oppressed as the king's soldiers. The room began to swim; Margery intended to say, "I don't understand." Instead she said, "You are very dangerous."

"So we are more alike than you think," said Julian. "I was in my thirtieth year when I fell so sick that I was expected to die. My first instinct, however, wasn't to send for a priest."

"Why not?"

"Because in my experience people die a little faster as soon as the priest comes," Julian replied coolly. "It's common politeness. My case was different. God appeared to me every day, ending only when I was well again."

"I've heard tales."

"I know. It became the tattle. But you and I know how life overturns when God speaks."

The old lady paused, but not from shyness or a desire to keep things to herself. She was overwhelmed, even now, forty years later, by the light that had streamed into her body then. She had left her sickroom, as if floating above the earth, and beheld the cosmos reduced to the size of a hazelnut. In that vision, seeing that all of creation could fit in the palm of her hand, she knew that God was in everything. If he was in everything, he must be in the sinner and his sin and even the Devil himself.

"I was amazed to see sin in a new way," she said. "It is not our shame. Sin will become our worship."

Margery, who thought she was long past being shocked, felt more than shocked at that moment. She almost panicked. "You cannot be praising sin," she said weakly.

"I praise all of God's creations. It can't be that one part is perfect and the other part diseased. We are pained by knowing that we have sinned. That pain was given to us to show where we have lost love. If we listen to our own pain, we will find a way through to love once more. Sin is repaid by bliss."

Julian took long enough to say these words that Margery could calm herself. She looked at her hands and noticed that she had emptied her cup of wine. She was beginning to understand, because her own pain had turned to ecstasy—not always, but more than a few times.

"Sin is in God's plan," said Julian. "We are led by every sign, by everything that happens to us, toward love. That is why all is well. That is why all shall be well. What I told you is absolute truth. Pain comes and goes. We sin today and forget tomorrow. What abides forever is love."

Margery didn't disguise that she was overwhelmed; she began to sob. There had always been a touch of humiliation when tears overcame her in public. Now she wept freely, and it felt as if grains of poison were being dissolved and washed from her heart.

"I was so afraid to lose my soul," she murmured when she was able to form words.

"Too many people have told you that your soul was in danger. Before you believe anyone, ask if they have ever seen their own souls."

It seemed to Julian that she had revealed enough. The effort exhausted her, and, besides, she was a realist. Half of Norwich had made its way to her door; most of them broke down crying when she spoke. But she didn't observe that Norwich had turned into a gleaming city of saints.

Margery reached out in the darkness and took the old lady's hand, even though it meant separating it from the rosary. Julian drew it back.

She said, "Don't think I've blessed you. You bless yourself. Your soul will never take rest in things that are beneath itself."

My soul blesses me. Even when I sin? thought Margery, but she didn't say it aloud. She could barely take in this new view of sin. The trip back to Bishop's Lynn hadn't become shorter while she sat there. She rose; the two of them exchanged nods. As she walked out into the coolness of late twilight, Margery had no thoughts. A silence lingered inside that calmed her. In the coach on the way home, she wrapped herself in a blanket and tried to sleep as it jounced along. She wanted to envision a world where all shall be well. It was difficult. To imagine that all is well already was impossible. After awhile Julian's image seemed to fade away.

To outward appearances Margery Kempe kept wandering restlessly. There was a particularly holy relic in Danzig she had to see, a chalice that overflowed with Christ's blood every Easter. But she was haunted by indelible words from Julian: "You will never be free until you see your own soul." She found herself on an invisible pilgrimage. A woman in white might be seen anywhere as the years passed. When she was too old to travel, Margery became calmer, but for the day she died.

Witnesses recall that she became excited at the last. With a faint cry she reached out her hand, grasping feverishly for an object hovering over her bed. No one else saw it, however, and she passed away without a word. Whatever had aroused her spirit was between herself and God.

Revealing the Vision

Turning to a Christian mystic after looking at Eastern mystics feels more familiar. We are used to terms like "soul" rather than "Atman," Jesus rather than Shiva. But behind this familiarity God is departing from the reassuring fatherly images of church sermons. Not everyone is in favor of the divine disappearing act. The pull of old images is strong, and breaking away from them is wrenching. Violence can ensue. The romance of being in the world but not of it—which is the essential romance of mysticism—clashes with harsh social reality.

I can't help but feel that Julian of Norwich is the most touching figure in this book. She wasn't martyred; there is no evidence that she suffered any persecution. We have no record that she was lonely, even though she lived away from society in rural seclusion at a time when the deep forest crept to the edge of even sizable towns in England. What makes her so touching is the gaping distance between Julian's inner life and the brutality of life around her. It took a long time before scholars stopped calling her era the "Dark Ages" and adopted the more polite and clinical term the "Middle Ages." But how much darker could an age get?

The Black Death, which Julian witnessed early in her life, was a holy terror, literally. We can hardly imagine it—not just the shock of seeing corpses piling up in the streets, as up to a third of a town's population died in a matter of days, but also the terrifying conviction that God was indeed bringing down his wrath. Scapegoats were sought out and killed—witches, Jews, and heretics. Death's scythe swept with unstoppable savagery. Against this background, imagine a woman hearing this message from God: "All *shall be well*, and all *shall be well*, and all manner of things *shall be well*."

These words are the ones Julian is remembered for in the annals of Catholic mystics, a fair share of whom were women. But in England in the fourteenth century, Julian stands out in a ravaged landscape full of violence, disease, the Peasants' Revolt, and strong-handed clerics who sometimes supported their own private militia. Julian's only rival is Margery Kempe, who would not be remembered, since the Church didn't pick her up, except that she published a memoir, the first published book written by a woman in English.

They met when Julian was old and Margery middle-aged, and in imagining what they said to each other, I've raised the central issue that hovers around mystics: Are their revelations real? Once you are canonized, made officially saintly, the matter is settled by the book. But for everyone in this book, with few exceptions, hearing from God led to an outcast's status and general suspicion. In Julian's time, every life was entangled, one way or another, with religion. This meant, without a doubt, that countless people claimed to be divinely inspired, just as countless local churches claimed to have precious relics like a piece of the True Cross or the spear that pierced Jesus's side.

It doesn't help if a mystic receives messages that disagree with the religious powers of the day. They often do, as if God chose the humblest to correct the errors of the mightiest. Here is a sample from Julian that couldn't have pleased the local bishop:

> God showed that sin shall be no shame to man, but worship.
> For right as to every sin is answering a pain by truth, right
> so for every sin, to the same soul is given a bliss by love.

The language is archaic, but the import was shocking at the time: sin isn't something to be ashamed of. God is sending you pain to show you where the truth lies. Therefore, sin is ultimately a way to find bliss through divine love.

Do not be ashamed of sin? As everyone around her knew, sin was a universal condition. It linked every person to the fall of Adam and Eve. No less important, it created the durable mixture of fear and devotion that enabled the Church to amass vast wealth. Every cathedral is a monument to redemption and sin, tightly holding hands. Margery Kempe was tormented by not knowing where she fell in this bargain. Was she a sinner who must devote every penny to pilgrimages—she was incredibly well traveled for a woman, visiting the main sites throughout Europe—for fear that she was damned? In her mind, Margery seemed to feel this way, and we are told cryptically that, when she was very ill, she confessed such dreadful things that her confessor ran from the room, refusing to absolve her or to tell anyone what she had said in his ear.

Or was Margery genuinely visited by God? There are doubting mystics, after all, and one imagines her trying to get Julian to clear away these doubts. Which she did, after a fashion. Unable to detect whether Margery's various visions, fits, sweats, and public exhibitions were really from God, Julian took a simpler course. She said that since Margery devoted herself to charity and other holy works, the outcome of her strange state, half ecstasy, half madness, was goodness in the end.

The fourteenth century is far away, but our existence has enough fears and threats that "All shall be well" needs explaining. To the modern mind, calling this an article of faith is hardly a defense. Nor is Julian saying that all shall be well when we die and arrive in heaven. What was revealed to her can best be described as a state of awareness that is much more expanded than ordinary waking awareness. Placed in that state spontaneously, Julian saw sin, evil, and suffering in an entirely new light:

> Truth sees God, and wisdom beholds God, and of these two comes the third: that is, a holy marveling delight in God, which is love.

This new kind of seeing represents her experience of being united with a divine presence that transformed her. The actual visions lasted only a few days, but their effect was permanent (reminding us that people today who have near-death experiences report that, having "gone into the light," they return with no more fear of death).

Julian's new perspective revealed truths that by now will seem familiar to readers from earlier chapters:

In God's sight all men are one man, and one man is all men.

Suddenly is the soul united to God when it is truly at peace in itself.

We may never come to the full knowing of God till we know first clearly our own Soul.

There is no mistaking that some mystics bring warnings from God, but Julian isn't one of them. Her message is that God contains no wrath and that "we are His joy and His delight, and He is our salve and our life."

It was also made clear to her that awareness of God implies a journey from suffering to unity, again a common theme in this book. How is this journey undertaken? The ingredients are familiar and Christian. Julian advocates prayer and contemplation, and her chief mission is to reinforce faith in God's love. This can feel disappointing. After the rush that comes when reading the great mystics, readers can feel let down. "What about me?" is a natural question, and often there is no answer. Or rather, the same conventional answers are given over and over. In the East the advice shifts from prayer to meditation. Still, each seeker is left to walk the path alone.

I think it's healthy to turn disappointment on its head by realizing that inspiration isn't empty or momentary. In Julian and her like we have evidence of personal transformation. We witness the workings of a different state of awareness. Above all, the spiritual path acquires a human face. She is someone who had to figure out, as every seeker must, how to live in the world with such extraordinary knowledge.

The more cosmic Julian becomes, the more extraordinary her state seems. A famous passage in her text, *The Showing of Love*, begins with a tiny, everyday object:

> He showed me a little thing, the quantity of a hazel nut, lying in the palm of my hand, as it seemed. And it was as round as any ball.

Being in a new state of awareness, Julian perceives that she's holding the earth in the palm of her hand, much like William Blake several centuries later seeing the world in a grain of sand. Blake also speaks of holding infinity in the palm of your hand. Julian uses the image to support her view of the divine:

> I looked upon it with the eye of my understanding, and thought, "What may this be?" And it was answered generally thus, "It is all that is made."
>
> I marveled how it might last, for I thought it might suddenly have fallen to naught for littleness. And I was answered in my understanding: It lasts and ever shall, for God loves it. And so have all things their beginning by the love of God.

The way that Julian connects the humble and the universal has given her message its staying power. I doubt that anyone could read her experiences without feeling close to her. The three surviving manuscripts of her book have been printed, as I understand it, for meditation in convents. There is no doubt that it exists as a document of Catholic faith.

What inspires us today is a direct account of an ordinary person suddenly seeing with the eyes of the soul. Throughout the evolution of God, people yearn for transformation. Each religion is like a training program for dropping the shell of mortality in order to live in the gleaming sheath of immortality. When religions insist that only one training program works (and disbelievers will be punished as heretics if they say otherwise), immortality gets lost in dogma. But each mystic who attests to her or his transformation gives hope. Julian of Norwich found transformation in a setting of death and strife. But she is closer to us than Eastern mystics, and so her familiarity makes our own transformation seem more possible.

7

GIORDANO BRUNO

"Everything Is Light"

The Church sent a larger-than-average gondola to pick up the prisoner in Venice. A twisted sign of respect? The glistening black hull was wide enough for four men. It was outfitted with chains to bind the prisoner's chest and manacles for his feet. Dressed in a dirty brown shift, the short, erect man stood quietly on the lowest step of the quay, letting the waves of the Grand Canal wash over his bare toes. The guards assigned to him were watching from inside the prison, where they were keeping out of the cold. Two other men stepped out of the boat, a jailer with keys dangling from his belt and a young Dominican priest, who kept staring down nervously.

"Get in," the jailer ordered roughly. "Don't move until I have you chained in. We don't need a fool jumping ship."

Not looking at the jailer, the prisoner did as he was told. He focused his attention on the young Dominican.

"Your first?" he asked.

"I don't know what you mean, brother," said the young priest, who was having a hard time getting back into the boat as it swayed on the water. He wasn't coastal born. This might have been the first boat he ever met with.

The prisoner faintly smiled. "I should have been more specific. Your first excommunication? Inquisition? Conspiracy against the innocent? And don't call me brother. I've been defrocked several times, when it suited them."

"This one's a talker," the jailer grumbled, nodding to the gondolier, who pushed away from the palazzo steps. The dawn sat on the horizon, blessing Venice the way wealth and beauty expect to be blessed. By now the prisoner was shackled and bound. He sat in the middle seat of the black lacquered boat with its grandly carved prow.

As they glided past a row of waterside palazzos, no one noticed an onlooker wearing a nightcap who had appeared at an upper window of one palazzo, no one but Bruno, the condemned man they were carting to Rome. Tilting his head, he shouted with unexpected violence.

"I've been despised by bigger men than you! I've been despised by kings. Tomorrow I will be despised by the Pope. Traitor, coward!"

The man in the upper window scowled and backed away out of sight.

"Quiet down. Honest folk are sleeping. I don't want to have to gag you," warned the jailer.

"Honest folk are sweating between incestuous sheets, half of them," said Bruno. He laughed to see the look on the priest's face, then leaned forward confidentially. "That man who was staring down at us, he has no conscience. I was his friend, his teacher. But he condemned me to the bishop anyway, for spite. I woke up in his house one morning to see five ruffians storm the room. They thrust me into his garret before the officials came. He'll go back to sleep now, and at noon he'll pay for a special Mass. Just in case being a Judas irks God a little."

The young Dominican had been forewarned about the prisoner's silver tongue. He was determined not to respond, but it was a long row to the mainland where a prison cart awaited. The gondolier, who was fat and belched garlic fumes, pulled lazily on his oar. He was in no hurry.

"God is just. Perhaps you will find mercy," said the priest, judging his words carefully. The jailer was in the employ of the papal see, and he had ears.

Bruno twisted his mouth. "Don't give yourself away. Sympathy with a heretic is the same as being a heretic."

"And are you a heretic, then? Do you hate God?"

"God?" Bruno eyed the young priest. "The last duke I served took an interest in me personally. He sat at my feet for months. Then he concluded that I had not a scrap of spirituality in me. I took it as a compliment, although the duke was shocked. He drove me away from court by night in a cloaked carriage and hoped never to set eyes on me again."

Bruno paused. "You think me very confident for a condemned man."

"Not condemned yet," corrected the priest.

"As good as."

The canal soothed the waves that rolled in from the Adriatic. If you judged the Church by the magnificent domes that rose around them, you'd think Venice was paradise. A better paradise than Eden, since this one was swathed in silk and gold.

Bruno fought the sway of the boat to sit bolt upright. "Can you smell the corruption? I was being tried by the bishop of Venice, but that wasn't safe enough. Now Rome demands my body. We both know what they intend to do with it. Have you ever heard your own bones crack? Nasty. Pardon me, I realize that the clergy isn't used to hearing the truth."

The young priest wanted to retort that his whole life was devoted to the truth, but he shrank back. The prisoner's rashness pushed at him like a fetid wind.

For the rest of the trip over the water, no one in the gondola spoke. They landed at a small stone quay that was deserted except for the prison wagon.

Before he could be hauled into it, Bruno jerked on his chains.
The jailer's attention was caught. The Dominican had already
climbed up to a seat on top.

"I want to say good-bye," Bruno said.

"Good-bye to who? There's no one about."

"If you're blind."

The prisoner enjoyed being an enigma, clearly. He knelt on
the bare ground for a long moment, placing his cheek against the
earth. He couldn't blame the earth for his troubles. Perhaps the
times were to blame. The plague scoured his village when Bruno
was a boy, under the shadow of Vesuvius near Naples. Turks
raided the countryside and hauled away slaves. Your sister or
daughter might disappear overnight. Crops withered, as if so
much ill fortune deserved nothing less.

Despite any such curse, the real blame was in his nature. Giordano Bruno's soul was inflamed by anger, zeal, curiosity—many
things—yet his insatiable appetite for fame is what goaded him
into insanity. Insanity made him the most notorious heretic in
Europe. Not a simple insanity either, like the visions that poor
wretches had, screaming about Satan with a goat's head and fiery
eyes. Bruno wanted to be the most notorious heretic in Europe.
He wouldn't be satisfied until the Pope sent for him personally,
and then what?

They would have a brilliant conversation. Bruno would rise up
and dazzle the Holy Father with his arguments. What were his
faults in the Church's eyes? He held that the earth moved around
the sun. So did Copernicus, a Catholic, while Aristotle, a pagan,
said no. Bruno had written other controversial things: that infinite
stars shone in the sky, each one a planet with human life on it;
that all things were made of God, not just by God; that in every
man, even the grossest sinner, divine light is present.

These notions were not heresies. They were truths. They had
their own divinity, if only you opened your mind. Bruno could already see the admiring look in the Pope's eyes as he unwound his

defense. A torrent of eloquence climaxed gloriously as the Holy Father shrank into his ermine-trimmed robes like a frightened child, while Bruno, brandishing his fist, cried, "See? I have proven it beyond the shadow of a doubt. I am not the heretic, since I worship the truth. You are!"

He felt a kick in the ribs that wasn't soft. "Get up. You've kissed the mud long enough," the jailer growled.

Bruno's fantasy was reluctant to vanish. Staggering to his feet, the most notorious heretic in Europe fixed the jailer with icy arrogance.

"Take me to Rome, immediately. I have things to say."

The jailer, who was not just a clod, appreciated the act. He gave a mocking bow and opened the door to the prison wagon. Bruno stepped inside, ignoring the stench that filled the dank interior, which was lit by a single barred window on the door. There were no seats. He sat on the filthy straw-covered floor while the jailer chained him to two iron rings hanging from the side of the wagon.

"Apologies. We left Your Honor's satin cushion behind."

The door slammed shut, and soon the transport was bouncing on the hard stone road that led down to the water. The January chill pierced the cracks in the wagon boards, but he thought better in the cold. His manacles were mercifully loose, and except for the stench Bruno wasn't in any great discomfort. This was all a hopeful sign. The Church wanted him back. It wasn't going to subject him to such degraded suffering that he couldn't keep his mind intact.

Even better, he was not pursued by the demon of despair. Even at that moment, sitting in the filth on the wagon floor, Bruno appreciated being alone with his thoughts. They were his one consoler, as they had been since he ran away to become a monk at fifteen, almost thirty years before. *I am as safe as my thoughts*, he told himself.

The Inquisition in Venice had been going his way. He would have won, but one day the courtroom was vacated, and the accused was informed that his case had been transferred to Rome, by direct order. Even though the demon of despair never visited Bruno, it brushed him lightly when he heard the announcement. *Rome means death.* He quickly swept the fear from his mind. He would talk about the stars one more time. *Look at them. See what I see.* The revolving heavens would save him before the Church brought heaven crashing down on Bruno's head.

The journey to Rome took two days. The prisoner wasn't fed or let out of the wagon, even for the call of nature. He slept hanging from his chains. A weaker man would have doubted that the Church still cared for him. To Bruno, these privations proved the opposite. His mind was so feared by the authorities that the court wanted him to be fatigued. They would find him more compliant that way. This belief redoubled when the wagon had almost arrived at the destination. The wheels stopped with a lurch. The door was flung open, and in the brilliant sun of the south Bruno's eyes were dazzled.

He heard a horse stamping in the dust, then a shadow blocked out the sunlight. In jumped a stout man who made the wagon boards groan. Bruno blinked. The door slammed shut, and they were off again.

"Greetings." In the dimness Bruno recognized the black cassock and sash of a Jesuit. "I have the honor of escorting you the rest of the way, doctor. We'll have you out of these unfortunate bonds soon. Water?"

The Jesuit fumbled for a moment and then held a silver beaker to Bruno's lips. The prisoner drank from it, but not desperately. If he was being greeted with dignity, Bruno would keep his as well.

"Where are we going?" he asked when his mouth was moistened.

"To the *castello*. A room awaits."

"Ah."

Bruno was too weakened to summon more than a syllable. The *castello* meant that he was going to a most feared place, the Castel Sant'Angelo, a huge circular bulwark on the bank of the Tiber. It was built as the tomb of the emperor Hadrian centuries ago, but he wasn't the first man to enter and never emerge again. Certainly not once the Inquisition took over the castle as the place for torturing suspected heretics.

If the Jesuit relished the shudder he had produced, he never indicated it. He held the silver beaker to Bruno's lips until he had drunk it dry. Next he produced a folded napkin and undid it to reveal some good bread and cheese, which he fed to the prisoner with surprisingly gentle care.

"It's sad that such things should go on between educated men," said the Jesuit. "I would not use the word 'inquisition' in your presence, except that you realize, with your clarity of intellect, that it refers only to an inquiry. *Quaero, quaerere, quaesivi, quaesitum.* Latin is so much easier."

From another mouth this turn of pedantry would have amused Bruno, but he felt a chill.

"We have assembled some papers," the Jesuit went on. "Sign them, make a few modest statements before the Curia, and by nightfall we will share supper on the piazza. The whole unfortunate affair will be cleared up."

Bruno nodded without reply. None was expected, apparently. The wagon, the chains, and the stench of his own excrement spoke for themselves. Any escape route would be eagerly seized.

The dirt road turned to stone paving, then to round cobbles. The door was thrown open, and the jailer, after letting the Jesuit out (the priest had pressed a perfumed handkerchief to his nose by now), unlocked Bruno and bodily hauled him into the outside light, which was now growing toward dusk.

"A coin for your kindness," Bruno said. "My footman will pay you."

The joke produced a scowl from the jailer. The water and scrap of food had raised Bruno's spirits. The huge stone drum that loomed over him wasn't so frightening anymore. The castellated roof looked less like jagged fangs, the great iron doors less like a maw. Once inside, he was led to a well-lit room with a bed and chairs, not a cell. Moments later a servant in Vatican livery brought in a tray with steaming soup in a tureen.

The prisoner, if that is what he was, ate alone. Just before falling exhausted onto the bed, he was visited again by the solicitous Jesuit.

"Someone will bring you a suit of clothes in the morning. Throw the rags you're wearing into the fireplace. The necessary papers can wait until after breakfast."

They exchanged smiles, although Bruno was cynical enough to know that he was being toyed with. He gave a shrug inside. Recantation? He had done it often enough to escape prosecution. He might even delay signing the documents. He enjoyed being put on trial, to tell the truth. It was pure theater, and the stage belonged to him. In Venice, his case had been important enough that the assigned judges weren't a row of hand-me-down Jesuits sitting like crows over a corpse, but the bishop himself. For seven months Bruno had argued his case along clever lines.

"Your Excellency, if I have made mistakes regarding Our Lord, give me paper and time. I will recant everything. But these mistakes were accidental."

The bishop, who ate in the same banquet halls that welcomed Bruno and seduced the women he met there, looked doubtful.

"Accidental? You have theology. You took your vows as a priest."

"When I was a mere boy. I did not mean I am without God. But God comes to us in many ways, not to be reasoned. He came to me as a brilliant, shining light that revealed the secrets of the natural world, not the world hereafter. I am a thinker, an observer, a philosopher. My mind is astonishingly abstract. Was I not almost made professor of mathematics last year at Padua?"

This was a good card to play. The times were not ignorant, and the Church had moved with the times, recognizing after a long, bloody struggle that the universities added to God; they were not his enemy. Bruno had mixed himself up in the struggle. If the year had been 1393 instead of 1593, he would have been secreted away and killed immediately. At least now the Church paused to reflect before it condemned novel ideas.

"The chair in mathematics went to Galileo in the end," remarked the bishop with a tone of respect.

"And Galileo is no more a priest than I am," Bruno reminded the court. "He turns his eyes to the stars, and so do I. Does it offend God if a man examines his handiwork with awe and wonder? The font of reason cannot hate reason. It glorifies Our Father to have creation explored by the mind of man."

Yes, he had done well in Venice. The doubters were silenced. If his old friend had not turned murderously jealous, Bruno would have won.

Morning came, and with it the new suit of clothes and the promised breakfast. Bruno ravenously tore at the bread and bacon, washed down with good grappa. He almost wept to see sunlight pouring in through curtains instead of barred windows. He had his back to the room when he heard the solicitous Jesuit enter, but when he turned around, there was no Jesuit, just two guards in polished steel helmets.

"Where are the papers?" Bruno asked. His mind already knew that he had been tricked.

Without reply the guards rushed at him and pinned his arms to his side. One muttered to the other in a rough dialect Bruno didn't understand. They dragged him into the corridor, allowing him to shout out protests without gagging his mouth. A door studded with iron bolts stood at the end of the corridor. One guard grabbed a smoky torch from a wall sconce while the other shoved Bruno through the door. The flickering flame was just bright enough to keep him from tripping down the stone stairs that appeared at his feet. The circular stairwell took four twists; at the bottom stood a hooded figure with his arms folded over his chest.

Rome means death.

Bruno refused to allow the thought to take hold. "This is a mistake. I've agreed to recant. Someone should have told you."

Without a word the hooded figure gave a nod, and Bruno felt his arms jerked backward. He winced as ropes were knotted around his wrists. The two guards grunted and went back up the winding staircase, taking the torch with them. They left blackness behind, and despite his best efforts Bruno might have felt terror at that moment, except that the hooded figure opened the shuttered lantern he was carrying by his side. Its flickering beam led them down several corridors, around two corners. Bruno tried not to listen for groans.

The hooded figure unlocked a small door and swung it open, stepping aside as Bruno stooped to enter his cell. It wasn't entirely black inside, thanks to a narrow sun well dug from the surface above. Before Bruno could turn around to say something, the door behind him slammed shut, and a lock clanked mercilessly. With a moan the most notorious heretic in Europe sank to his knees.

There was a knock on the door when they came for him. Bruno promised himself to show courage in the face of torture, but he quaked anyway. Then he realized that torturers wouldn't knock. Someone was giving him time to pull himself together. Still bound, he did, as best he could, and opened the door to see the solicitous Jesuit, a bland look on his round face.

"May I?"

Bruno bowed and stepped aside. By the light in the sun well, Bruno knew that he had been in his cell for a night and a day. No one had brought food or water. He wouldn't complain. The Jesuits wanted to shock and demoralize him. If that was their game, he had to figure out one of his own.

"I had a bishop as judge in Venice. I expect no less here in Rome," he said, getting in the first word. Boldness in the face of degradation, that would be a good tactic.

The Jesuit examined the cell carefully, as if he expected to find an upholstered chair in the corner. Being stout, he was winded from the long twisting stairs.

"If it comes to a trial," he said smoothly, "we will supply a cardinal. But this isn't a trial, I assure you. The Holy Office has earned a reputation for cruelty, but really the Jesuits are the most learned and knowledgeable of all the brothers in Christ. We understand, and where we do not understand, we educate."

"Do the Jesuits consider me uneducated? That would be novel," said Bruno.

"Indeed. But not all of your learning seems directed toward God."

Bruno began to feel more at ease. This was sounding like a debate, and he excelled at debating. A guard appeared at the door. He loosened the ropes that bound Bruno's wrists behind his back. The muscles had grown so weak that his arms flopped by his side once they were loosened, feeling cold and lifeless. But after a moment Bruno could rub his hands together. He practiced this while the guard led the way up the stairs to the main hall of the castle.

The Jesuit motioned toward a side room, where four other Jesuits were waiting. They didn't line up behind a bench like a tribunal, but sat around in comfortable chairs. The room gave off a warm smell of mocha and anise rolls, as if Bruno were slightly late for breakfast. He felt a gnawing ache in the pit of his stomach. Out of the corner of his eye he saw one of the Jesuits wipe his mouth with a linen napkin.

"Ah, good. We shall talk. We shall all be comfortable," this priest said. He was older than the others and apparently in charge.

Boldness, Bruno reminded himself.

He pointed to a bowl filled with fruit on a side table. "We all want this to end quickly. My defense is simple. I need an apple."

The Inquisition had been examining heretics since the twelfth century, enough time that nothing surprised them. Bruno could have begged, pleaded, wept, or cried out to God. Thousands of doomed unbelievers had done so, but he was the first to ask for an apple, if he correctly read the surprise that he caused. Without waiting for anyone to move, Bruno strode to the table and whirled around, holding up the cold fruit, which had been spending the winter in a cellar.

"Who made this apple? The Creator. How did he make it? Red, round, crisp, and sweet. Tell me, have I committed heresy by saying those words? Does 'red' offend God's ears? Is 'round' against canon law? Are 'crisp' and 'sweet' evil incantations used to summon the Devil?"

He held the apple higher as his gaze sternly swept the room. "No, of course not. I have described what is to be seen in this apple, as I have described what I see in the skies. I lecture on mathematics and many other subjects. Kings have summoned me to teach them my famous methods in memory. Queen Elizabeth of England may be a damned Protestant, but we didn't discuss theology. She is growing old, and she wanted instruction in how to remember the names of all her courtiers. I politely obliged."

Several of the Jesuits nodded, just the way the bishop of Venice had. So it was theater once more. Bruno paused for a second to gather his dramatic powers, but the senior priest interrupted.

"We don't care."

"What?"

The priest rose to his feet, padded over to the coffeepot, and poured a steaming cupful into his demitasse. "We don't care how clever you are. You defended yourself in Venice by claiming to know nothing of theology."

He wheeled on the prisoner with a bland expression and two cutting words. "Not here."

Bruno felt strong enough to hold back his anxiety. "You are saying that this apple offends God?"

"I am saying that you offend God. Or are you so vain and puffed up that you've forgotten your own words?" Balancing his cup in one hand, the senior Jesuit pulled a paper from his waist-band, squinting a little as he read it:

"'The true aim in life should be illumination, true morality the practice of justice'."

"Yes, I wrote that, but what could be wrong—"

The priest cut him off. "Let me finish. 'The true redemption should be the liberation of the soul from error, so that it can reach union with God'."

Bruno saw that his accuser had screwed up his face, but his own words moved him, and he blurted out, "Beautiful!"

"Horrible," the Jesuit snapped back. "Can you stand there hear-ing your vile heresy and not see hell?"

Bruno felt the blood drain from his face. Suddenly the room was colder, and he swayed as if his spine had softened.

"No," he muttered softly.

The senior priest eyed him with an indecipherable look. Taking his seat, he nodded to the solicitous Jesuit, who seemed to function as bailiff.

"Giordano Bruno, the defendant," he began, assuming a formal voice as he stood up. "Witnesses have sworn that you returned to Italy to teach magic and initiate students into the supernatural arts. You traveled in Protestant lands to preach against the one true Church. You converted to Calvinism to curry favor and then suffered excommunication by the Protestants when they could no longer abide your lies. Your books teach a new religion that you call 'light,' which is an abomination to the correct faith established by the blessed Jesus Christ."

The accusations would have kept on unfurling, but the senior Jesuit raised his hand.

"As you can see, Bruno, apples won't save you."

The others smiled at the witticism. Bruno felt the urge to scream, but desperation hadn't blinded his reason. His predicament tightened around his throat. He had followed the divine light. He had believed that all sins are steps away from the light, all redemption steps toward it. He longed for the day when he would be one with God. Nothing else mattered.

There were heretics as numerous as fish in the sea, damned by false witness, conspiracy, intrigue, and jealousy. A few saved themselves, if they knew which way to twist. But Bruno was doomed by something far worse. He had cursed himself before God by seeing the truth.

He was right about one thing: when the torturers came, they didn't knock. The Holy Office ordered soft torments at first. He had a rag stuffed in his mouth while water was poured into his nose. From the outside this looked like nothing, but to the victim it created a panic unto death. Water gave way to steel tongs, hot coals, rocks pressed on his chest. The torturers never pressed Bruno so hard or heated the coals so hot that he was in danger of dying.

The first year was spent this way, breaking his body. When Bruno was dragged before the four Jesuits again, still seated in armchairs before the fireplace, they asked if he had anything new to tell them.

"I would like a diploma in pain. You can't say that I haven't applied myself."

So the process of breaking him continued. To the Holy Office, torturing a heretic had a spiritual purpose: mercy. Was it not merciful to force out demons, so that a purified soul might stand before God? This kind of mercy ran a few risks. Among the accused, a few would be innocent, yet they tended to confess every kind of horrible sin even before their last fingernails had been plucked out with pincers. The guilty too made lurid false confessions once they were hung from leather straps until their shoulders dislocated. It was necessary to keep on hanging them until their confessions were reasonable. So the logic went.

After the second year Bruno was shrunk to a collection of seeping wounds and scars. He could no longer walk, and it was hard to understand his speech because it was generally expressed as animal moans. The Holy Office reconsidered the case. The accused had refused to recant, despite all persuasions. Fear of the rack would reduce him to begging, and during those times he would confess to a few pitiful errors. But the heresies in his books were too many and too flagrant. Worse, the people had sympathy for him. The word "martyr" was being whispered.

One day Bruno looked up to see a new priest, lean and young, standing in his cell. The clanking lock and the creak of the door hadn't awakened him immediately. Bruno spent uncounted hours sleeping; the difference between night and day meant nothing anymore. The only reason he sat up was that the newcomer's habit wasn't Jesuit. His swollen eyelids prevented him from making out anything more.

The priest, a Dominican, knelt beside the iron cot. "They've allowed me to visit you and bring food. Here." He held out a basket of provisions. "I'm deeply sorry for you, brother. Ah, I forgot. You didn't want me to call you that."

Pain never left him, but as his eyes cleared, Bruno recognized the young Dominican from Venice.

"They're trying a new tactic. You're it," Bruno said.

"I'm not one of them. Do you know how dangerous it is for me to say those words?"

Bruno gave a dry, hoarse laugh. "So the tactic is to be subtle. Good. Talk on." With a feeble kick he knocked over the basket. "Take your Judas offering when you go."

"You must eat."

"Only the living must eat. I am already dead. It has just taken a long time for the news to reach God."

Carefully the priest gathered up the spilled bread and sausage, putting them back in the basket. "We never really met. I'm Father Andrea. I'm here to console you."

Bruno held out his hand, made crooked and deformed by bones that were broken too often to heal. "Console this," he said.

Father Andrea's eyes widened. "Do you have no faith left at all? 'Even faith the size of a mustard seed—'"

Harshly Bruno cut him off. "You dare? Get out!"

He threw the basket at the priest's head, sending the provisions flying. They looked at each other silently, the only sound being the scurry of rats, who couldn't believe that food suddenly fell from the sky.

Father Andrea murmured, "I am your only hope."

"The dead don't need hope."

And so the first meeting ended. But the virtue of patience was strong in the Dominican. He returned every day. He was willing to sit for hours while Bruno turned his face to the wall, refusing to acknowledge his visitor. Finally, one day was different. When the priest entered the cell, Bruno was pacing back and forth restlessly, as if his legs had healed overnight.

"I will talk with you. Do you know why?"

Father Andrea smiled. "You have care for your soul."

Bruno laughed. He sounded bizarrely merry. "No. I understand immortality now, for the first time, and I need to tell someone before they kill me. Something so precious cannot go to waste."

The priest looked crestfallen, but his patience didn't falter. "Go on."

Bruno became more animated. "I will unfold something stupendous. You see, I have gone beyond death. As the body withers, the soul expands. More and more I am blind to this world. It is dissolving, vanishing like a wisp of smoke. Last night, God held out immortality to me."

Bruno's rheumy eyes burned and overflowed with tears. "But I didn't take it. I've returned to tell the world what I know. You must pay attention. Do you understand?"

This mixture of vanity and madness made Father Andrea's heart sink, but he kept quiet.

"The secret of immortality lies with God," Bruno began, "but what is God? In these times, no one is safe who asks that question, even though it occurs to every child. The only difference is that I never stopped asking. I couldn't."

Sorrowfully Father Andrea said, "Perhaps it was a good question with evil consequences."

"I don't believe that. To question God is to move closer to him."

"And closer to danger."

Bruno gave a wry smile. "No doubt. Try to accept that I was not led by Satan when I questioned God. I am a man of the age, and in this age we want to know everything. My obsession with God brought answers, and the Jesuits cannot force me into denying that these answers were divine."

Bruno raised his hand. "I know you want to object, but let me finish. If everything was made by God, then God is in everything. We cannot limit the Infinite. Therefore, God is in every creature, every hill and tree, and every person. Why don't we see the God in us? Because the light has been pushed away by ignorance and error. This much I realized before I was betrayed in Venice."

Father Andrea couldn't control himself. "The Church teaches none of this. You are stepping on sacred ground, where you don't belong."

"Peace. I have only a little more. When I was thrown into this hole, I despaired. Not for my life, because it befits a wise man to accept death calmly and sometimes to seek it. Yet in my agony something else happened. As my body was destroyed, the light shone brighter. The joke is on the Jesuits. Their torments stripped away all my fears, for nothing can be worse than the worst. Beyond the horror of pain I found the light I have searched for, and I was bathed in it until, all at once, *I became the light.*"

The fervor in Bruno's voice caused the priest to bury his face in his hands; the prisoner was spelling his own doom. Bruno tugged at Father Andrea's arm, making him look up.

"You live for the truth, yes? If your vows mean anything, report that you did not see madness in my eyes or the burning gaze of a demon. The light is the truth. It is in all things, and when we know this, we can work back to the light. Nothing else is needed. The stink and hypocrisy of the Church are meaningless. I should have excommunicated the Pope long ago. But the light embraces even the worst among men. Even a Pope can be saved."

After this, the Dominican paid no more visits. He was bound to report Bruno's words to the Holy Office. They had enough evidence to condemn him then and there. But Bruno's cause was becoming scandalous, and the Jesuits retreated into silence. No word was issued about the proceedings, and for seven years his imprisonment continued. There were more tortures, more interrogations. To the immense irritation of the tribunal, Bruno stood firm in his refusal to recant. It would have taken a brave lawyer months to untangle the convoluted charges against Bruno, which kept changing—bravery was needed because the lawyer could find himself thrown into prison too. Bruno had no lawyer at all. He lapsed into stubborn, weary silence, listening apathetically to the rigmarole of obscure Latin. On the days when he had just been tortured, his head lolled against his chest; he sat in court half conscious and moaning.

Finally the day came when people had forgotten the scandal. Seven years into his trial, Bruno was hauled before a cardinal, just as the senior Jesuit had promised that first day. The flash of red in the prelate's costume glowed in the dim courtroom.

"Does the prisoner have anything to say before the sentence is pronounced?"

Bruno was a gaunt shell, with no bone left unbroken. He raised his head. "Nothing."

The court wasted no time with solemn gestures. Bruno was sentenced to burn at the stake immediately, after a spike was driven through his blasphemous tongue and his heretical mouth was closed with an iron cage.

He listened with a pensive look. "I believe you are more afraid to sentence me than I am to hear it," he said.

This was taken as one last impudence from a man who was determined to be reckless his entire life. The cardinal rose, casting a contemptuous glance. If he replied to Bruno's taunt, it was not recorded.

The burning took place at the Campo de' Fiori, a large and crowded flower market. Business stopped only briefly for the spectacle. The iron cage clamped around his jaw prevented Bruno from crying out, although his body writhed in the flames. An impudent priest—or perhaps an impostor who had stolen a cassock—dared to jump on the woodpile to hold a crucifix before Bruno's eyes. He turned his head away, and Vatican guards quickly pulled the priest off the pyre to drag him from the scene.

When the heretic's body was consumed to ashes, the crowd had scattered. An unknown member of the clergy took a handful of ash and scattered it to the winds, where it disappeared in the Roman twilight like a thin wisp of smoke.

Revealing the Vision

With the life and death of Giordano Bruno two worlds crash into each other, and the reverberations are still with us. Faith and science began as enemies, because facts threatened to depose faith. This threat was clear to the Church authorities who pounced on scientific breakthroughs as if they were heresies. A fact cannot be a heresy unless you force it to be. One can conceive of a Church that welcomes science as a new way to glorify God's creation. The Church could have permitted God to be a rational Creator working through natural laws. This wasn't the Church that Bruno tried to accommodate, either by blending in as a monk, teaching as a professor, or prodding as a scientist.

One problem with all of his tactics was that Bruno had many mad ideas—his aristocratic pupil in Venice betrayed him to the Inquisition, because Bruno refused to teach him the supernatural arts. Bruno considered himself an expert in these arts; he toyed with "magical mathematics." You have to pick through a jumble of fantasy and speculation to arrive at Bruno's revolutionary spirituality; but once you arrive, his insights still amaze.

He saw what other mystics had seen, that nature is a field of light emanating from the Godhead. But what makes Bruno revelatory is that he depended, not on faith, but sheerly on the mind to see what he saw. He stands for the human mind as a part of God's mind. Today we still struggle over whether spirituality is consistent with reason. To be a scientist doesn't automatically make you an atheist. But it does send you into the swampy ground where faith can sink under you like quicksand.

When Bruno was burned at the stake on February 17, 1600, it was a bright morning bustling with flower sellers in a busy Roman market. One can almost imagine housewives in aprons buying winter roses. His case had grown infamous, so what came from the crowd was probably a mixture of jeers and tears. It was the final curtain in a long, cruel, slow drama that had lasted seven years. Bruno was important enough as a thinker to survive this long; his recantation meant something to the Pope and the Holy Office.

And the court's judgment, holding that Bruno had denied the divinity of Christ, wasn't a mistake. He had flirted with the Arian heresy, which questioned whether Christ was equal to God. But it's unlikely that this was more than a passing phase in Bruno's mental journey—which was fickle, daring, inspired, ridiculous, noble, and bizarre, depending on where you try to pin it down. He is remembered today as a martyr for intellectual freedom, especially by scientists, who group him with Kepler and Galileo, brave followers of the new astronomy that began when Copernicus declared that the earth moved around the sun.

One thing Bruno wasn't is a scientist. In his lifetime he was best known for a system of mnemonic techniques that interested even kings and queens, such as Elizabeth I in England. As a personality he wasn't able to please those in power, however, and he managed to alienate every court he attached himself to, sometimes getting driven out of the country. He was a contrarian, and those who remembered him said he was introverted and inclined to be melancholy.

In the end, after his gruesome death, the piteous tale of Giordano Bruno became an symbol, but an ambiguous one. I was drawn to the mystical side of him. Inspired by the new discoveries being made in the stars and planets, Bruno's mind took astonishing leaps. He was convinced that there were infinite worlds; life existed on these worlds and perhaps even angels. Instead of being fixed on the seventh day of God's creation, nature was constantly in motion. In fact, the cosmos was probably expanding at a fantastic rate, which means that creation is a continuing process. Taking such leaps enabled Bruno to sound amazingly like a contemporary of ours, as when he writes:

> Everywhere there is incessant relative change in position throughout the universe, and the observer is always at the center of things.

That's Bruno putting on his scientist's cap, but there was not enough science in his day to warrant such a daring leap. His real journey was toward the transcendent, the field of light that in his mind was merged with God, nature, and the starry night sky:

> The Divine Light is always in man, presenting itself to the senses and to the comprehension, but man rejects it.

As the future unfolded, the domains of science got sorted out. Astronomy was separated from astrology. Evolution replaced Genesis. So it's natural that Bruno can't be a martyr for both camps—unless. In that small word "unless" another revolution could be taking place. As modern people, we inherited the scientific revolution. The conquest of superstition is part and parcel of that revolution, as is the separation of reason from unreason. It sends a shudder to read that more witches were burned in England after the death of Shakespeare in 1616 than before; such hysterical persecution wasn't just happening in Salem, Massachusetts.

For four hundred years we have moved away from Bruno's field of light only to come full circle. The unit of light is the photon, and physics recognizes that all interactions responsible for matter and energy in the cosmos involve the photon. In other words, human beings exist in the field of light, and our bodies, quite literally, came from stardust. Going even farther, some farsighted physicists wonder if the universe has a mind; to them, it acts like a living being as it evolves and develops more and more complex forms. The human brain, so far as we know, is the most complex thing in existence. Was it really a product of random chance over the past 13 billion years? To believe in randomness as the only creative force in nature, one physicist quipped, is like saying that a hurricane blew through a junkyard and built a Boeing 777.

I lament that the two key words "intelligent" and "design" got hijacked by religious fundamentalism for the purpose of defending the creation story found in Genesis. There is no doubt that Genesis is actually a creation myth, and a beautiful one. It exists to tell us about ourselves at a mythical level; for that, it doesn't need to be rejected. More fascinating is a liberated view of intelligence and design, which could lead to a cosmos reborn.

Bruno was a witness to the last time that happened. In the rebirth of the universe thanks to Copernicus, Bruno had the most expanded vision of possibilities. He makes statements that could be straight from Shankara and the ancient Vedic tradition in India:

> I understand Being in all and over all, as there is nothing without participation in Being.

It is our loss that Being has ceased to be a mystery, as it was for Bruno and all mystics. "To be" seems like a given, a blank. "I am" simply means that you are present. Being suddenly acquires its mystery once more, however, when you dip into modern physics and discover that the entire universe emerged from a void. This theme arises frequently as we touch on the visionaries in this book, and yet it must be emphasized that the void that preceded the universe is a fact. Everything that looks solid and familiar is actually the product of mystery.

The noted English neurologist Sir John Eccles makes this point with stark clarity: "I want you to realize that there exists no color in the natural world, and no sound—nothing of this kind; no textures, no patterns, no beauty, no scent." Every quality in nature is the opposite of reassuring; it belongs to the reality illusion that we surround ourselves with. When two lovers hold hands, it seems as if two warm, pliant objects are enfolding, but that is pure illusion. Every sensation is created in our own awareness from invisible properties like electromagnetism. In fact, the atoms that are the building blocks of the universe have no physical properties at all; therefore, nothing made of atoms can be physical either.

Bruno was a rare combination of mystic and rationalist, which enabled him to grapple very early on with the reality illusion. He had been thrown out of the Dominican order, but remained intent upon God, and he assumed that when he talked about nature, he was talking about God at the same time.

> There is no being without Essence. Thus nothing can be free of the Divine Presence. . . . Nature is none other than God in things.

Is that last sentence literally true? Looking for "God in things," we no longer apply the lens of Christianity, yet there is no doubt that the search remains the same. What lens do we need? There are many answers floating around the scientific and spiritual community; some optimists believe the two will join together once they recognize that they are after the same unicorn: a vision of God and nature that erases all boundaries and yields the final answer to nature's riddles.

If that happens, Bruno's tale will find its justification, not as a martyr's tale to be pitied, but a seer's to be celebrated. To redeem him fully, we have to accept another of his visionary sayings: "It is manifest . . . that every soul and spirit hath a certain continuity with the spirit of the universe." Bruno saw this truth with a courageous clarity we can only envy. In time God was allowed to become a rational Creator. The Church regretted its persecution phase, and today it is permissible to preach that facts glorify God's marvelous works. But as he evolved to make peace with gravity and thermodynamics, God is still frowning over stem cells and the first days of life in the womb—or so the Church holds. The truce between faith and facts remains uneasy.

8

ANNE HUTCHINSON

"Spirit Is Perfect in Every Believer"

The mother stood on the shore with eleven children gathered around her and spread her arms.

"Behold Leviathan!"

It was hard not to behold a beached whale, and much harder not to smell it. The stinking carcass was an unusual find, washed up from the schools of whales that spouted like an Italian fountain garden off the Massachusetts coast. The local natives (who were feared as "the savages" no matter how peaceful they acted) had rushed to the scene ahead of the colonists. They lacked boats big and strong enough to launch into the teeming pods. But when a dead whale washed ashore, a time of plenty had arrived.

Some braves straddled the back of the massive gray beast with long spears, slicing off swaths of flesh that flopped with a smack on the sand. Women knelt with small stone blades to carve away chunks of meat for drying.

"Do you know what this means?" the mother asked, addressing her flock like a teacher.

"It means their tribe will eat this winter," said Bridget, one of the older daughters.

"If they don't rob our barns first," muttered Francis, one of the middle sons, who resented being dragged across the sea to please God. Dreaming about a sweetheart in England, he had spent the summer digging rocks out of the so-called soil on a farm outside Boston.

The mother frowned. "Think not of this world. Surely this is a sign."

The Hutchinson brood, which was excited to see their first dead whale, quieted down. They knew, even down to the tiniest, that their mother could find a sermon in anything. She had already found one as they picked their way over the rocky beach. It began, "And the Lord said to Joshua, 'Take up twelve stones from the river Jordan'" and continued until they reached the spot where the whale lay stewing in the unseasonal heat.

If Anne Hutchinson could make a sermon from stones, she would feast—theologically speaking—on a whale. She pointed at it, entirely ignoring the smell, the half-naked savages clambering around, and the possibility that visitors from the Puritan colony might not be welcome.

"What is Leviathan?" Anne asked. "The Bible tells us."

"One of the seven princes of hell," a boy in the back piped up.

"And is this dumb creature before us a prince of hell?" asked Anne.

"He could be a princess, if he's not a he," suggested Katherine, one of the youngest girls.

Anne smiled. "The Bible speaks only of princes, child." She decided to answer her own question, since the urge to sermonize was growing impatient. "No, this creature is not a prince of hell. But the Bible tells us that Leviathan was guilty of pride, and thus is pride fallen here. No fish is prouder than the whale, which rules the sea. Yet this one was smitten, and now he has become carrion for any passing dog."

None of her children complained as Anne discoursed. They had arrived in the New World the year before, 1634, to join the new Eden that God had ordered them to populate. Back in England the only reality they had ever known was Puritan. A serious and godly reality, in the extreme. Everyone they saw at church was exercised over the corruption of the Anglican clergy. All hated the papists and reviled King Charles for marrying a Catholic queen, or whore, as the Puritans openly called her. Nobody crossed themselves or prayed to saints, as their Anglican neighbors did. None of them venerated the Virgin Mary or knelt before the cross as they entered a pew.

But the oldest Hutchinson children did know that having a sermonizing mother was unusual. The most ambitious preachers in Boston, in their long black frock coats, gave Anne Hutchinson a wide berth when it came to scripture. She was past forty, not young and no longer of girlish features. It would never have occurred to her to wear makeup to disguise her years, just as, being a Puritan, she wore honest black and brown. Fancy colors were vanity. But her face glowed when she recited scripture; in repose she showed the strain of bearing fourteen children and burying three. Since she wore a tight cap that covered her hair, the lines in her face stood out. So did her piercing eyes.

At this moment, without preparation, she began reciting twenty verses on Leviathan from the book of Job, beginning, "'Can you pull in the leviathan with a fishhook or tie down his tongue with a rope? Can you put a cord through his nose or pierce his jaw with a hook?'"

Her husband, William, came up over the dunes; he had lingered behind to arrange the return coach to Boston. Winded and unprepared for the stench, he stopped to catch his breath. He was close enough to hear Anne reciting, and it made him smile. He had money, many children, and, rarest of all, a wife who knew as much as any man about the Bible. The younger daughters giggled when their mother reached this verse: "'Can you make a pet of him like a bird or put him on a leash for your girls?'"

Anne was a tolerant preacher, unlike some, and she merely

raised a finger. "Here is what I want you to especially notice, my dears. 'Who would approach him with a bridle? Who dares open the doors of his mouth, ringed about with his fearsome teeth?'"

She paused expectantly, and when none of her children spoke up, their father filled the breach. "What your mother means," he said, half walking, half falling down the steep dunes, "is that Leviathan guarded the mouth of hell. So the whale's enormous mouth was given by God as a sign of the trap that awaits all sinners."

"Nothing less," said Anne. "How marvelous is the book of Creation, and how blessed that God has opened it to us."

William liked the look of contentment that spread over her face. She saw God's hand in everything, which was the Puritan way. To trip over a curb or drop an egg meant that you needed to examine your spotted soul. Calamity and persecution had made the Puritans search for the tiniest grain of sin in themselves. The farmers joked that every spring brought a new crop of stones in their fields. It was a grim joke at that, and secretly a few saints, as they called each other, doubted if God approved of their errand in the wilderness.

The first to throw their fate to Providence, the Pilgrims had landed fifteen years before, in 1620. Prying sod from the ground to build huts, they couldn't have foreseen Hutchinson's fine white timber house in the center of Boston. Their grim records from that first year were terse, but horrifying.

In December, bitter weather had set in, far worse than anything known in England. On December 25, the hardiest settlers departed the *Mayflower* to live on shore. The date wasn't significant, since they didn't observe Christmas, which was invented by the papists in Rome.

Six people died that month, eight more in January. Seventeen perished in February. What was killing them? For some, it was voluntary starvation as mothers gave their rations to their children. Thirteen of eighteen married women died; only three children did. The rest died of scurvy or of a plague no one could name. They would simply whisper "the sickness" when another fell victim. God was not smiling.

Still the settlers built their crude shelters and still they prayed, every waking minute that could be spared. It wasn't until the first day of spring that the last Pilgrims came off the boat, and even as March warmed, thirteen more died. Burials were conducted at night under the cloak of darkness, for fear that the savages would become bolder if they saw how the number of intruders had dwindled. (Not that the Indians showed their faces; that first winter they lurked like shadows in the forest.) Looking around the Plymouth graveyard, the survivors counted forty-five graves, almost half their number. The mouth of hell, reflected William Hutchinson, had opened on that beach too.

Unless it was the mouth of heaven. When they were alone he'd consult Anne, who had a gift for reading God's tests and rewards. The family spread a cloth on the hill overlooking the beach, picking a spot away from the smell. It was a pleasant outing, and the children got a surprise at the end, a bit of honey to pour over their bread. But as clouds moved in from the sea and they quickly rose to pack up and retreat to the wagons, a fleck of color caught Anne's eye.

Katherine, who tended to be dreamy, had taken a pink ribbon from her doll's dress and tied it into her own hair. Anne stared for a second, controlling her anger.

"Give that here, child," she said, holding out her hand.

Katherine knew that when Mother spoke in a flat, quiet voice, something bad had happened. She handed over the offending ribbon and forced herself not to cry. The walk back to the wagons was somber. The clouds had quickly gathered into a gray blanket overhead; drops began to fall.

They were lucky, and the shower was light, not enough to penetrate the homespun cloaks they bundled their heads in. Addressing no one in particular, Anne said, "Jezebel. We shall speak of her. Anyone can go first."

None of the other children spoke up, since it was obvious that Katherine needed to answer, even if she was barely seven.

"Jezebel was an evil queen who worshipped idols," said Katherine. "And she was an adult."

Seven wasn't too young to hear about adultery, but perhaps too young to be focused on it. Anne let the mistake pass. "The queen tried to kill the prophet Elijah," she said, "but the Lord killed Jezebel instead. Nothing escapes his eye, even the most innocent transgression."

Fingering the pink ribbon, she unfolded a tale of miracles and gore. Jezebel, the wife of Ahab, was intent on destroying the God of Israel, so that her false god, Baal, might be victorious. She gathered 450 prophets of Baal to contest one prophet of the Israelites, Elijah. Empowered by the Lord, Elijah proposed a simple test to prove who was the real God. A fire sacrifice would be mounted. The 450 prophets of Baal built an immense pyre of offerings and prayed to Baal to send fire to set it alight. Their voices arose in a loud chorus of pleading, and when no fire came, they cut their flesh with knives. But even the blood of priests brought nothing from their god.

Elijah had built a small pyre, and to show his supreme confidence he poured a beaker of water on it three times. Lifting his eyes, Elijah asked God to send down fire, and in an instant the pyre was ablaze. Jezebel was foiled; she never forgot the insult.

"She plotted against Elijah," said Anne, "but her evil was to no avail. In time Jezebel was trampled to death by horses and her body eaten by dogs."

"Except for her skull and the palms of her hands," interjected one of the boys, who was eager for biblical tests.

"Except for them," nodded Anne, taking Katherine's doll and tying the pink ribbon around its waist again. The little girl had images that night of dogs chewing on the corpse of a bedizened queen sporting pink ribbons in her hair.

The gore didn't disturb mother or child. As a child herself in

England, Anne had heard bloody readings from books of martyrs. They fascinated her, and she could calmly munch on a teacake while looking at engravings of a saint's disembowelment. It was only natural to sympathize with martyrs since her own father, a preacher with outspoken Puritan leanings, had been imprisoned and convicted of heresy for defying official church authority. The family was in sore deprivation during the period when he was under house arrest.

The worse the Puritans were persecuted, the more righteous they became. The line between themselves and everyone else became hard and fast in the New World. A commonwealth had been established to look out for everyone's good, but the saints, as they called each other, would never be like the strangers, as non-Puritans were known. No one kept the line more definite than Anne, until she made a mistake and suddenly being a saint was not so scandalously easy as before. For now, the crisis was waiting in the wings, not yet ready to occur.

It would be awhile before the newborn baby, crying and thrashing as it entered the world, asked, "Am I saved or am I damned?" For the moment, he was simply beautiful. Anne wrapped the infant in swaddling clothes and handed it around. The mother, exhausted from labor, had fallen asleep. But she was safely attended. At least ten other women assembled for the birth, in an informal ceremony known as a gossiping. They cooed over the new little boy. Anne, as leader of the group, was well satisfied. She knew that there was a danger that the mother, the child, or both might die in the coming weeks. It was important to have pure attendants to keep that from happening.

"Send word to the father, all is well," she told one of the women, who scurried from the room. Anne was in her element and happy to be there. She looked around.

"In what condition is this child come into the world?" she asked.

The other women knew that they were about to hear a pronouncement, and they were eager to.

"First, it is born into freedom from oppression and the reach of kings, unlike our dear Lord, who was forced to flee Herod's wrath," Anne began. If anyone in the room wondered how Boston could be out of the reach of King Charles, she didn't say so. Defiance to the crown was a popular stand.

"In its condition, this baby arrives in the company of the righteous," said Anne. "We have determined our own fate, as a free congregation. But none of this will matter if a baby carries the stain of sin into this world. Look at him. Where is the stain? What has he done, weak and helpless as a kitten, to deserve God's censure?"

This was the nub of the question, and one could hear a nervous cough in the background. But the women would protect her, no matter what she said in that room. The Puritan men knew this, and Anne counted on it. The newborn had been passed around the circle and came back to her. She kissed its forehead. To the women around Anne this was all but a benediction.

"So he is saved?" one of the younger women asked.

"I hope so," Anne murmured. "But Christ spoke to me to tell me that I am saved, and that is a path open to everyone. Spirit is gracious, and spirit is perfect in every believer."

Christ had spoken to her personally? The women in the birthing room were awed.

An outsider could be forgiven for taking Anne innocently. Grace and spirit were common coin in every church. But to the Puritans these were loaded terms, fraught with danger and hope. Those sojourners who had braved the ocean crossing were betting their souls in a cosmic wager. To the naked eye the Puritans had landed in a trap, exchanging the familiar world of home for a savage wilderness. But home was a fouled nest. Here at least they could sit apart as the elect, favored by God to build a city on the hill.

With one sticking point. When strangers, non-Puritans, landed in America, they could strike out individually and damn the consequences. The saints could only succeed by holding together.

Every Sunday Boston's preachers leaned over the pulpit dangling torment and damnation. "Work, work, work! Toil ceaselessly for your souls, brothers and sisters. If any of you slip, the fiery pit yawns open for us all."

The sticking point is that you never knew if your toil had succeeded. Original sin was an invisible stain even on the freshest newborn baby, and for the rest of his life only God knew if that baby was one of the elect or one of the damned.

Anne had grown up knowing no other theology. Her father took her by the hand one day when she was seven or eight. He wasn't yet the firebrand who would get thrown into prison for his sermons against the bishops. The family lived peaceably in London, and it was a short walk to the Thames.

Her father pointed to the south across the brown sluggish water. "Tell me what you see," he said.

Anne craned her neck over the parapet that lined the shore. "Little boats, big boats. Men fishing. And those pretty flags," she said, pointing to the theaters in Southwark, on the opposite bank, that ran up their pennants on sunny days to signal that a performance would be held. They were woven of bright colors and sported emblems of lions and mythical beasts.

"Not pretty flags, my child," her father corrected. "Across the river is Sodom, where sin brazenly announces itself. There, the wicked tempt those who are an inch away from turning wicked."

Nothing showed the divide between the elect and the damned as much as the theaters, which in the eyes of Puritans were a sinkhole of depravity. Diversions and entertainments were diabolical tricks. Even on the rare occasion when a decent religious drama might be staged—not the disgusting works of a Devil's disciple like Shakespeare—the theaters were surrounded by inns where drunkenness, gambling, bearbaiting, and cockfights took place every night. An honest citizen could be ruined simply setting foot in the streets. True to their name, cutpurses roamed the crowds with their knives at the ready, quick to cut a victim's money purse loose and run away.

Anne's father looked grim. "I promise you, child, one day God will wipe this iniquity off the face of the earth or he will send us to a place where virtue can prevail."

It frightened Anne to hear such things. Fear for her soul stifled the other side of her nature, which wanted to take one of the small skiffs across the river to see for herself what iniquity looked like—to tell the truth, it might look like fun. That was only a momentary fancy, if it existed at all. But Anne took something else away that day.

"Am I an inch away from turning wicked?" she asked.

Her father smiled. "Of course."

Only those two words. He didn't turn their stroll into a sermon, but Anne felt struck to the heart. "Of course" she was in peril of being damned; her father could tell her so with a satisfied smile. Growing up, Anne never mentioned to him what his words did to her. Events moved quickly and tumultuously. Her father was in prison and out again, transferred to a remote living in Alford, far away from London in Lincolnshire, where he would cause no trouble. But he kept railing against the bishops, and then the meager living was snatched away and he was put under house arrest. The ups and downs never ended. If Anne hadn't married two years after her father suddenly died, she might have wound up a poor servant.

Anne grew up knowing travail, but each blow had a divine meaning, as all tests do. The meaning was that God would not wipe the new Sodom off the face of the earth. He was showing through every setback and outrage against the Puritans that they must seek a world elsewhere. No other choice was possible. Yet when they arrived in the colonies, the elect were throwing the dice. Raw nature posed worse travails than any bishop back home.

London was scourged by bubonic plague, but this new place was scourged by "the sickness." London had cutpurses, but the colonies had savages. The only hope was to be more rigid, strict, and vigilant than ever.

"Why are we so sorely tested?" the preachers railed. "Because we are so close to the goal. God must scour every spot of sin before he admits us into the company of the blessed—it is just around the corner." It was a message no one disbelieved, or if they did, they fled Boston when no one was looking and never returned. The wilderness would deliver judgment on them soon enough. The only threat that shook the Puritans came unexpectedly, from within. Anne Hutchinson had been visited personally by Christ, and he showed her another way.

There was no question of accusing her publicly, not at first. The Hutchinson house, which stood very near the governor's, attracted more and more people who wanted to hear Anne unfold God's grace. These were not just women from the gossipings, although it helped that Anne attended almost every birth as midwife. Preachers rode in from surrounding towns. The freemen of the colony, being the most important church members, elected a new governor every year, and for 1636 it was young Henry Vane, barely thirty, who supported religious tolerance—he made a point of spending evenings at the Hutchinsons'. On a pleasant night as many as sixty people might pass through their open door.

Eyes were always watching outside the door, however. Some of those eyes belonged to families that felt the colony was their private possession. They had settled first, invested their money in shares, and prevailed in ensuring that Massachusetts would be strictly Puritan. Newcomers were feared. There was pressure on the crown to change the original charter, which allowed almost anyone to settle in the Bay Colony. The old guard tightened its control over Boston.

"Tolerance is all well and good," they muttered, "until we are tolerated out of existence."

Boston was too small for the two factions not to pass on the street every day. One elder and former governor, John Winthrop, was the thorniest and most outspoken among the old guard. If anyone first uttered the word "sedition" about Anne, it was he or a man clinging to his coattails.

"Don't tell me I must stop speaking because one old stiff-neck thinks he is mightier than God," said Anne. She was resolved, but so was Winthrop, and it was worrisome that he had got himself elected deputy governor, which gave him a place from which to attack young Vane, freshly arrived from England.

"He won't last. I'll wager he won't even stay," Winthrop declared behind closed doors.

When William Hutchinson went about on business, pleasant greetings in the street turned to curt nods and then nothing at all. Passing Winthrop was like a winter's blast.

"He says you offer the easy path," William said one night after company had left. He stood in his nightshirt beside the narrow bed he shared with Anne, tucking in warm stones wrapped in cloth while she made sure the candles were safely out.

"Easy? In England I could walk out to look at the moon in December and not risk freezing to death. There's no easy path here," said Anne.

"You know what he means."

"He means that God wants every settler to break his back until John Winthrop says, 'That's almost enough, brother. Just ten years more, if you please.'"

William bit his lip. "I only say this. Don't tread on him unless you know what you do."

Anne had such calm self-assurance that she might have replied, "Let him try treading on me. It's the same as treading on God." A grain of humility made her keep the thought to herself. Yet no one could doubt that Anne's defense was the Bible and her fierce knowledge of it. Scripture was a tangled skein that she unraveled easily, moving from the prophets to the Gospels, from King David to the king of kings, without having to find the passages with her finger. A marvel of a godly woman—unless you happened to hate her.

Winthrop had a long, narrow face designed for disapproval, so it was impossible to tell that his mood was darkening. But he never stopped burrowing in one tunnel or another. After his term of one year, Vane was sent packing back to London, and Winthrop once again became governor. The preachers who sympathized with Anne quailed, except for a few.

Standing at the gangplank before his ship left, Vane regarded the town of Boston.

"Built on three hills, but it's not a city on a hill, is it?" he murmured. "The new Jerusalem isn't before me." A dream was quickly vanishing.

Vane promised Anne and her followers that he would get a new charter from the king to overturn the colony. Brave words, but soon Vane was caught up in his own brand of sedition. Revolution was his calling now, and what awaited him was beheading.

Not that Anne foresaw this or the other calamities in the future. The first came swiftly enough.

"There's to be a trial," said William, weeks after Vane had departed.

"For what?" said Anne.

"The worst. Heresy."

"Send the court a message. If they want a fair trial, they should charge themselves with heresy at the same time."

Puritan trials were simple affairs. The defendant was burdened by guilt even before being told the charges. The process of getting a confession took almost no time. Winthrop stood up with the intent of flattening Mrs. Hutchinson like all the others.

"You hold assemblies in your house, a thing that is not tolerable to God and not fitting to your sex," he began. "You trouble the peace of the commonwealth and our churches."

"I don't hear a legal charge yet," Anne rejoined.

"I've named them, and I can name more."

"I haven't heard one. What have I said or done?"

Her steadiness flustered Winthrop. "You are part of a faction that—"

She cut him off. "What faction? When did I join?"

Winthrop searched for words. "It is generally known that you entertain these people."

"I asked you before—name my legal offense."

She was tearing him apart with tiny cuts, nitpicking every blustering accusation.

"Your opinions are against the word of God. They may seduce innocent souls who come to hear you. If you keep on, our only course is to retrain you or put you away from us."

Anne almost smiled. "You may, sir, if you have a rule for it from God." At thrust and parry Winthrop was hopeless.

He knew it and exploded. "We are your judges, not you ours!"

Anne had a reply, but the trial was hastily adjourned as night fell. They couldn't get her to confess, which baffled everyone; courts had no other job. William left with high hopes. Winthrop had walked into a disaster.

But Anne was somber, and that night her husband fell asleep without his wife beside him. It wasn't like her to pray all night, but then this was the most extraordinary night of her life.

The next morning she seemed changed, and it wasn't simply the exhaustion of exercising her soul.

"My dear," said William gingerly.

Anne set her jaw. "It's all right. I know the truth. God tells me that I must speak it."

She stood up in court before the magistrates could say a word against her.

"If you give me leave, I will tell you what God has revealed to me. The ground of my belief is that He has blessed me. He has shown me how to hear the voice of Moses and the voice of my beloved Jesus. I can hear the voice of John the Baptist and the voice of the Antichrist."

A judge spoke up. "How did you know it was the Spirit?"

"How did Abraham know it was God who told him to sacrifice his son?" said Anne.

"He heard an immediate voice from heaven."

"Just as I do."

They knew they had her then. Revelation was the rock of Christian belief. When Christ was taken away, the new faith would have died if the apostles had not heard from the Holy Spirit. Unfortunately for Anne, worshipping the old revelations wasn't the same as believing the new ones.

The judges leaned forward, pressing her to repeat what she'd said, but Anne refused.

"You have power over my body, but the Lord has power over my body and my soul."

The atmosphere was tense and quiet. She was speaking things no one could disagree with now, and her followers saw a glimmer of hope. If only she had stopped there. But she didn't.

Turning to Winthrop and the others, Anne raised her voice. "I assure you, if you continue with this trial and the course it is taking, you will bring a curse down upon you and your posterity. *The mouth of the Lord hath spoken it.*"

A collective groan went up, followed by consternation. Anne's followers believed her message and trembled. Her enemies were glad to have heresy so plainly revealed. Only a few kept silent, probably out of cynicism. They knew that her condemnation was inevitable. The old guard had won. But whoever they were, every observer believed in divine revelation. They had to doubt. Had Anne Hutchinson delivered an inspired message, or was she playing the same guilt game that no Puritan could escape, including herself? Whichever it was, Anne condemned herself out of her own mouth. Winthrop declared that Mrs. Hutchinson was delusional; the court found her guilty of sedition.

She barely noticed the sentence of banishment when it was pronounced. She spoke up once more, mildly.

"I desire to know the reason why I am banished."

Winthrop replied, "The court knows the reason and is satisfied."

In her heart Anne wanted to go and so did the ministers who believed in tolerance. They scattered north and south, founding new towns as far away as Maine and Connecticut. The old guard tightened the rules, making it illegal for any to house a new settler under their roof for more than three weeks. After that time, a magistrate would decide who belonged and who didn't. Faith and politics had found a way to forge the same manacles.

Anne led her family into the wilderness with eighteen others. Did she hear the voice of Moses then? The group founded a new town in Rhode Island, a safer place to hear revelations. Looking out over the sea, which still teemed with whale spouts, Anne worried that Winthrop's faction would reach out and swallow up the new settlements. She and the younger children pressed farther south, beyond any English charter. Even then the spirit wouldn't let her rest.

William was the lucky one, dying before they moved again. Anne never saw a new city. She landed in the forest among scattered dwellings just north of the Dutch colony in New Amsterdam. She was uprooted from her own people. God's eye was upon her, of that she never wavered. His eye was upon her when she heard her voices. It was upon her when she read the book of Creation. It must have been upon her one night in 1643 when the local Indians, enraged by how the Dutch had misused them, attacked the house.

All those who had gathered around Anne, including six of her children, were murdered that night. The horrifying news spread that their scalps had been taken, and worse, a young daughter named Susanna, only nine years old, had been captured by the Indians. Captivity was a fate no female could regard without dread.

Legend has it that in the confusion of the attack, young Susanna ran away and hid in a large cleft rock in the shape of a tortoise shell or a whale's humped back. Leviathan hid her from the worst of the savagery, until she was found by the attackers and whisked away into the forest. By then the raiders were over their murderous mood. Telling the story in later years, the settlers took to calling the cleft formation that the girl hid in Spirit Rock.

The Hutchinson family that was left in Boston never ceased their search for Susanna. She had been a babe in arms when her parents sailed to the colonies. The Indians raised her in captivity— she rarely spoke of any details—and after a few years they traded her back to the English. She returned to Boston. To bridge the unspeakable gap when Susanna had been gone, she was treated like an unknown person and reintroduced into polite society as someone fresh and new. She lived to marry and bear children; she died of old age.

Who can stop the mind, though, from conjuring up images of Anne's last night? The house would have had only a few windows, left open after a hot August day. Then it came. The sound of glass crashing, the pounding footsteps of the invaders, the children's cries, all were mixed with a sight we can be certain of—the enraged Anne standing her ground as she ordered her killers to leave in the name of God.

Revealing the Vision

To the earliest settlers in New England, God was giving humanity a second chance. The moral rottenness of Europe could be left behind for an unspoiled landscape that was extravagantly called a new Eden. It thrilled the souls of these radical Protestants to be rewriting the fall of humankind. They had complained bitterly about the corruption of the Catholic and Anglican churches, although their zeal for purity in all things had made them the butt of ridicule, including by Shakespeare. (A character in *Twelfth Night* mocks, "Dost thou think because thou art virtuous there shall be no more cakes and ale?") Yet this fervent optimism ran into several crushing obstacles that spoiled the apple. Not a serpent, but stubborn human nature and the trials of bleak New England winters came as crushing blows to some Puritans, while others turned flint hard and scraped out a bare living that was more like God's punishment than a reward. The deity was not allowing an easy birth for the new Adam and Eve.

We don't live in a world where Satan is watching if you go to the movies. Our souls are not in peril when we indulge in a hot fudge sundae. But the Puritans felt keenly that the enticements of pleasure were created to tempt the righteous to fall. The first Massachusetts colonists were overwhelmed by new settlers with different, more lenient beliefs, but the old Puritan strain, with its prudery, guilt, hellfire, and damnation, stuck in the collective mind. The New World was indelibly marked as puritan, with or without a capital *P*.

We cannot look upon the Bay Colony as a grim curiosity. Salvation lies at the heart of being a Protestant. Anne Hutchinson, like everyone around her, believed that God was intimately near. Under his gaze, every soul was naked. It was up to each believer, then, to enter into a soul bargain with the Lord, and the bargain could turn fatal at any moment. The slippery slope to hell was much easier to find than the steep stairway to heaven. From our easy vantage point, the setup was a kind of abusive relationship, since the Father's love could only be kept by acting the part of a perfect child, no matter how often God became enraged and visited random punishments without giving a reason for them.

Punishment in the first years of the Pilgrim settlement wasn't random—it was constant, and the more people perished from starvation or the mysterious malady recorded as "the sickness," the more rigid the mind-set became that looked for sin as the cause of misfortune. Anne Hutchinson shared with everyone a belief that reading the "book of Creation" would reveal signs of inner failure and weakness.

She would be the perfect martyr if we didn't have the transcript of the 1637 trial in which a kangaroo court ensured that their local gadfly was banished. Everything condemned by the old guard in Boston (remembering that "old" meant landing in the New World four years ahead of anyone else) became revered in American history. Tolerance, however imperfect, replaced sectarian bigotry. Free speech became a right written into the Constitution. Eventually the rise of the women's movement made Anne look even better.

Unfortunately, we do have the trial record, which reveals that the defendant was either delusional, a fanatic, or seriously misguided in her spiritual quest. Hearing Anne curse the judges who were about to condemn her meant, in the eyes of Puritans, that she wished eternal damnation upon them. Not the picture of a gentle prophetess guided by Jesus whom we might like to embrace. But a woman who came out publicly to announce that she heard the voices of Moses, Christ, John the Baptist, and the Antichrist would be greeted just as hostilely today as she was then. How can we revere revelation and be deeply suspicious of it at the same time?

This was a crucial dilemma for the whole movement known as Protestantism. The endless—and to our eyes pointless—battles over heresies, the gruesome persecution of witches, and the split-

ting off of contentious new sects prove that an intimate relationship with God is two-edged. If you are the sole authority of God's
word, no other authority can deny your truth. Going back to the
earliest days of Christianity, it appears that knowing God directly,
which was called Gnosticism, was probably part of the faith
during the decades right after the crucifixion. So were the ten-
dencies that burned in Anne Hutchinson's heart: resistance to authority, the right of women to preach, and a hunger for revelation.

As the official church rose, it set itself against Gnosticism, and
when the emperor Constantine put the imperial seal on Christianity as the state religion in 313, one of the first campaigns of
the early bishops was to wipe out the Gnostic heresy—in fact, for
centuries all that was known about the Gnostics came from the
fervent condemnation of their enemies. Power politics has never
found a way to keep its fingers out of religion, as Anne Hutchinson discovered, with fatal consequences. Yet gnosticism with a
small *g*, the belief that God can be contacted by anyone, can
never be extinguished.

A passage in the New Testament contains the seed of trouble.
In the Americanized King James Version, 1 John 4:9 sounds in-
nocuous: "In this was manifested the love of God toward us, because that God sent his only begotten Son into the world, that we
might live through him." But the first phrase can also be trans-
lated, "In this was manifested the love of God in us." Christianity
has worried over what "God in us" means. Anne Hutchinson took
it to mean that the Holy Spirit was equally in everyone, a message
that recurs among all the world's mystics. But sin exists in all
people too according to the tradition stemming from the fall of
Adam and Eve. So how do the two poles of good and evil relate in
our divided nature? This is a question that extends far beyond the
curious, grim band of Puritans struggling to survive in the wilderness.

Somehow Christ's death, which redeemed the world of sin,
didn't wipe sin out. This fact is apparent to the naked eye, yet to

believing Christians, all murder and violence that followed the crucifixion is different from the murder and violence that preceded it. The difference is salvation. By surrendering to God through his Son, your sins are forgiven and your soul redeemed. Thus the death of a single individual marked a turning point in the history of the world. Non-Christians accept no such turning point, but that's in the nature of religions, to mark exclusive territory for their version of God. The Christian God is waiting for sinners to take advantage of a cosmic bargain that defeats all evil for all time; the choice is ours.

For the Puritans, the cosmic bargain was so palpably real that they began to examine it under a microscope, reading the finest of fine print. (The faction represented by John Winthrop even called itself the Legalists.) How was the contract fulfilled? Did you accept God's word at face value or did he have to prove that he accepted you? Was a newborn baby, always in danger of dying very quickly, an unredeemed sinner, or would baptism take care of that? If not baptism, then what? Because the cosmic bargain was written in invisible ink, these minute but life-altering details became rife in Protestantism long before the Puritans sailed.

Just as Europe had splintered over theological niceties, the American colonists continued to divide, and out of the original meager settlements tiny bands of renegades melted into the forest to found new towns from Maine to New York, all wanting to breathe their own air and worship their own version of the Protestant God. We shake our heads today that anyone was willing to risk starvation and death over a delusional issue like infant damnation, but when your soul is at risk, such niceties lead to eternal damnation, should you forget to obey the fine print.

Anne Hutchinson set herself against legalism with breathtaking certainty. She declared that "laws, commands, rules, and edicts" existed only for those who were blind to the light. The path to salvation was clear to "he who has God's grace in his heart." She emerges on the "good" side of the fanatical struggle, but her plea for grace didn't actually win. One person would never be enough, however holy her life, to convince the world that sin was entirely forgiven simply by knowing it inside. What actually triumphed was Winthrop's conviction that you have to work hard to earn God's favor—this was the doctrine of "sanctification"—which to him was a self-evident truth. If you didn't work hard, you would certainly fall into ruin, and that could hardly be a sign that God loves you. Therefore, even if you don't feel saved or particularly favored by Providence, your hard work proves that you are willing to strive toward salvation. Faith found a visible outlet. As the Protestant work ethic prevailed (interestingly, the phrase is synonymous with "Puritan work ethic"), John D. Rockefeller Jr., the world's first self-made billionaire, could take triumphant advantage. When asked where he got his riches, Rockefeller smoothly bypassed his ruthless business tactics, which led to the ruin of many competitors, by saying, "God gave me my money."

Anne Hutchinson can't be seen as victorious, but she is representative of a division that troubles human nature. Faith remains invisible, no matter how many good works we do, including charity and selfless altruism. This implies that God hasn't retracted the curse laid on Adam and Eve. Guilt has shifted, however, becoming a psychological issue rather than a religious one. Still, in times of crisis, the possibility of an angry God always rears its head, and too often violence in the name of appeasing God breaks out. What can please God more than attacking his enemies, who are obliged to return the favor since they believe in their own version of God?

Where does that leave grace? Perhaps where it always was, as a private communication between God and each person's inner world. Anne Hutchinson died a violent death, and it's not hard to imagine her enemies feeling justified—the heretic got the divine punishment she deserved. But the secret of grace is that they never would have known whether they were right. Grace, if truly received, brings complete peace. The path of hard work, on the other hand, never loses its anxious worry; the instant God is seen as demanding something, he might never be satisfied. In the harsh climate of Puritanism, Anne Hutchinson spoke severely:

> One may preach a covenant of grace more clearly than another. . . . But when they preach a covenant of works for salvation, that is not truth.

Many of the world's wisdom traditions agree with her. As for those that don't, they inherit an anxious existence that turns faith in God into a risky gamble.

9

BAAL SHEM TOV

"To Live Is to Serve God"

Avraham Gershon, son of a great rabbi, couldn't believe that God was so clumsy. His timing was terrible. There was no other word for it.

"Wait for a proper man, a man who has something to give. You can't marry this nebbish. I forbid it," he fumed.

His sister, Chanah, was distressed. Hands folded in her lap, she kept her gaze on the floor. "He's a teacher, and people love him, they say." She hadn't actually set eyes on Yisrael, although she had been told the name of her betrothed.

"Love?" Avraham snorted. "Tell me, how do you make soup out of that? I won't give him any money, be sure of it."

Avraham stared out the window. By the Christian calendar it was 1716. Spring was breaking in Poland. The czar couldn't take that away from the Jews.

Chanah was meek-voiced, but stubborn. "So I must obey you before I obey my father? Where is it written?"

"Our father is dead," snapped Avraham. "He meets this nobody while traveling to preach in the *shtetls*. He foolishly promises his daughter's hand, and then what does our father do? He eats a chicken leg, feels a bit off, and dies in the night. Ridiculous."

The old rabbi had gone to the outlying villages, the shtetls, because there had been an outbreak of messiah fever. A movement, in fact. He went to talk sense to the people, especially the ignorant, who couldn't read or write. Some had started to worship a dead rabbi from the Ukraine, whispering that miracles were done in his name. But instead of breaking the fever, their father must have gotten infected. It was some kind of joke, really, or a trial. After he returned home, all he would say was that he had given Chanah to Yisrael ben Eliezer.

The groom-to-be, who was poor as a turnip digger, was due that afternoon. The day was ominously bright. He'd be on time and smiling. Why not? His bride was one of the choicest catches in the prosperous town of Brody.

Avraham glowered. "And don't talk to me about what is written. A woman—an unmarried woman, in fact—has no right to speak of the law to a man."

Avraham had his back to his sister, and when she didn't argue, he felt a flicker of hope that she might listen to him. But when he turned around, she had already crept out of the room. He could have ordered her back. Until she married and became the responsibility of her husband, she was under the authority of her brother. Avraham sighed. He wasn't a monster. He wanted her to be happy.

Like other prominent Jewish families they kept a goyishe maid, a Christian, who did the chores on the Sabbath, when all work was forbidden to Jews. The girl lit candles, sliced the bread, even opened and shut doors. This one, named Marya, entered. A man was at the kitchen door, a peasant who wouldn't leave, although the cook had dumped some slops on his feet.

Avraham almost ordered the peasant to be beaten from the door, but he stopped himself. A righteous man is weakened by anger. If he performed an act of charity, he reminded himself, some good might come of it. With old Rebbe Ephraim dead, his congregation was subject to poachers. The fickle were already drifting away. The rabbinical court that Avraham had inherited settled fewer lawsuits. The familiar noise of wives weeping over their faithless husbands and neighbors accused of stealing eggs had quieted down. The silence made Avraham nervous. He went to the back door, fumbling for a zloty to give as alms.

The beggar was a young man, under twenty, who wore shabby clothes, but didn't smell. Avraham held out the coin, hoping he wasn't showing charity to a drunkard.

The beggar smiled. "Reb' Gershon?"

"How do you know my name?"

"Shouldn't I know it if we are going to be related?"

Smiling more broadly, the beggar opened his arms. Avraham involuntarily stumbled backward.

Not to be rebuffed, the beggar saw an opening and slipped past his future brother-in-law into the kitchen. "The road. It's hard on the feet," he said cheerfully. Since he wore no shoes and had walked to Brody with his feet wrapped in rags, this remark made sense.

"What is that smell—noodle pudding, kugel?" he asked.

"The road. It's harder on the stomach," said Avraham drily. "We were expecting you. Only not quite like this."

"I know, I know," said the groom-to-be apologetically, unable to take offense. He turned to the cook, who was fumbling with her greasy apron, unsure how to react to the intruder, who was clapping his arms around himself to get warm.

"I forgive you for dumping cabbage scraps on me. What's your name? I am Yisrael ben Eliezer, and it would be a blessing to find out how well you make kugel."

Avraham jerked on the young man's arm. "It doesn't matter what her name is. You'll get fed in time. Come."

Yisrael rubbed the soles of his feet against his pants legs, to wipe off the layer of mud caked on them. He followed Avraham into a parlor filled with warmth from a crackling hearth. The visitor seemed awed. What were the walls lined with? It could be silk.

Instead of walking immediately toward the fire, Yisrael ben Eliezer closed his eyes, and his smile assumed a different, unusual shape. Praying? Avraham Gershon couldn't believe it. This nobody was thanking God for the existence of a working fireplace.

"Before you ask, she's not coming down. It's not a match," said Avraham firmly.

"That's too bad. I heard about your father's death, peace be on his memory." Yisrael's tone was sympathetic, as if he hadn't heard the bad news about not getting his hands on Chanah's dowry.

"Oh, I almost forgot," he said, reaching into his leather coat, which was patched and stained. He brought out a small bag tied with string. "What do you think of that?"

Avraham frowned. "What is it?"

"Seeds. For planting. By God's mercy none of the village wheat got moldy over the winter."

With a humble but ceremonious gesture Yisrael handed the bag to his host.

"You're in a town. We buy flour. We don't plant wheat," said Avraham slowly, as if addressing an idiot.

"Isn't it time someone did? Not you, of course, but the wretched poor. I saw them on the way into town. There are Jews with nothing to eat living in the shadow of the synagogue," said Yisrael, his voice growing sober.

The house was not so big that two men's voices didn't carry upstairs. There were light footsteps outside the parlor, and before Avraham could keep the groom-to-be from setting eyes on her, Chanah appeared. Yisrael grinned as if he'd seen the gates of paradise fly open.

"I am Yisrael," he managed to stutter.

Chanah said nothing, blankly staring. Her brother began to cheer up. The groom-to-be was obviously not a promising sight, particularly when he turned around and took off his traveling coat. His black suit was so old it looked shiny enough to see your reflection in.

"Yisrael thinks it would be a good idea to plant crops around the synagogue," Avraham remarked brightly.

"What?" muttered Chanah.

Their visitor coughed lightly. "Not quite, dear brother. I think it would improve the lot of Jews starving in town to move to farms where they could raise food. Their children are dying. It would be better all around." Yisrael turned shyly to Chanah. "Do you agree?"

Avraham inserted himself before his sister could reply. "She has no opinion on the matter. None at all."

His rudeness was miscalculated. Chanah took pity on her shabby suitor and stepped forward. She told him her name. Yisrael beamed. Dinner that night was sturgeon soup and latkes, an uncomfortable affair as Avraham sulked. Yisrael slurped down the broth without any etiquette. In between he talked enthusiastically about the plight of the Jews in the rural countryside.

"Your father was on a righteous mission, in his own mind. The messiah, here in Poland? Of course in the shtetl one hears about this miracle rabbi all the time. He has a growing following."

"What's his name?" asked Chanah, who had to fill in the gaps while her brother, keeping the wine to himself, stared at his glass before refilling it.

"Sabbatai Zevi. He was considered very holy. I wish I had been alive to see him."

"What good is there setting eyes on a charlatan, or perhaps this Zevi was even mad," muttered Avraham.

Yisrael bent over his soup. "You never can tell," he said mildly.

"Wouldn't we know if the messiah had come?" asked Chanah.

Yisrael shrugged. "Nothing says that he would know himself. God hides the truth as much as he reveals it."

Even though his brain was foggy, a light struck Avraham. "You didn't encourage our father in this madness, did you? No, it was you. It had to be." Avraham lurched to his feet. "And now you dare come here?"

"Brother!" cried Chanah.

"Stay out of it. I work night and day to convince people that Ephraim of Brody wasn't out of his mind. A great man suddenly babbles about the messiah? If he picked this bag of bones to marry you, he must have lost his reason entirely."

"Where I live, almost everyone goes hungry. Is that a sin?" asked Yisrael quietly.

"I wouldn't know," snapped Avraham. "Ask God why you suffer. Ask your false messiah, why don't you?"

After throwing down his napkin and carelessly tipping his glass over, Avraham stalked out. He banged upstairs. In the ensuing silence Chanah looked thoughtful.

"What did happen to our father? Can you tell me?"

"I'm not sure I'm permitted. But I could tell you once we're married," said Yisrael. "Husband and wife are one." Despite the disturbance, he didn't push his plate away, but kept eating. There was little doubt he hadn't seen such a meal for a long time.

"You make it sound like a dreadful secret," said Chanah.

"It's a secret, but not dreadful. More joyful, I would say." Yisrael looked around hopefully, and Chanah rang the bell. They might as well bring in the noodle pudding, even if she couldn't eat a bite. Her nerves were frayed, yet she felt as if the world had suddenly turned on its axis.

Here was a very unpromising groom-to-be, who couldn't eat properly at a table. But Chanah had heard a secret from her father that wasn't shared with Avraham. Utterly impoverished, Yisrael yet was beloved of villagers because he could heal in the name of God. Such a rabbi was called Baal Shem for his miraculous works. It wasn't for table manners that the great Ephraim of Brody had selected Chanah's husband. He saw him with the eyes of the soul.

Every word that a Baal Shem said was of utmost importance, and Chanah did her best to grasp wisdom from Yisrael's ordinary remarks, not because she respected him—she hardly knew him—

but because she was committed to following her father's wishes. This was to be her husband, even if his secret, once revealed, were a good deal less than joyful.

Avraham kept his word. After driving Yisrael from his house, he disowned his sister and refused to give her a penny. Chanah kept her promise to God and her father. She wed the Baal Shem under the canopy with no one present who knew her, much less willing to give her away.

She had shamed Avraham and their family, but he relented slightly at the end.

"Your husband goes around town dressed like a peasant," he said, "and if that's his life, he needs a horse."

So they started out their new existence with a horse as their only worldly possession. The first few years were spent in grinding poverty. Yisrael was reduced to manual labor, digging clay to be made into bricks. Chanah found a wagon to hitch the horse to and made deliveries to even poorer families who had no horse at all.

And the secret was revealed, almost as soon as they had slept with the marriage sheet between them and Yisrael had deflowered his bride without seeing her.

"Do you remember when I made your brother so angry, talking about the news of a messiah?" he asked. Chanah nodded. "I said, 'You never can tell,' and he stormed out of the room. I had a reason for those words."

Chanah felt faint. She was cold in her wedding bed, in a rickety hut where the wind whistled through the walls, and suddenly a feeling of loneliness overcame her. It would be too much if Yisrael believed the messiah had come. Couldn't he wait to tell her in the morning?

Seeing her distress, Yisrael went silent. They lay there as he stroked her cheek, but it was only a short pause.

"Be easy. I am not in the messiah movement, but I do have secret beliefs."

What he unfolded was strange to Chanah. It had to do with mystic Judaism, Kabbalah. Nothing about that made her anxious. Avraham was considered an authority on Kabbalah, which was widespread in that region.

"The Jews cannot be abandoned by God," her brother declared. "He has left us messages about our fate. The messages are hidden, that's all."

Chanah was used to getting up in the middle of the night and spying her brother, bent over in the dark with a sputtering candle by his side, poring over the Talmud, searching for secret numbers and codes. It wasn't her place to think about such things, but now she had no choice. It helped that her husband's arms were warm when he wrapped them around her.

"God has every reason to destroy the world," Yisrael said. "Have you ever wondered why he doesn't? There is enough sin, even among the good Jews, to make God abandon the human race. This problem worried me very much as I grew up.

"The answer doesn't lie out in the open, like hay drying in the sun. It must be hidden on purpose, and if so, where can it hide? In the hearts of those who know."

"And you are one of those?" asked Chanah.

"If anyone asks whether I am one of them, I can only say what I told your brother: you never can tell. The secret is buried that deep."

"This makes no sense. Anyone who keeps a secret knows that he is keeping it," Chanah objected.

"Not this kind."

Begging her to be patient, the Baal Shem unfolded a cosmic scheme. As he delved into Kabbalah, the young Yisrael discovered the most mystical number, which was thirty-six. Why? Because it has been revealed that thirty-six righteous men have been appointed by God to keep the world from being destroyed. Exactly that number, no more and no less.

"The Lamed Vav," said Yisrael. "You must remember this. Our whole life together depends upon it."

It seemed like something a child could remember, since *lamed* was the thirtieth letter of the Hebrew alphabet and *vav* was the sixth. *Why would a grown man be obsessed with—?*

Yisrael cut off the thought before she finished thinking it. "When do we know for certain that God spoke? In the Torah, when the world first began. Our fathers heard the truth from God's mouth. For example, when Sodom had fallen into depravity, God raised his hand to wipe it out and everyone who lived within its walls. But Abraham beseeched God to save the people. God agreed on one condition, that Abraham find fifty righteous men in Sodom. Abraham searched the city in vain, and when he couldn't find fifty, he begged God to change his demand. God then asked for only ten righteous men, yet even then there were not ten to be found. He asked for only one righteous man, and he was found, by the name of Lot."

"And still Sodom was destroyed," Chanah reminded him.

Yisrael was too excited to be interrupted. "What matters is that God found a way to keep the human race alive. He is doing the same thing today. Has sin decreased? Has the messiah come to save us? No, so we must save ourselves. That is what the thirty-six, the Lamed Vav, are doing. In secret they are the righteous men who keep God's wrath at bay. Isn't it wonderful?"

Chanah thanked the Lord that Yisrael hadn't blurted out these ideas when he lived under Avraham's roof courting her. The last thing she needed was two Kabbalists fighting over who had the magic number. She went to sleep exhausted, but happy. If this was her husband's joyful secret, it wasn't hard to keep and nothing to be ashamed of.

She soon found that the secret was far from private. The Baal

Shem, although only eighteen years old, had a fervent following. They called themselves "the righteous," and they all accepted his belief that the thirty-six must exist, secretly and unknown to anyone else, or else the world would end. It might be a strange belief, but it was all they talked about; therefore, it was all that Chanah heard.

One July day she was scrubbing clothes by the river. It was a scorching day; she was bent over a rock squeezing soap out of the heavy washing. There wasn't an extra penny to hire a peasant girl to do the drudgery, as they had in her father's house. To any passerby, Chanah herself looked like a peasant girl.

The woman next to her kept babbling about the thirty-six, until Chanah blurted out, "What good do they do us? We are two penniless Jews thrashing clothes against the rocks. This is salvation?"

Word got back to the Baal Shem, naturally. Chanah knew it would, and she braced herself. Whatever he threw at her, she was determined to throw it back. He came in that evening and sat down at the table without a word; he kept silent as she ladled out the watery cabbage soup and cut the black bread.

They ate like that, saying nothing, but not anxiously. Chanah knew her husband well, and he wasn't angry. She waited for his reaction.

Halfway through, Yisrael smiled. "I don't slurp, have you noticed? That was one of the three promises I made when you married me. This girl was brought up in a nice home. She doesn't deserve slurping."

Chanah knew he was getting at things sideways, so she played into the game. "And what were your other two promises?"

"To love my dear wife and to keep her safe. Only I can't keep you safe."

The Baal Shem pointed out the open door, which let the breeze in since their hut had no windows. "Out there are enemies. The czar to the east, the Germans to the west. If I ride a horse three days from here, what do I see? A burned-out land where the Turks have killed everyone. The Turks! They crossed the whole Black Sea to find some Jews and wipe them out."

Chanah bit her lip, never having heard him in such a dark mood.

"I know that God wants to keep us safe, and I know I am too weak to help. That was why He sent the vision of the thirty-six to me, so that I would not lose heart. I would see that he knows everything and his children are cared for."

"But I thought you were one of the thirty-six," said Chanah. "Your followers worship you. I just assumed."

"I'm sorry, but no. The Lamed Vav are hidden among us. They never reveal themselves. They may not even know their holy mission. All they know is that God wants them to lead the holiest life possible. To live is to serve God. This has been revealed to them in their hearts."

Although she was listening, Chanah couldn't help smiling to herself. Her husband worked night and day to get people to believe in the thirty-six, and he wasn't even one of them! He had taken on a thankless, foolish task. She saw that clearly. The only redeeming feature was that maybe it was a task that God had willed.

As Chanah grew used to her life, God played a new trick. Her brother, moved by his sister's poverty, agreed to set Yisrael up in business, but the business Avraham chose was tavern keeping. This was not permitted for a Jew and totally opposite to the righteous life Yisrael set for his followers. But the Baal Shem shrugged off these objections, saying that it was in the spirit of the law to show kindness to everyone, including sots and the morally weak.

Tongues were set wagging for other reasons. "The rebbe and his wife, they are still like newlyweds," the gossips whispered behind Chanah's back. "He keeps her up all night, can you imagine?"

This was true, but not in the sense they meant. The Baal Shem prayed long into the night. Chanah got out of bed barefoot and came to him with a candle in hand.

"What are you asking for, night after night?"

"Nothing."

"How can that be?" she asked.

"I want to leave myself and go where God is. If I pray with enough love, he lets me into that place, and then everything is perfect." He smiled innocently. "Forgive me. I must sound very selfish to you."

"It can't be selfish to seek God," she said. Sometimes before she left Chanah would kiss her husband on the forehead or touch his chest. His skin would be hot if he had prayed long enough. He called this "the burning," a bodily sign that he was in a state of ecstasy.

Their life was lived so close to the bone that Chanah kept wondering how he could pray without asking God for a small boon or relief from suffering. She embraced her own private thoughts. For instance, she thought that her husband should ask God directly if he was one of the thirty-six. Wasn't it better to know, once and for all? But if she hinted at such doubts, Yisrael shook his head and refused to discuss the matter.

As he grew older, a gift came to him, and to all the Jews in that region, which shifted between Poland and the Ukraine, depending on which ruler was greedy enough to fight for it.

"The government needs us now," the Baal Shem told his followers. "The Turks have been driven out, and the land they invaded was devastated. They killed everyone they could find and left them to rot in the streets."

He caught himself and turned to Chanah. "I'm sorry if you would prefer not to hear this."

Whatever she might have preferred, the men in the group shuffled their feet, and Chanah knew she wasn't wanted. The Baal Shem told her later that the region in question, Podolia, having been depopulated by the invaders, was in sore need of farmers to move in. The Polish authorities were taking a lenient view and invited the Jews to settle.

"You see how God looks out for us?" said Yisrael. "Land for poor Jews, but even better, a place for new ideas."

This new land became seed ground for his followers, who became known as the Hasidim. The name meant that they were pious, but also loving and kind. Is human nature so easily changed that each Hasid was suddenly a saint? Their skeptics were not convinced, but the peasants began to trade tales about the Baal Shem. He went to any house where there was sickness and provided herbs and a holy message to fold inside an amulet. These were mystic names of God that could heal.

Avraham took note when he traveled to visit his sister. "So, your husband was playing a part with his shiny black suit. There's a magical creature behind his humility. A miracle rabbi, they say. You must be proud."

At that moment the Baal Shem walked into the room. "Pride is the only sin that is unforgivable. We know this from the fallen angels, no?"

Avraham didn't want to start a fight. He rode around the countryside, and the ignorance of the Jews who had come in from everywhere—Russia, Poland, the Ukraine—amazed him.

"All I hear is messiahs and miracles. The most preposterous tales are circulated. Is this fairyland?"

What he said wasn't pure prejudice. Somehow, by being released from the oppression of the towns, these Jews had released their fantastic imagination. Every fallen tree that blocked the road could be the mischief of a golem or dybbuk, unholy spirits walking the land. Eggs that failed to hatch were the work of gremlins, and when winter was dark and deep, ghosts were spied dancing among the snowflakes.

"You encourage these superstitions?" Avraham accused the Baal Shem.

"What should I do instead?" Yisrael replied.

"Don't pretend with me. You know what makes us Jews. One and only one thing—the law. Without the law, we would have disappeared from the face of the earth."

"Then let me ask you," said the Baal Shem quietly. "Has anyone ever loved the law?"

Avraham was stymied. The words "love" and "law" didn't belong together. God didn't mean them to, which went to show how nearly insane the Baal Shem must be. As he parted, Avraham told Chanah that he pitied her, but could no longer protect her.

"Mark my words. Pious Jews should leave this place. Here the Talmud has died," he declared.

Avraham was right in his world, where the law, as interpreted by generations of scholars, made the Talmud a lifeline to God. In its books were preserved every wise and holy thought that was lawful. But there is another kind of lifeline, which has nothing to do with the law. People can believe in legends that uplift their hearts. Something precious is thereby kept alive.

"You never can tell" had turned into a useful philosophy as the Baal Shem gradually became enveloped in myth. When he left a farm or shtetl, wisps of legend trailed behind. A fox broke into the henhouse, but instead of biting a chicken on the neck, he saw a mezuzah nailed to the doorpost. Suddenly the fox started to pray, and he left without snatching even a chick.

"You see? The Baal Shem told me to nail a mezuzah to the henhouse, and I had no idea why. Now I know," said the farmer with a knowing nod of the head. True? You never can tell.

As his fame spread, the Baal Shem moved from one place to another, doing good works and gathering disciples. But at home he never seemed to change, and since women did not attend the prayer house, Chanah had little notion of her husband's reputation. It astonished her to get up some mornings to find offerings left at their door—a bunch of wild roses, a loaf of festive challah.

"Wouldn't it be a sin if they are starting to worship you?" she worried.

"Cut the bread, put the flowers in a vase," he said. "We might as well have something nice while I pray to God for an answer."

Yet it wasn't these offerings that made Chanah uneasy so much as the awe that everyone showed around the Baal Shem. There was no question of offending God. The Hasids lived up to their name as pious men, and even their worst enemies couldn't fault them, since the Baal Shem demanded the strictest observance of prayers and rituals.

Unable to shake off her nagging curiosity, Chanah wondered which of the men she could question without being found out. One day after Sabbath, the Baal Shem emerged from the prayer house trailed by his disciples. It was his custom to take a pleasant drive into the country to break the Sabbath, and Chanah was waiting with her best shawl around her shoulders. On this day, however, he didn't greet her. Calling for a wagon large enough to hold all of his immediate followers, her husband gave Chanah a nod that told her nothing, and off the men went, leaving her behind.

They returned late the next night. Chanah was waiting up to hear the whole story, but the Baal Shem kissed her on the forehead, saying, "I know what is in your heart. Just this once, seek out the youngest follower, who is barely a boy, and tell him it is no shame to satisfy your curiosity."

The next morning Chanah ran off to find a boy named David, who had just celebrated his bar mitzvah the week before. Considering himself a man, he was reluctant to tell tales about the Master, but after a good deal of persuasion, he unfolded the story.

The men had gathered as usual to celebrate the beginning of the Sabbath together. Out of respect for the Baal Shem, the atmosphere was quiet and restrained.

"I'm sure you know," said David, "that he reads the secret workings of the world. He knows why things happen and what is the will of God. So even the slightest gesture of the Baal Shem contains mystery within mystery."

Chanah, who certainly did not know this, concealed her surprise and asked for more of the tale.

As the Baal Shem was about to say the prayer over the wine, he suddenly burst out laughing. This wasn't a mild chuckle, but a full, deep laugh that startled all of the disciples. They waited for an explanation, but the Master resumed the prayer, only to burst out a second time, and then, when this eruption subsided, a third. Everyone sat there dumbstruck, but no explanation was given, and the rest of the Sabbath proceeded as if nothing unusual had happened.

Upon setting foot outside the prayer house the next day near the end of the Sabbath, however, the Baal Shem said, "Come." He called for a wagon, and they all piled in. Only instead of a pleasant ride, the journey took all night, during which the Baal Shem said nothing. The next morning they arrived at a nondescript village.

As soon as the Master set foot outside the wagon, all the Jews knew that something important was happening. The elders rushed up in a pack and asked to what they owed such a surprise visit.

The Baal Shem looked them over, and said, "I know you are good Jews, but the one I need to see is Shabti."

"Shabti the bookbinder?" asked the lead elder. "He's a simple soul with no learning. He crawls between heaven and earth without anybody noticing."

Somewhat offended, the elders sent for Shabti, who arrived cap in hand. "I know that I sinned on the Sabbath," he confessed. "How you should know it is beyond me, but tell me what penance I must do to atone, and I will obey your judgment."

The Baal Shem waved his hand. "Before we get to that, tell everyone what happened."

Stammering and red-faced, Shabti began. "God be thanked, I've earned a living all my life, never having to ask anyone for anything. My only goal is that on the fifth day of the week I have money for my wife to go out and buy what she needs for the Sabbath—flour, fish, candles. But as you see, I bear the weight of old age, and last week I had nothing to give her, not a penny even to keep a light on the table.

"I sighed and resolved that God wanted me to fast this Sabbath. So be it. I told my wife that she must wait for me at home while I went to prayers. We have good neighbors with kind hearts. They would see no light from our house, and then they would run over to offer candles and bread and the rest. But I won't take alms. I ordered my wife not to accept charity, and when she promised me, I went off to prayers with a heavy heart."

Shabti was so devout that he began his prayers at the tenth hour of the day before the Sabbath and went home after sundown the next day. Walking home in the dark, he saw a light in the window, and as he entered, the smell of fresh bread and baked sturgeon filled his nose.

His wife stood there with a glowing face and, it being the Sabbath, Shabti didn't have the heart to be angry with her. She had shown a woman's weakness and taken alms. He sat down to pray over the wine when she spoke up.

"This is the most splendid holiday we've had in years. The wine seller was astonished when I asked for his best bottle," she exclaimed.

Shabti couldn't restrain himself and was about to rebuke her, when his wife threw her hands up. She hadn't disobeyed him at all. Instead, when she was left alone in the house with only half a candle left, his wife decided to clean everything from top to bottom, as seemed suitable before fasting. She chanced upon an old chest full of yellowed clothes, remnants of the innocent years when they were newlyweds.

"Who would think? I lifted a tattered blouse imagining that I might still be able to smell a trace of perfume on it," she said. "Out tumbled a gold button, and I remembered losing it long ago. I rushed off to the goldsmith, who said that it was very fine work, the kind of work nobody does nowadays. He gave me so many coins for it. What do you say—a miracle?"

Shabti was astonished and overjoyed. He started to pray over the wine, but he was so happy that he burst out laughing and whirled his old wife around the room in a dance.

"I knew it was wrong in the eyes of God, but I was so overcome with joy that I did it twice more," Shabti confessed. "So how bad is my sin, Master?"

"God is offended when we do not feel joy," said the Baal Shem. "When you laughed out loud, he rejoiced."

Young David gave Chanah a serious look. "So you see? The Master saw all of this unfold in the secret workings of the world. He was so glad at Shabti's joy that he burst out laughing three times, every time the bookbinder did."

Tears came to Chanah's eyes, and it was hard not to embrace David, but she didn't want to give away that she had never heard such things about her husband. He, of course, knew what David would tell her. When Chanah returned home, the Baal Shem smiled with the same innocence as ever, accompanied by the familiar shrug. You never can tell.

His fame only grew, until the day he died, barely sixty-two. Chanah had preceded him, or she would have been celebrated the rest of her days. In the Baal Shem's eyes, he was surrounded by good Jews, each one a recipient of his mystical blessing, a ray of light sent from God through the Baal Shem's soul.

He never asked for veneration. "What have I done? The sun didn't exactly stop in the sky. And God has sent a messiah to laugh at me."

Just before Baal Shem's death, a strange figure had sprung up in that region, a miracle rabbi named Jacob Frank. He formed a cult

around himself, declaring that he was the messiah. He traveled
with a gaudy retinue who were styled as his twelve disciples.

So the Hasids found themselves caught between the Talmud-
ists on one side and the Frankists on the other. They were too
mystical for one camp of enemies and not mystical enough for the
other. The sparkling new messiah made a spectacle of himself in
all the villages that had once stood in awe of the Baal Shem. It got
to the point where Frank, it was said, wanted his followers baptized.

A shocked Hasid ran into the aged Baal Shem's house to tell
him this terrible scandal. The Master took it philosophically.

"What the Jews will believe and what they won't," he murmured. "Has there ever been another question?"

Revealing the Vision

For the Christian world, the arrival of the Messiah changed the course of history, which will lead inexorably to an end point on Judgment Day. But the resurrection also influenced the past, since it justified centuries of waiting. Jesus proved that the wait wasn't in vain. Judaism continues to wait, but history doesn't, and so there is mounting tension between modern life and the archaic portrayal of Yahweh in the Bible. God needs to be kept current. Otherwise, a religion can collapse from within. This problem was met in Judaism through the long tradition of learned commentaries recorded in the Talmud. If scripture didn't comment directly on how to run a business in Berlin or buy from the vegetable stalls in Warsaw, a learned rabbi would fill in the blanks with an interpretation. Law never stopped working.

But where does this leave love?

Updating the rules isn't the same as salvation, or even the same as knowing that God is still paying attention. On that score, reassurance comes from mystics, of which Judaism has its own rich tradition. Mystics reveal God's love here and now, and love is above the law. But can love prevail? This question was most acute for Jewish visionaries like the Baal Shem Tov. He rose at a time of ferment, when social turbulence almost always meant trouble for the Jews—they would be blamed and persecuted as a matter of course. For centuries, ever since the Romans destroyed the Temple in Jerusalem, survival meant strict adherence to the law, and even the Kabbalah, the mystical interpretation of Judaism, belonged within the grasp of learned commentators, not a rural rabbi who lived like a peasant among peasants.

At first the vision of Yisrael ben Eliezer seems cryptic. Even his title is enigmatic. *Baal* means "master," and *shem tov* means "good name." Other rabbinical teachers had been given the honorific title of Baal Shem; Tov was added specifically to refer to the founder of Hasidism. His name can be read two ways, as a "master with a good name" or as a "master who practices wonders with the name of God." The Baal Shem Tov was the most renowned of miracle rabbis, preaching his vision of the Lamed Vav, thirty-six righteous men who kept God from destroying the sinful world, age after age. By association he became one of them, but that wasn't his intent. In fact, since pride was the only unforgivable sin and humility the purest mark of righteousness, the Baal Shem Tov held that anyone who publicly declared himself to be one of the Lamed Vav must be a fraud.

The two false messiahs mentioned in the story did exist at the time, giving us some idea of how tumultuous Eastern Judaism must have been. The Baal Shem Tov set himself firmly against such claims, yet ironically almost everything known about him consists of wonders, miracles, and saintly deeds that are considered legendary. Throughout the illiterate peasant shtetls his name is associated with healings, being saved from disaster, and finding good luck in the midst of misfortune. Always there is the theme of simple faith as the highest virtue. But the legends grew out of an undeniable truth, that myth nourishes the yearning soul. The Tzadikim, the hidden righteous sects, thrived in Polish Judaism, and the Baal Shem Tov exemplifies their kindness and purity.

Beyond the time, however, his vision was panentheistic, embracing God in everything. It also can be accepted as including all faiths, since the thirty-six did not have to be Jewish. Creation glowed with the same divine presence—the light of shekinah as it was known in Hebrew—and even sinners were included. As history unfolded, the Hasidic movement remained ultra-Orthodox. It turned inward, and the universality of the Baal Shem Tov was obscured, if not lost altogether.

Even so, he remains a spiritual icon, a kind of parable anyone can identify with. It is the parable of the wanderer, the lost son who cannot find where he belongs. This was a painful issue for Jews scattered in the Diaspora. To be the chosen people and yet suffer more than people who were not required enormous faith.

And there was even stronger pressure to conform to the law, whose rules and rituals bound Jewish identity together. In that sense the Baal Shem Tov wasn't a rebel, but part of the ongoing anxious question about what it means to be Jewish.

To him it meant joy. Hasidism is about the end of anxiety, and in various sayings of the Baal Shem Tov (it is hard to separate the true ones from the fictitious) he repeats how wrong it is for Jews to be discouraged and downcast. His own illumination made him see the possibility of perfection in everyone:

> Your fellow man is your mirror. If your own face is clean, the image you perceive will also be flawless.

The reason he emphasized prayer and total observance was not to conform to the law, but to open a way for purity. The world as reflected in the eyes of a pure soul is perfect, the feeling it arouses is bliss, a sure sign of connection to God. The implication for impurity was just as obvious:

> But should you look upon your fellow man and see a blemish, it is your own imperfection that you are encountering— you are being shown what it is that you must correct within yourself.

The Baal Shem Tov was appalled by cynical teachers who pawned off fake miracles, and even more appalled by the rise of a self-proclaimed messiah, Jacob Frank, who eventually went so far overboard that he wanted his followers baptized, like Christians. It's easy to forget that when the New Testament was written, one of its aims was to prove that Jesus of Nazareth was a good rabbi, fulfilling the law rather than breaking it. The Baal Shem Tov appears to reach across such boundaries also, as when he quotes Leviticus:

Do not seek revenge or bear a grudge against anyone
among your people, but love your neighbor as yourself.
(19:18)

In a broad sense, everyone is a wanderer trying to find a right-
ful place in the world; the spiritual dimension comes when you
ask if your place is to serve God, which implies that "place" is not
fixed by your home on earth. In the shtetl, popular teaching was
done through familiar analogies. Besides his purely mystical message, the Baal Shem Tov follows in the long tradition of making
God human:

When a father punishes his child, the suffering he inflicts on
himself is greater than anything experienced by the child.
So it is with God: His pain is greater than our pain.

This wasn't meant as a way of making suffering inevitable. As
one can easily understand, there was a strain of Jewish theology
that already made suffering inevitable. How could it not, to a
people who had been outcasts for over seventeen centuries when
Yisrael ben Eliezer was born? Instead, the Baal Shem Tov uplifted
the simplest of lives, prefiguring Leo Tolstoy's ideal of the peasant
being closest to Christ. The poorest are the servants of God, and
the Baal Shem Tov believed that to live was to serve God. Therefore, the poor show everyone else a profound truth:

The wholesome simplicity of the simple Jew touches on the
utterly simple essence of God. . . . When you hold a part of
the essence, you hold all of it.

For almost anyone today, this is an uncomfortable message. We
no longer see the poor as God's beloved children; a gloss of
shame and pity covers our eyes when we look on unending pov-

erty. The Baal Shem Tov taught in a different age, still very close to the medieval, where poverty was an inescapable fact of life. After he spent an afternoon scything wheat with the peasants, Tolstoy the nobleman could retreat to tea, a manor house, and velvet cushions. The Baal Shem Tov spent some early years under conditions close to slave labor, and even when famous he never attained real creature comfort.

Panentheism turned the Jewish predicament on its head. Instead of living nowhere, searching in vain for a home, Jews could look around and see the whole cosmos as their true home. In Hasidism, nature constantly delivers messages from God. No event is outside his gaze; nothing should be considered an accident.

> Everything is by Divine Providence. If a leaf is turned over by a breeze, it is only because this has been specifically ordained by God.

Naturally, this rings true with the vision of a Puritan like Anne Hutchinson. The Baal Shem Tov founded a movement to purify the faith, and because he desperately needed confirmation from God, an absent deity was inconceivable. God must be watching at all times, sending signals of approval and disapproval via everyday events. Anne Hutchinson was enthusiastic about finding sermons in stones, and so was the Baal Shem Tov.

Even today, when Hasidic communities are tight enclaves all but invisible to the general population, there is a theological bond between them and fundamentalist Christians: the bond of reading God's private telegrams wired directly to the pure of heart. The evolution of God at this stage is more a reminder that he is still paying attention. Each person must decide how to live under the gaze of eternity. Ancient and modern history are linked by that duty.

10

RABINDRANATH TAGORE

"I Am the Endless Mystery"

There was a hue and cry when the Ouija board arrived. The youngest girls in the family squealed with delight, while a house-maid cut the twine and peeled off the brown wrapping paper. It didn't seem strange that such a parcel had come all the way from London to Calcutta. Everything arrived in the post except for cook's daily supplies, which she ran to the market for as the sun rose.

"How many do you cook for, anyway?" the vegetable seller asked as he packed long beans and okra into a sack.

"Don't be nosy," the cook said tartly.

No one knew what went on behind those walls. Before they reached school age (or before they found a husband, if they were girls), the Tagore children never left the compound.

"Run, run!" the boys cried, galloping down the halls to round up all fourteen children. The youngest, Rabi, didn't run. He re-mained where he was most days, staring out a grated window at the city he was never allowed to set foot in.

When one of his older brothers, Jyotir, appeared at the door, Rabi turned his head. (Jyotir's full name was Jyotirindranath, just as Rabi's was Rabindranath, but they all used shorter nicknames.)

"What is it, this thing that came?" Rabi asked. He liked hubbub, being a normal boy. But a natural reserve kept him from joining in.

Jyotir was beside himself. "A telephone line to the dead! Can you believe it?"

With that kind of buildup, it was impossible to resist the new thing, although it was disappointing to look at, a flat varnished board about the size of a serving tray on which large letters and numerals were painted. No matter. Rabi knew exactly which of the dead he wanted to talk to. The hours passed slowly. It was a lucky day, though; their father, Debendranath Tagore, who was rich, would come home in the evening before leaving again on one of his endless trips.

If only he knew more about the scene he left behind when he stepped out the door. It's a misfortune when a child falls prey to cruelty. The misfortune doubles when cruelty comes masked with a lie. It's always the same lie: "This is for your own good."

Behind his father's back anyone felt free to give Rabi a casual smack. When they held his head underwater in the tin washing tub, the house servants would make sure to lift Rabi up before he blacked out. He sputtered and gasped, wondering why they were smiling.

"You'll thank us one day. We are making you strong," they said. They all took pride in how moral they were, and strict in their religion too.

The boy had good instincts and saw that this was a lie. Little good that did him. The Tagores lived in a huge house, isolated from the outside world behind a high wall, yet the twisted maze didn't mean there was room for escape. Every wing had resentful chambermaids, a bossy governess if a new baby had arrived, overworked sweepers, and outdoor gardeners—there was no end to his punishers. Since the boy was gentle and soft, the blows he received were bewildering as much as painful. But his mother had petted him, so he resolved to show that he wasn't a whiner.

The one kind servant he could hide behind was Kailash, the old groundskeeper who seemed as dusty and worn out as Calcutta itself. Kailash was a joker, always hanging around the gates to tease whoever came and went.

"What a beautiful sister you have," he'd say when a girl arrived with her wizened grandmother. Or "How perfectly the gods have blessed you," if a vain middle-aged dandy showed up without the gray hair he had the week before.

As he handpicked fallen leaves off a patch of perfect lawn (kept immaculate to show the colonials that an Indian could out-British the British), Kailash thanked God that he wasn't a beggar on the streets. He never skipped a daily offering of marigolds to be laid at the feet of the Krishna statue standing with a seductive smile at the back of the garden.

"He protects me. He protects us all," Kailash explained when Rabi was four and old enough to be curious about everything.

"How?" the boy asked.

"By keeping the demons away, the *rakshasas*."

Two of the worst *rakshasas*, starvation and disease, roamed just beyond the high wall, and the old part of the city where the mansion stood had become degraded into a place of thievery and prostitution. Rabi didn't know why Krishna didn't protect them too, but when he heard shrieks and swearing outside his window at night, there was every reason to make the compound a privileged prison. He clung to Kailash also out of need. His older brothers and sisters were married or at school or surviving on their own. Their father had huge estates to attend to around India, and his travels, which lasted months at a time, created a vacuum.

"It's a servocracy around here, old man," Jyotir said, when he found Rabi crouching one day under a palm tree nursing a fresh bruise. Rabi didn't understand this new word, or why Jyotir laughed, since he had just made it up. But he knew well enough that those on the bottom could royally hate those on the top.

The best thing about hiding behind Kailash was that the old man spun tales that were addictive. When in the mood, he wove garbled romances involving Rama, Sita, and Krishna, with any passing Western hero—a Galahad here, a Lochinvar there— thrown into the mix. These last came to Kailash's attention when he lingered under a window while novels were read aloud to the assembled children. Learning was a constant business in the Tagore mansion, stepped up whenever their father came home, since he was a great one for history, astronomy, music, and paint- ing, just to scratch the surface. His talk was a scattershot barrage of facts. Did Rabi know that the year he was born, 1861, Lincoln went to war to free the slaves? It was the same year that the czar freed the serfs in Russia.

Rabi's head swam. He had never seen a slave or serf. Were they like untouchables? But after hours of studying, he always had an appetite for Kailash's romances, since the old servant was canny about naming several of the noble princes, swains, and warriors "good Sir Rabindranath." One tale stuck in Rabi's mind, about the two epic lovers Prince Rama and his beloved wife, Sita.

"They were rich and beautiful. Life was too good," Kailash said solemnly, "so Lord Rama was banished to the forest for fourteen years."

Rabi, who wasn't interested in filler, said, "Get to the part about the golden deer."

"There was a deer made of gold, which means that you would starve to death before being able to eat it."

Rabi stamped his foot. "That's not the story. You forgot the demon."

Kailash, whose memory was growing somewhat feeble, sud- denly remembered. "Ravana, the king of the demons, set eyes on

Sita and fell instantly in love. He wanted her desperately, so he devised a trick. He ordered one of his magical servants to create a golden deer to lure Rama to run after it with his bow and arrow.

"The trick worked. Demons are hateful, but clever. Rama's brother was Lakshmana, and he was a better brother even than the ones you have. He had joined the couple in the forest, and now he drew a circle on the ground around Sita.

"Don't leave this circle," he ordered. "My duty is to protect you, and while Rama and I chase the golden deer, you will be safe here."

"She won't do it," said Rabi, who enjoyed predicting parts of a tale that he knew by heart.

Kailash sighed. "Too true. When the brothers were gone, Ravana disguised himself as a beggar, crippled and bent over and whining, 'Oh, kind, kind lady, won't you give me a scrap to eat?'

"Sita took pity on him and stepped outside the circle. Bang! The king of the demons turned back into himself again. He snatched her up, and off they flew in his magic flying chariot."

Rabi nodded wisely. "Men will learn to fly soon."

Kailash shook his head. "Don't you believe it. That's the same as asking Ravana to come back again."

Despite the thrill of Sita's kidnapping, they both knew that it was only a matter of time before Rama hunted Ravana down to dispatch his ten heads and twenty arms. But one day Rabi refused to hear the tale again. An eavesdropping servant had gotten wind of it, and the next morning he and two others grabbed Rabi out of bed. They drew a chalk circle on the floor and plunked him in the middle.

It was just after dawn, and nature called, but when the boy got up to use the chamber pot, the servants hit him with sticks.

"Be a good little Sita," they teased. Another trial he kept to himself.

Later that month, the old man Kailash suddenly died of fever.

Being seven, Rabi was more curious than grief-stricken. What did it mean to die? Where was Kailash now if not hanging around the gates to joke at the expense of rich people?

And that same evening brought the arrival of carriage lamps, and servants, bidden by Rabi's mother, rushed with torches to unload the master's luggage. Debendranath embraced his wife and looked at their brood with happy satisfaction. His pride in so many sons and daughters was like an iridescent bubble that none of them wanted to burst by telling him about the servocracy. He strode into the parlor trailing instructions and promises after him.

"I've planned a trip to a hill station near Nepal. Who wants to go? And we are getting a piano for the Westerners when they come to the house for music. Oh, I have some toffee in my valise. Tell the cook it's not for boiling; we'll eat it after dinner." And so on, each word like a gift dropped from a benign benefactor. The Ouija board was also a gift, but their father raised his eyebrows when he saw it set up neatly on a tea table surrounded with cushions for the children to sit on.

"Ah, that. Did I order it? I must have."

He was such a curiosity seeker that there was no chance he would ignore the supernatural contraption or send it back. The Tagores hurried through supper to cut short the suspense before they telephoned the dead. Rabi was the pet, and his request was honored first.

"Kailash. There's no way he won't have a joke for us. Being dead won't stop him," he said.

His father agreed and sat down before the board, placing his fingers lightly over the planchette, the little device that skated over the board to spell out words as the dead sent them through. The grown children weren't believers and struck poses of knowing boredom. The instruction booklet said that every participant could lay their fingers on the planchette, but their father decided that only Rabi would be permitted at first.

They dimmed the lights and took their places on the scattered cushions. The room, although far from the kitchen, captured the warm smell of saffron and naan bread. Rabi might have grown drowsy if his nerves weren't set on edge.

"What happens now?"

His father screwed up his eyes staring at the instructions in the near darkness. "Call upon one of the dead by name."

So father and son put on a solemn face, sitting across from each other with their fingers poised on the planchette.

"Kailash, it's me. Are you there?" Rabi called, addressing the air over his head, the most likely place where heaven might be located.

At first nothing happened, but gradually the planchette started to quiver, and then with surprising speed it moved to the word "Yes" embossed on one corner of the board.

"You moved it on purpose," accused his father.

"No, I swear," Rabi blurted out.

"We don't swear in this house. I believe you. I didn't move it either. How odd," his father murmured. "Ask the old rascal a question. What do we have to lose?"

Rabi didn't hesitate. "What's it like to be dead?"

The other children laughed, but his father nodded in agreement. What better question could one ask of the dead?

The planchette started moving again, and as it paused over various letters, they realized that Kailash wasn't going to abridge his answer. Someone ran to fetch pencil and paper. Rabi was too busy calling out letters to group them into words. Suddenly the message was done, and everyone around him was smiling.

"What is it?" he asked.

The paper was passed to him, and it read, WHY SHOULD YOU GET SO CHEAPLY WHAT I HAD TO DIE TO FIND OUT?

"Cheeky monkey," their father muttered, but behind his amusement Debendranath was a little impressed. The game went on as other children crowded Rabi out of the way. Kailash refused to communicate anything more, and Rabi went to bed that night clutching the paper. It felt to the boy not like a scrap of scribbled words, but a scrap of his only friend returned to life. Or had Kailash managed to die without dying?

That night Rabi saw an endless ocean in his dreams. A tiny speck bobbed on the waves, which turned out to be a rowboat. Kailash was rowing, looking as dusty and worn out as he had when picking leaves off the lawn, and his passenger was Rabi's mother. He was sure of it, although the woman never fully turned her face to him. The next morning the boy awoke with gummy eyelids, as if it were possible to cry while you were fast asleep.

When he was eleven, Rabi got to see the hill station his father had promised him. They made their way north by slow degrees, stopping at several estates the family owned. As their carriage passed, the local farmers would leave their plows and run up to the road to prostrate themselves in the dust.

"Are you their god?" Rabi asked, but his father didn't reply. He didn't even smile in his indulgent way, which he usually did if the boy asked a clever question.

Up and up the northern roads winded as they neared the Himalayas. Rabi stuck his head out the window, despite the cold April air, breathing in this green world of deep gorges and waterfalls. Dense forest would suddenly break out into vistas of the high peaks. He'd never seen snow, but he could feel it on his shoulder just by staring at the white caps on the mountains.

They switched from the train to a horse cart, and then a town, called Dalhousie, rounded the bend. Rabi burst out laughing. It was a cluster of gingerbread houses that comically duplicated a quaint English village.

"Homesickness," his father whispered.

The hill stations were built for British families as a summer retreat, an escape from the terrible fevers that killed many women and children if they risked staying in Delhi or Calcutta. But after his initial surprise, Rabi was blind to everything but the natural wonder of the place. Being shut up in a mansion all his life, he had fantasized about the world he couldn't enter. Now it exploded in every direction, and the vastness made him dizzy. He had the strange sensation of being the center of everything he saw, an invisible point of awe.

There was something else too. He had been given the sacred thread, which was a major step to manhood for all Indians. The ceremony, called *upanayana*, was ancient and solemn, a rite of passage that Lord Rama would have knelt down to receive. Priests chanted mantras in an atmosphere of incense, fruits, and flowers; there was a sacred fire into which offerings were made. Rabi felt as if the fragrant fumes were lifting him up. When the three-stranded cotton cord was laid across his shoulders, he trembled. A faint shock went through his body, and with wide eyes he gazed at his father, who understood.

"It's real. Invisible things can be real," his father murmured.

Rabi believed him. It was like the cold dusting of snow on his shoulders. He felt it when he read about the mountains; images formed in his mind, mysterious and vivid, even before he set eyes on the real snowcapped peaks. But he wondered why the sacred thread always seemed to rest on him now.

They stayed in the hill station for three months, in a rented bungalow with mountain grandeur outside the window and a frigid stream close by where father and son bathed every morning. He was given biographies to read and history books, astronomy lessons (which Rabi loved, since he could take the star maps out at night while gazing at the wondrously clear sky, like black crystal), and tables of Sanskrit verbs. Rabi knew no other life, so none of this seemed unusual, not even the meager food and long hours of meditation that his father imposed. The shared routine was their bond.

One day they were out for a walk when his father recalled something.

"You asked me if our people thought I was a god?" His father always said "our people," because he disliked words like "peasant" and "servant."

He pointed to a ragged boy squatting by the side of the road. He was a Dalit, considered untouchable by tradition and long prejudice. The boy stared at the ground, making himself invisible until they passed. When Debendranath gestured to him, the Dalit hesitated. On the rare occasion when an upper-caste stranger gave him a small coin, it was always thrown at him so that no contact would be made. Some Brahmins went home and bathed if the shadow of a Dalit fell across them.

When the boy got close enough, Debendranath said, "Sit with us. I want to tell my son why you are a god."

Startled, the Dalit stammered, "But I need a bath."

He blushed for uttering something stupid. He wasn't happy in the first place to be in the presence of rich strangers.

Rabi's father held out a water bag. "Drink and rest in the shade. My boy is interested in gods, and we can't disappoint him."

The Dalit did as he was told.

Debendranath turned to Rabi. "Why is this boy a god? If you were his mother, she would say that he is exceptionally beautiful, like a temple statue. Our eyes wander to beauty naturally, without being told to. Beauty has a power of its own, whether in a lovely young girl or the tree we are sitting beneath."

The Dalit gaped, but Rabi was used to his father's way of talking. The only thing that made him squirm was the reference to pretty girls.

"Nature is rich in beauty," his father went on. "We don't ask why. We simply accept it. But what happens when the beautiful girl departs and is out of sight? What happens when we leave the temple and its statues? Beauty still lingers. Our eyes have nothing to see, yet something lingers in the heart. We feel touched, and if something is beautiful enough, we feel inspired."

Rabi couldn't grasp every word, but he knew what his father

meant. When he went to sleep at night in their bungalow, the darkness was filled with a presence like perfume. He had even told his father about it.

"I call this the scent of beauty," his father said. "If you follow perfume wafting down a dark alley at night, it can lead anywhere. It could even lead to danger, but we follow anyway. Similarly, we trail after beauty, hungering to find its source. For surely to be in your mother's arms is better than simply remembering her scent."

Rabi's mother had stayed at home, but he had no trouble remembering the patchouli she wore. If he shut his eyes, the scent came back by itself, like a voice from a faraway land.

Debendranath looked over at the Dalit, who was holding the water bag halfway to his mouth.

"You can drink from it," Rabi's father said, nodding. The boy hesitated. It didn't seem possible that he wouldn't contaminate the water. But the day had grown fiercely hot, even near the mountains, and he gulped down a few big swigs. Rabi was silent, sunk in thought.

His father said, "Heed what I'm saying. Beauty makes us follow it. Everyone knows this, but most cannot see the mystery. They think that the way to pursue beauty is to run after the next girl who intoxicates them. Or perhaps money intoxicates them instead, or power. But beauty is a mystery because it comes from God. I brought you to the hill station so that you can see God everywhere. But really all you see is the scent he leaves behind. Or call it his secret messages."

"What do the messages say?" asked Rabi, who liked puzzles.

"They say, 'Follow me'," his father replied.

"Where?"

Without answering, his father lightly tapped Rabi in the middle of his chest. "You cannot possess God. The mystery remains endless, all the days of our life. But you can feel it inside and cherish that feeling, like a precious pearl."

The Dalit was bored, having never heard such talk. He wasn't interested in Rabi, although the two boys were about the same age. Without a doubt the stranger's son would pelt him with rocks the moment his father's back was turned. The two strangers grew quiet, a good time for the Dalit to escape. He put down the water bag skin and crept away.

"He's afraid of us," Rabi said when he noticed what had happened. The Dalit was still in sight, but a good fifty yards down the road already.

"He'd be much more afraid if you told him who he really is. People crave to hear that they are part of God, but when they hear it, they feel ashamed. A pity."

His father had retreated into a kind of bemused detachment. Rabi knew this mood very well. It was predictable, in fact. Every time his father waxed passionate about a subject, immediately he seemed to be sucked into himself. The retreat didn't make him sad, but he would be unreachable for moments or hours. Rabi understood, since he was much the same way. So they let the Dalit escape without handing him a rupee. Father and son gazed at the clouds gathering like misty fleece over the far peaks. Since the mystery is different for everyone, nobody can tell if they were thinking the same thoughts. At least they shared the same sky, which was enough.

God, Rabi found, was like chasing a train. On the way to the station your carriage is blocked by a cowherd. By the time you make it to the platform, red-faced and breathless, the train is gone, leaving only wisps of smoke and the acrid smell of cinders. But you must get to Delhi, so you push on to the next station, and there too the train has just left. The same thing happens town after town, until you only meet up with the train when you have traveled all the way to Delhi and find it sitting in the yard, grinning at you. The difference with God is that most people reach death before they reach Delhi.

Death in the family had been the problem all along. After the old servant Kailash, it was Rabi's mother, who was taken when he was thirteen. Then it was his father, but Rabi was over forty by then, so the world considered it natural. Another old man, this one rich and famous, received an obsequious obituary. The world had no idea. Rabi had not just grown up under his parents' noses. He had seen life and love through his mother, as he saw mind and service through his father.

Where did these gifts come from? Where did they go?

He sat on the porch overlooking the grounds of his estate. No one called him Rabi anymore, only Rabindranath. People murmured the name as they bent to touch his feet. Everything revolved around him—a family, a school, the local farmers, the struggle for Indian independence. In all this busy round, Rabindranath knew only one thing: he was chasing the train to Delhi.

When the becalmed air of noon settled over the activity on the estate, he liked to dictate. He was doing it that day.

"I slept and dreamed that life was joy. I awoke and saw that life was service. I acted and behold, service was joy."

Tagore paused, glancing over at the young male secretary squatting on the porch. "Did you get that?"

The secretary nodded and smiled. The heat wasn't too suffocating near the cool manor house, and he was privileged to serve Bengal's greatest writer. Rabi had grown into that. The secretary modestly bent over his notepad, ready for the next line. What was he really thinking? Maybe nothing. Maybe he sat at Rabi's feet in silent awe. It would do no good to ask him. We are all mysteries to ourselves, and when we start to think, we are eavesdropping on messages sent from beyond.

That could be the next line, but it flew out of Tagore's mind before he could voice it. A pretty young woman had run up dressed in a sky-blue sari trimmed with gold thread. She was a niece, the daughter of one of his brothers, so she dared to grab him by the hand and pull him away.

"Not so fast," he protested. It was a joke, because everyone marveled that, at fifty, he had a boy's restless energy. He played at letting his niece drag him reluctantly across the lawn. The performance couldn't start without him. The dancers today were children from the local village. He worked constantly to improve their lot.

Many were Dalits, which was ironic. Tagore had written countless poems and stories about untouchables. Readers were shocked at the inner lives of these creatures and moved by their struggles. It was a new way of looking at people whose shadow used to make them cringe. The money from the stories helped pay for the school where Dalit children could be raised up. It must have been the first time in history that money came from loving untouchables instead of working them to death.

The hall was noisy when he stepped in; it instantly grew quiet. The parents who had come with their children shushed them. He mounted the stage and held a piece of paper close to his eyes. Any gathering expected some words from Rabindranath Tagore, which were received like scripture. Hadn't the king of England knighted him? But Sir Rabindranath sent back the honor as a protest against colonialism.

Now he recited slowly, knowing that for three-quarters of his audience, who couldn't read or sign their names, many words would be difficult.

When the lotus opened, I didn't notice and went away empty-handed.
Only now and again do I suddenly sit up from my dreams to smell a strange fragrance.
It comes on the south wind, a vague hint that makes me ache with longing, like the eager breath of summer wanting to be completed.
I didn't know what was so near, or that it was mine.
This perfect sweetness blossoming in the depths of my heart.

A grateful murmur went through the hall. Whatever they didn't understand, the people felt. A few started to applaud, the ones sophisticated enough to know that you can clap for poetry; it wasn't really scripture. The children rushed noisily on stage in their costumes, and the sitar and drums were already starting before Tagore took his place in the front row.

His niece looked over at him with concern. He knew that look very well. Since 1905, the year his father died, death's nose had sniffed out the others he turned to for love—his wife, then two of his children. A tragedy. Everyone said so, and they worried for him. But was any of it real? The question penetrated his grief, and when he went to sleep at night, he sometimes imagined the smell of cinders. Dangling death from his fingers, God was racing ahead.

Which was why death pervaded so many of Tagore's Dalit stories. The people he grew up with, the rich and the good, didn't know how their closest servants died, except that it must be like dumb animals, silently suffering, then whining briefly before they closed their eyes. In the Tagore family Kailash had died that way, but not another old man whom Rabi loved. He died extraordinarily.

Srikanath Babu was like a plump, round fruit on legs. He had a shining, clean-shaven face and a bald head as smooth as a mango. Kailash had wooed Rabi by building romantic tales around him, but Srikanath Babu was the boy's first critic, and the most perfect he ever had. Nothing Rabi wrote was greeted with anything less than ecstasy.

"Ah, I could sing those words going to heaven!" Srikanath Babu would exclaim.

So feverish was his enthusiasm that, before the precocious boy had finished reciting a new poem, the old man would jump up, run to Rabi's father's room, and burst in to sing the first lines. Many of these poems were *kirtans*, or devotional songs. A lover of music, Srikanath Babu was never seen without a sitar in his lap. By his side always stood a smoke-filled hubble-bubble, as the locals called a hookah.

Srikanath Babu sang peculiarly as he strummed his sitar, because he no longer had a tooth in his head. Amazingly, this too was a cause for joy.

"Why should I trouble my poor mouth with sharp fangs?" he said.

He could not tolerate to hear about suffering and death. Rabi's brothers knew how to torment Srikanath Babu to the point of tears. They had only to read him legends of Prince Rama or the warrior Arjuna in which a character was pierced by arrows or hacked with a sword. Srikanath Babu would thrust his arms out, as if pushing away a snake, and beg them to stop.

The day came when Rabi's father was a bedridden invalid enduring his final illness. He was resting at his leafy river estate near the town of Chinsura. Srikanath Babu was desperate to see him one last time. He himself was very ill and could only walk with the aid of his grown daughter. The two of them took a train to Chinsura. There was great anxiety about undertaking such a journey. Srikanath Babu was able to see only if he took his fingers and held his eyelids open for a moment.

He survived the trip, though, and was taken immediately into Debendranath's sickroom. Srikanath Babu lifted his eyelids and wept at the sight. He could hardly speak, and in fact left without saying a word as the patient slept.

"Didn't you want to greet him?" his daughter asked.

Srikanath Babu, who was humming softly to himself, shook his head. "I touched the dust of his feet. That was why I came." Two days later he died in the little cottage by the river that they had provided him.

Death had undone everyone in Rabi's life in a different way. Most were at peace, but one, the wife of his brother Jyotir, smiled one day, gently pointed out weak spots in a new poem of his, and then took her own life in the night. Each time he was unable to escape a spell of dark depression. At the same time, he wondered more and more what it meant to die. There were things you had to know if you wanted to unravel life's secrets—love, truth, beauty, but also death. He jotted down any thoughts that might bring him an answer, and the astonishing part was that when he felt close to the mystery, so did his readers.

Sometimes he touched on the tenderness wrapped up in sorrow:

My heart beats in waves
on the shore of the world
And writes its name in tears
with these words:
"I love you."

But more often he wondered at things no words could express:

What do I long for?
Something that is felt in the night
But not seen in the day.

He must have been sunk in such thoughts, because the next thing Tagore knew, the hall was filled with the sound of clapping. The performance was over. Proud parents were smiling. The children onstage were bowing; the musicians staring around, impatient to get to tiffin, their afternoon meal.

No one could rise before the master did, so Tagore smiled at the children and said, "Go, go!" Under a tent beside the hall treats were laid out on tables.

His niece waited at the door, renewing her concerned look. It would have helped more if she wore Srikanath's unquenchable smile. His jollity would have been foolish in another person, even idiotic. But people never mocked him behind his back.

"Do you ever think about God?" Rabi had asked as a boy.

"Always. What else is there to think about? The world takes care of itself, no matter how hard people try to run it."

"And what do you know about God?" Rabi asked.

"Only one thing," replied Srikanath Babu, puffing on his hubble-bubble. "God is an endless mystery."

Tagore patted his niece's hand when she tucked it into his arm. They started to cross the lawn to the refreshment tent. "Do you recall old Srikanath Babu?" he asked. "I seem to hear his voice today."

"How could I? I wasn't born yet," his niece said. She kept her eyes peeled for anything on the ground that might trip her aging uncle, as if she were escorting a Dresden doll to a tea party.

"He was very fond of me," mused Tagore. "And he came to a good end. But that's not what was on my mind. He taught me the only important thing I ever heard about God."

Tagore repeated to his niece the comment about God being an endless mystery. "It's funny that such a simple remark should stick with me, but it did, for years. And then I saw what Srikanath Babu really meant."

They had arrived safely at the tent, and his niece looked around for a chair where the Dresden doll wouldn't be disturbed. "What did he mean?" she asked absentmindedly.

"God has to be a mystery," Tagore replied. "Because the only one who could explain him is himself, and no one bothers to ask him anymore."

What was driving him? Restlessness. It had become an irresistible force. When Tagore arrived at a new place, which could be Buenos Aires or Shanghai, reporters milled around, craning their necks to get a better look. Here was something you don't see every day, a tall old man in flowing silk robes. He wore a long white beard, like an eternal grandfather or Merlin the magician. When he leaned into the microphones, blinking at the popping flashbulbs, he said uplifting things, which everyone wanted to believe.

"Love is not a mere impulse. It must contain truth, which is law."

That was his stock in trade, uplift. No one snickered, although some mentally rolled their eyes.

"Every child comes with the message that God is not yet discouraged about mankind. "

The voice was sonorous, the eyes remarkable, wide and liquid. But what world was Tagore living in?

Hitler was on the rise; the markets had crashed in 1929. What did the Indian sage have to say about things that matter in the real world?

"We live in the world when we love it."

Hopeless. At least Gandhi had a cause worth space on the front page. Tagore was on record as disliking mass protests, even for Indian independence. The reporters bent over their notepads, but everyone in the room knew that this would be a story filed under "local color."

Yet he never stopped his journey, lasting for decades now, to far corners of the world. Every poet is restless. The muse is a demanding mistress. But he had the mystery before him, always to follow, never to capture. Tagore wasn't blind. He saw the skepticism in reporters' eyes. He could envision them loosening their neckties after he left the room, glad that the sermon was over and they could escape to the closest bar for a drink.

Where had his restlessness carried him now? Somewhere near Potsdam, the map said.

"A pleasant place, serene," he murmured gazing out the car window. "Can I walk the rest of the way? The trees are reaching out."

The driver, who was a round-faced German, didn't want to say no, but he didn't want to deviate from his assigned duty either. The professor was sitting patiently in his small brown house with the red tile roof. A new batch of reporters was milling around, not just Germans but French, Poles, even some Americans, who had the best cigarettes. Trees could wait. But the driver let the old man out a little short of the path to the front door, so he could have his serenity.

Tagore took his time among the slender trees that seemed like maidens with their delicate leaves swaying in the breeze. He was seventy, and the forest meant more to him than did Hitler. The reporters would seize on things he said against Gandhi's total pacifism. "Did Gandhi want to invite Herr Hitler and Signor Mussolini to take whatever they wanted?"

The real world. It kept racing on its frantic pace, fueled by the next crisis. In such a world, what fuels peace?

He forced himself to abandon the forest and walked up the path to the house. Seeing him out the window, the professor adjusted his formal coat and stepped out on the porch. This was the moment. Cameras were raised. The great Tagore was shaking hands with the great Einstein. It was like a collision of planets.

In the hubbub Einstein leaned over and whispered. "I memorized a line of yours. 'We come nearest to greatness when we are great in humility.' I believe it."

Tagore smiled. Not because of a flattering quote. He sensed something. When you got close, the famous face of Einstein—the whirligig white hair, caterpillar eyebrows, and sagging eyelids—didn't prepare you for the secret he carried inside.

Tagore leaned over and whispered back. "I would memorize your words, but unfortunately they are all numbers."

They retreated inside, where there were tea and comfortable chairs. After a moment, a rare thing happened: two great men became genuinely interested in each other. Einstein didn't want to talk about world peace or the Nazis and the danger that would drive him out of Germany if it grew worse against the Jews. He had God on his mind.

"Do you think God is separate from us?"

"No. Human nature is infinite. It can reach the divine."

"How?"

"By merging with ultimate reality. We live in a human universe. Eternity reflects the eternal human. You have been busy hunting down time and space. I talk about the eternal human because without us, there is no time and space."

Einstein sat back. They regarded each other, and he saw immediately that something huge was at stake.

Forming his words carefully, Einstein said, "There have always been two views of the universe. One says that the world exists even if human beings were wiped off the face of the earth. The other says that there could be no universe without human beings."

Tagore nodded. "Quite right."

"But if no one was inside this house, that table would still exist."

"Why does the table exist?" Tagore asked. "Because someone perceives it. As an individual, you feel separate from the table, so it appears to be independent of you. But the cosmic mind contains everything. Nothing can exist unless it is perceived, and Brahman sees everything."

"In science we collect facts, and that leads to truth," Einstein countered. "Gravity existed long before human beings arrived, don't you agree?" Einstein's tone was certain. He was famous for once saying that he hoped the moon still existed even if he stopped looking at it.

Tagore shrugged. "If there is absolute truth outside what human beings can understand, it is unreachable by your facts. The universe exists as it relates to humans."

Einstein allowed himself a wicked laugh. "Then I am more religious than you are!"

Their words were taken down by a reporter and sent around the world. The conversation lasted three days. People were divided. It seemed amazing that Einstein, who had baffled the greatest minds with relativity, making time stretch like a rubber band, would ask a poet's opinion about the universe. Tagore's answers, it was agreed, were high-minded, but no match for science. The eternal human? The cosmic mind? A famous English philosopher wrote to a friend saying that he would have to avoid Tagore the next time he came to London. His ideas were too embarrassing, a rubbishy jumble.

But in the small house, with just the two of them, Einstein grew pensive. There was a famous Greek statue of Apollo that he had gazed at in the Vatican.

"If there were no human beings anymore," he said, "then the Apollo Belvedere would no longer be beautiful?"

"No."

"I agree with regard to beauty, but not to truth."

"Why not?" Tagore shot back. "Truth is realized through humans too."

Einstein kept talking because he wasn't embarrassed by Tagore. "The mind of God" was a phrase he had used himself. Religious people who worried about science as an enemy sighed with relief when he said that he wanted to know the mind of God. He didn't practice any religion, and he disbelieved in God the Father, the God of Jewish tradition. Yet *something* at the far horizon of the universe filled him with awe and wonder. It wasn't his brain that had unfolded relativity; it was wonder.

"Whatever God may be," Einstein said, "perhaps it is best that he stays out of reach. The unknown drives me on, and I solve the unknown through science."

"But even science is an activity of scientific humans," Tagore replied. "Your facts don't exist outside the man who sees and measures."

Einstein shook his head. "I cannot prove that my conception is right, but it is my religion."

In the end, two planets didn't collide. They slid past each other. In passing, they exchanged glances. If you looked, the air was breathable on both planets; the landscape wasn't alien.

Other news swept their meeting off the front pages. Worse

was coming to worst everywhere. People started saying that this depression was the Great Depression. Hitler grew more frightening by the day. The train was leaving the station full of the disillusioned. Tagore could wave at them from the platform if he wanted to. He was already being forgotten anyway.

But this wasn't his experience, which remained luminous. God remained elusive, but a radiance presented itself every day. Inside the radiance a voice whispered, "I am here." Tagore obeyed his restlessness until he couldn't. His body surrendered to illness; the days became a trial of pain. He was glad to be alone with the radiance, which didn't fade despite his physical agonies. Another world war came and spread untold catastrophe. He was nearly eighty. Death stood at the door, but didn't enter his room for two more years.

Tagore could meet death's eye, and therefore it had no power to do anything but wait. Words had to release the poet before life would. Tagore asked for someone to take down a poem one day, even though he hardly had enough energy to wet his lips from the water glass by his bedside. In a thready voice he began,

> I have given completely
> whatever I had to give.

He stopped, gasping for air. There was no letting go yet.

> In return, if I receive anything—
> some love, some forgiveness—
> then I will take it with me
> when I step on the boat . . .

Nothing more came. The bedroom was silent and still. The old friend who was taking dictation thought he heard a rattle in the dying poet's throat. It would be a shame if his final verse was cut short.

The old friend softly got up to fetch the nurse, only to be stopped by a movement he caught out of the corner of his eye. Tagore had made a weak wave of the hand. The thready voice returned, and the old friend leaned close to catch Tagore's faint mumble.

When I set foot on the boat
that takes me across
to the festival of an end without words.

Then nothing more. Death no longer waited courteously at the door. Outside, the breeze was reduced to a faint stirring. Barely enough to make the leaves tremble on the crest of the trees, barely enough to stir the hair of maidens.

Revealing the Vision

"Today the light of mysticism went out." The obituary for Rabindranath Tagore could have included that sentence when he passed away in August 1941. He was the last great mystical poet to achieve world fame, and almost the last mystic in the public eye. A momentous change had occurred as science replaced religion in modern life. Tagore bridged both worlds, thanks to his highly Westernized education at his father's knee. He would become a mystic in the line of Giordano Bruno, who made no distinction between scientific wonder and spiritual awe.

For Christians of the high Victorian era that Tagore was born in, the age of faith, already waning by the time of Shakespeare, still drew breath. As long as God couldn't be understood, he held power. Saints were like scientists who journeyed into the unknown and came back to report, through their mystical experiences, that God was real.

We take it for granted that faith is inferior to facts when it comes to deciding what is real and what is illusion. Tagore didn't accept this truism. He insisted that God's reality was not threatened by uncovering scientific facts. He wasn't stumping for faith, however. Referring to a mystical inner journey, he said, "You can't cross the sea merely by standing and staring at the water." Or by measuring the ocean waves with a scientific instrument, he might have added.

His mysticism wasn't dismissed for being out of touch, which is surprising. Tagore was writing to a worried world, and when people read *Gitanjali*, his book of rapturous songs to God, it was thrilling to find someone who was immersed in love for the divine, a love so all-consuming that it was like drowning.

Thou hast made me endless, such is thy pleasure.
This frail vessel thou emptiest again and again,
and fillest it ever with fresh life.

Readers were entranced. The intoxication of Rumi had returned, seven centuries later.

> This little flute of a reed thou hast carried over hills and dales, and hast breathed through it melodies eternally new.

For a time Tagore was a sensation. He was the first non-European to receive the Nobel Prize for literature, which came in 1913, only three years after *Gitanjali* was written and, even more astonishingly, only a year after it appeared in English. That same year he toured the United States and Great Britain, displaying the restlessness that carried him to every corner of the globe for the next twenty years.

The West's enthusiasm for Tagore was feverish, but it wasn't destined to last. His message of love as an eternal mystery didn't jibe with the unspeakable horrors of World War I. What was rapture compared with machine guns and armored tanks? In the face of criticism, Tagore's certainty was powerful. He stood in a spiritual tradition that went back five thousand years to roots in ancient India. He had inherited a profound view of life that had survived many catastrophes. Labeling this tradition with a single word—*mystical*—gives it short shrift. Everything about human existence, including love, death, truth, and beauty, needed the foundation provided by God. God justified the mystery of life. He gave human beings a soul and a lord to surrender to. The violence and conflict inherent in human nature found an escape in the belief that beyond war, crime, power struggles, greed, and evil deeds, we are essentially divine.

If Tagore's had been an isolated voice, I doubt that Einstein would have taken him seriously or even agreed to meet him. Their conversations, which took place over three days in 1930 inside Einstein's small house outside Potsdam, made the world listen. Lengthy verbatim accounts were printed in major newspapers. But this wasn't entirely the clash of religion and science.

Einstein was constantly consulted for his opinions about God. He was both brilliant and benign. Unlike Darwin, who was bitterly opposed to the conventional religious piety of the Victorian era, Einstein wanted God to exist in some form. He famously said, "Science without religion is lame, religion without science is blind."

In other words, Einstein held out hope for cooperation, not just compromise. People could see the horror of a godless world, and yet God needed to be compatible with modern life. When Tagore met Einstein, he was almost seventy and Einstein just past fifty. They recognized in each other two men who had thought deeply about the nature of reality. This is why, I think, they spoke as equals, even though Einstein would never become a religionist. Tagore had made a statement about love that turned into a major quotation: "Love is not a mere impulse. It must contain truth, which is law." Einstein was too much the physicist to allow "truth" and "law" to be used so loosely. Yet he went down Tagore's path farther than one would have expected.

Their points of agreement are striking. Both held that God was a mystery beyond complete understanding. To Tagore, this mystery was internal, wrapped up in the mystery of the human heart. To Einstein, it was external, poised at the edge of the knowable universe. Yet he agreed, surprisingly, that the material world couldn't be proven to exist. In fact, this point had been troubling modern physics, well outside the walls of the church.

Quantum physics didn't set out at the turn of the century to destroy the picture of the physical world that we receive through the five senses. There was no agenda to turn atoms into clouds of energy, to make time expand and contract, or to declare that the subatomic world was entirely ruled by uncertainty. However, by 1930 all of these things turned out to be true. Physics shocked itself, and Einstein wasn't the only quantum pioneer who looked with doubt and no small degree of dread at what he had uncovered.

He found himself forced to make a choice between two views of reality. One camp of physicists surrendered to the fact of radical uncertainty. Nothing was truly solid or even physical; electrons behaved like waves in one mode and particles in another. If the building blocks of the universe no longer had any fixed physical properties, turning into ghosts, then why believe that the universe itself was any different? Einstein, who freely said that he wanted to know the mind of God, could not accept a random universe where every event was a matter of chance. He believed that nature existed in an orderly, stable way, even though he couldn't prove it. His camp was much smaller than the camp that wanted to topple all absolutes, and by 1930 he was isolated, quickly turning into a semitragic figure. His great discoveries were already behind him. He was clinging to ideas that other great physicists, such as Niels Bohr, Erwin Schrödinger, and Werner Heisenberg, had shaken off ten years before.

The public, with its simplistic image of Einstein as the greatest mind in the world—if not of all time—didn't realize his actual position. But he laid it out for Tagore, and the irony is that the Indian mystical poet held a view that was much closer to quantum physics, as it eventually matured, than Einstein did. Tagore declared that the observer creates perceived reality, that absolute truth was unattainable through objective facts. His was a ghostly world too, just like the realm of subatomic particles. Ideas so radical that Einstein couldn't bring himself to believe in them turned out to feel quite natural to Tagore.

We should remember that Tagore was always more than a poet; in today's terms he was a polymath, and he had been brought up in a privileged household where the children were taught mathematics and the natural sciences. Such a background allowed him to make sharp replies to Einstein. The sharpest came when Einstein made the point that was the bedrock of his beliefs. A beautiful sculpture like the Apollo Belvedere, he said, would no longer be beautiful if there were no human beings to gaze upon it. But it didn't take an observer to create truth, meaning the truth about what is real and what isn't. If every human being disappeared, the table that sat in the room would still exist.

Tagore came back with a quick denial. If beauty depends upon human beings, so does reality itself. The table didn't take its existence from any single individual. Obviously there was still a table in the room if the room was empty of people. But the table needed something outside materialism—the cosmic mind—in order to exist. The chain of logic was very clear: we only know what is real through our consciousness. If anything is real outside our awareness, it will remain unknown. Because consciousness is so central—letting us see, hear, touch, taste, and smell the world—we must find out where it came from. Otherwise, we are like dreamers wandering in a world they take to be real, because no one has told them that they are asleep.

So where did consciousness come from? The only viable answer was that it came from itself. This is the mystical position, and few have voiced it as beautifully in modern times as Tagore when he portrays himself as a tiny speck in the infinity of God's creation.

At the immortal touch of thy hands
my little heart loses its limits in joy
and gives birth to utterance ineffable.

Thy infinite gifts come to me only
on these very small hands of mine.
Ages pass, and still thou pourest,
and still there is room to fill.

We are not alone, then, as conscious beings. God or Brahman or the universal mind—pick your own terminology—surrounds us. It is our source and origin. The only reason that we can begin to understand the universe is that its laws and orderliness aren't random. Every atom fits into a scheme that is innately orderly, not to mention beautiful, intelligent, loving, and all-knowing.

Because he worried about these things too, Einstein understood the logic of Tagore's worldview. Modern physics had already dismantled the physical world far enough that reality was looking more and more like a dream. Still, Einstein clung to what he called his religion: a belief that the universe was real as it appeared, not needing human beings to give it shape, form, color, sounds, and all the rest. It is quite moving to view Einstein in the midst of such confusing emotions. His doubts had placed him outside Judaism and quantum physics at the same time, standing on crumbling ground.

Tagore, on the other hand, never wavered. When he spoke of the "eternal human" and a "human universe," he was using deceptively simple words for complex ancient ideas. This was the inner journey of Buddha, Jesus, Lao-tzu, Zoroaster, Plato, Rumi, and every other spiritual seeker. For them all, the human mind reflects the divine mind. Thousands of years before Tagore, the Vedic sages had declared, "The world is as you are." There is no separation between what happens "in here" and "out there." Behind the shifting appearance of the Many—the wildly diverse activity in nature—stands the One. The One is higher reality. We see, because It sees. We are moved by beauty, because It contains infinite beauty. When we feel that we know something to be true, our minds have touched, just barely and for an instant, the endless scope of absolute Truth.

Tagore's story ends in a protracted, painful illness before he died in Calcutta, at rest from his world travels. Looking around, it's hard to find a conversation today that discusses reality and God with the same delicacy and respect that Einstein showed Tagore. The argument for his kind of idealism, where to live in the world is to love it, was defeated by a second world war and the looming atomic age. The victory of science is rampant; gurus stand in line behind techies. But the doubts expressed by Einstein haven't been resolved. The present point in God's evolution is ambiguous. Every negative trend from the past—a suspicious clergy, rigid dogma, the fight against tolerance—survives alongside positive trends that are just as ancient—a loving Creator, humans made in the image of the divine, direct contact with God's presence.

The horror of a godless world haunts millions of people. Technology races ahead, threatening to overwhelm us. Beyond the personal computer lies the promise of a quantum computer. Information doubles every two years. Smart phones rule. But God isn't susceptible to obsolescence. The divine speaks silently amid the din of shouting voices, and the miracle is that someone, somewhere, is still willing to listen.

Epilogue

"Are You There?"

Reading the stories of saints, sages, and visionaries creates a strange sensation, a mixture of inspiration and doubt. We are like a culture that once had telephones until they stopped working. We try to talk to God, only to hear dead silence on the line. "Are you there? Hello, hello. Is anyone there?" is the only thing left to say. With the connection gone, it's impossible to know if God is listening. Perhaps he or she is also asking, "Are you there?" from the other end of the line.

Before a connection to God can be restored, a vital question needs to be asked. Did people ever talk to God in the first place? The answer, if we are being logical, must be either yes or no. "Maybe" is a copout. No one would keep a telephone around that didn't work, not for the many centuries that human beings felt that God or the gods were listening. Someone felt a divine presence and heard it deliver messages from a higher reality. I've offered ten such people, and they are connected by a thread that runs through the history of spirituality. It's not faith that joins them, but consciousness.

Now that the age of faith is well and truly over, modern people make a reasonable demand. If God exists, we should be able to verify him. Holy words don't suffice. The authority of saints guarantees nothing in a fact-based world. To give the divine a free pass by claiming that God is above petty doubts doesn't reassure anyone who harbors those doubts.

God is reached through an inner journey, and the whole problem of proof could be settled if this journey could be verified. God once walked in the Garden of Eden in the cool of the evening, but no more. Ever since, the deity has left invisible footprints—until now, perhaps. Brain research has gotten sophisticated enough to peer into the working of minute areas of the brain, and neuroscience makes maps of regions that used to be terra incognita. Such maps can tell you which areas of the cortex light up when a person feels compassion, possesses strong faith, has a holy vision, hears voices, or prays.

"You are the light of the world," which Jesus said to his disciples, suddenly has a literal meaning. In fact, the areas of the frontal lobes associated with higher functions like compassion grow larger and stronger among Tibetan Buddhist monks who meditate on compassion. Certain brain frequencies in the delta band increase at the same time beyond anything seen before. God's footprints were not invisible after all; they were just hidden beneath the cranial bones in the soft gray tissue of our brains.

Making Our Own Connection

Where does this leave you and me as hopeful seekers? By showing that spiritual practice changes the brain, reality expands. The only reality anyone can know must register in the brain. Now atheists and other skeptics cannot reasonably claim that nothing is happening during spiritual experiences. The door is open for anyone who is eager for God. Or to be precise, four doors have opened. Looking back at the visionaries in this book, they followed four paths to reach higher reality.

The path of devotion has always been open to those who love God. As their love intensifies, they feel God's presence drawing near. That was easier in the age of faith. Daily life involved much prayer, and the local church was at the center of birth, death, marriage, feast days, Communion, and many holy days on the Christian calendar. As an inner journey, the devotional path is harder to take today. It involves an immersion in wonder before God and all divine works. Nature is regarded as a canvas that conceals the hand of God. The great advantage of the devotional path is its joy. The seeker worships in order to contact bliss. But as Rumi, the perfect devotee, shows, this love affair with the divine is as tumultuous as any human love affair, and just as prone to heartache. It is up to you to know at the level of feeling if God has touched your heart.

The path of understanding is the way open to the mind. It involves reflection on the great questions of life: Who am I? Why was I created? What does my existence mean? If only abstract answers come back, there is only dry mental investigation. But the mind can become passionate about God, and then it cannot rest without seeing through every illusion that blocks the way. All four paths are lifetime journeys, but the way of understanding may be the narrowest. You must have a strong intellect and unflagging curiosity. Thinking brings its own joys, but no one would say that this way is blissful. Taking Socrates as a model, one sees that society doesn't approve of gadflies and questioners of received wisdom. Yet there are people who cannot stop thinking about God, and knowing the truth about higher reality satisfies them more than devotional bliss can.

The path of service is the way of action, finding ways to do good in the name of God. Charity is one way to serve. Giving your time selflessly is another. But more than good works are called for. The deeper question is finding out which actions will draw you closer to God. Religions often fall back on the notion that God wants us to do certain things, such as obey his laws, to earn us approval from on high. I think that's mostly church politics, a way to keep worshippers in line. Being infinite, God wants nothing; therefore, he wants nothing from us either. Our limited self-love is nothing compared with infinite love. The secret on the path of service is to lose the ego, which serves only "I, me, and mine." To reach God, your service must be to life itself, which means serving all beings. Taking the Baal Shem Tov as our model, we see a humble existence that needs no reward, but derives inspiration from giving.

The path of meditation is the way of consciousness. Devotion begins with a feeling of joy. Understanding begins with a flash of insight. Service begins with an act of humility. But when you begin on the path of meditation, there is only being. In order to be, we need only one thing: consciousness. You are aware that you exist. Such a path would seem to be meager, if not threadbare. Being doesn't bring images of fun to mind. It brings nothing to mind so much as a blank. Which turns out to be the secret, because in that seeming blankness lies the beginning of everything. Consciousness is the womb of creation. Everything you will ever think, say, or do begins here. On the path of meditation, you open your mind to higher consciousness as your very essence. Taking Julian of Norwich as our model, we realize that this path is solitary, because meditation needs silence and self-communion. Its great advantage is that isolation doesn't have to be physical. You can meditate in the midst of an everyday life. Time is no obstacle when your goal is the timeless.

These four paths were set down in ancient India thousands of years ago. They have served—and been validated—for countless generations. I would also claim that they are universal ways to reach higher reality, not just Eastern ways. With the collapse of faith as a common inheritance, each of us must undertake the inner journey of our own choosing, but that was always true. Saints and sages once had more prestige than they do today. The voices they heard were not suspiciously labeled schizophrenic hallucinations, grand-mal seizures, or symptoms of a brain tumor. Those explanations arose in modern times in the wake of two world wars and the advent of the atomic bomb, which effectively corroded faith for millions—the medical rationale arrived as an afterthought, to justify well-entrenched doubts about a merciful, all-loving God. Yet the medical "evidence" rings hollow, because when we read the book of Job, Plato, St. Paul, or Rumi, their words mean something. They stir us deeply enough that we feel reconnected, however briefly and vaguely.

Living Proof

To satisfy science, what we need already exists: the feedback loop. Your body operates through countless chemical messages sent to trillions of cells; these messages create a response that the cells send back to the brain, and depending on what the response is, the next round of messages will change. The brain listens to feedback, and its connection to the rest of the body forms a loop. Now substitute God for the brain and human beings for the body's cells. The feedback loop remains the same: message and response. If you feel any impulse of joy, hope, beauty, or faith, its source cannot be outside your own awareness.

Divine messages occur within the field of consciousness. If God were outside human awareness, he wouldn't exist, not for us anyway. The scope of reality is infinite and eternal; this has always been part of God's mystery as well. But the infinite and eternal became enclosed in time and space with the big bang, and the same happened to the mind. If the mind of God became limited enough to enter the minds of ordinary people—which is what Job, Plato, St. Paul, and Rumi are all about—that isn't a miracle. Nothing in the infinite fields of matter, energy, and information that create the visible universe can be known until they are reduced to the human scale.

Einstein respected the cosmic mystery enough to say that what astonished him most wasn't the universe, but the fact that we can know it at all. With the same attitude, some farsighted scientists today have begun to recognize that consciousness is a proper field of study and research (largely thanks to breakthroughs in brain scans like the functional MRI). Some even go so far as seeing spirituality as inherently human—our brains, our genes, and therefore our thoughts are set up to seek God. This is a startling claim against the background of science as the great opponent of religion. We don't have to look upon it as a claim at all, just a hypothesis.

Let's call it the "soul hypothesis" for short. It can be stated without using any reference to God, as follows. We are conscious beings who want to know where our awareness came from. Only consciousness can understand consciousness; hence the long tradition of the inner journey. The saints and sages of the past were Einsteins of consciousness, explorers into the nature of reality. They were testing the soul hypothesis, and if these explorers came back with the same findings, century after century, culture after culture, why not give their findings credence?

Their findings are startlingly similar, in fact. The mind, they said, is like a river. On the surface there is constant motion and turbulence; reality can be described as constant change as the river flows through time and space. Just below the surface, however, the river grows slower and calmer. There are no waves, and as you dive deeper, the turbulence on the surface ceases to register. Stillness prevails, and at the very bottom of the river, if it is deep enough, the water doesn't move at all, or just imperceptibly.

Our connection to God, then, is like that between a wave and the still depths. A river is all one thing, flowing water, yet reality on the surface appears very different from reality down below. The great discovery of our Einsteins of consciousness was the revelation that all consciousness is the same. There can be no separation from God if this is so. God cannot die or abandon or stand aloof like a watchmaker unconcerned after he set the cosmic mechanism in motion. We are essentially divine, because God is just another name for the origin and source of consciousness.

We are back to the feedback loop now. If God's mind is an infinite version of our mind, all our thoughts are movements within the divine mind. Whether you call yourself a believer or an atheist is irrelevant. Consciousness never stops sending messages to itself, waiting for a response, and then adjusting the next round of messages. We possess a soul insofar as we realize that we are part of the feedback loop. The only difference is where you put your attention. Some people are content to remain on the turbulent surface of the river. They are fascinated by the constant activity, the ups and downs; life is a river-rafting trip. But nothing prevents a few people from focusing their attention on another level of consciousness, where calm, peace, wisdom, silence, and the vastness of the cosmic mystery reside.

My mind returns these days to Rabindranath Tagore. I chose him as a modern explorer in consciousness, and there is poignancy in his restless wandering. He was born four years before Lincoln was assassinated and died four years before the first atomic weapon was exploded at the Trinity Site. As much as anyone in history, Tagore felt the desperate need for humanity to hear a message of eternal love. Instead of bodhi trees and burning bushes, God's vehicle was the press conference dockside when Tagore's ship landed. Amid the barbaric terrors of the twentieth century, how strange those reporters must have felt scribbling notes about what he said.

"Let your life lightly dance on the edges of time like dew on the tip of a leaf."

"Love does not claim possession, but gives freedom."

"Music fills the infinite between two souls."

What? Tell it to North Korea and Iran. Tell it to mass murderers in the Congo, or the six million who perished in the Holocaust. Fear and horror do very well if you want to break every possible connection to God. When a person gets sick, trillions of cells receive distorted, toxic messages, and if the cells perish, they might doubt that the brain exists or has their best interests in mind. The breakdown of a feedback loop leads to isolation. If you ask "Is anyone there?" and get no reply, it's only natural to feel helpless and hopeless. The answer, now and always, is to test the soul hypothesis for yourself.

There are more enticing clues than ever. Brain research has provided the traces of consciousness as heightened activity in the cortex. Quantum physics long ago dismantled the reassuring world of solid objects and neatly connected cause and effect. There are abundant reasons for believing that the inner journey isn't foolhardy or a mass delusion imposed by organized religion.

It may be necessary to look nervously over our shoulders to see if science is nodding its approval. Ultimately, however, the poets and visionaries, the outsiders and mystics who constitute the motley crew of our spiritual past knew better. Being conscious, we are never away from the divine, even for a second, even during the darkest night of the soul. Somewhere inside, we all yearn to reconnect, and if we sit quietly, during those moments when life's richness is too overwhelmingly beautiful to ignore, we know that Tagore was profoundly right:

> Love is the only reality, and it is not a mere sentiment. It is the ultimate truth that lies at the heart of creation.

Ah, we realize, someone is on the line after all.

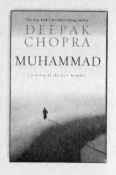
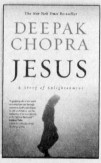
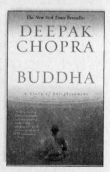
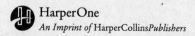